The Fiction
Writer's
Toolkit

The Fiction Writer's Toolkit

A Guide to Writing Novels and Getting Published

Bob Mayer

© Copyright 2001 by Bob Mayer
First e-reads publication 1999
www.e-reads.com
ISBN 0-7592-1436-0

Table of Contents

Preface

Point of view is the most critical style element in writing. It is also important in reading this book. I've been making a living writing for well over a decade and with each year and every new manuscript come new lessons learned. Over that time period I've also taught writing novels and getting published at various workshops and for numerous organizations. I've seen numerous ideas, stories and manuscripts in the course of teaching, helping other writers, and judging contests. I've been published by four different American publishers, ten foreign publishers, worked with over a dozen editors, and have had two primary agents.

The pages that follow are my experiences and opinions. They were born out of my desire to give those I taught something solid when they attended a seminar or class. I've been in numerous writing seminars and classes and walked out with nothing but some vague words that seemed to blow away under the harsh glow of my computer screen when I sat down to write.

Too many people lament the state of publishing and the "crap" that fills the shelves in the local bookstore. My goal in this book is not to complain but to explain; to tell you about the craft and art of writing and the business of publishing so you can accomplish your goals.

The world of writing is a very diverse one and there is a place in it for just about everything and everyone. Keep that in mind when you read what

I have to say. Just because I'm not a big fan of self-publishing or fee-charging agents doesn't mean there isn't someone out there who would benefit from either or both of those.

The bottom line is **I write because I enjoy it**. I write because nothing can beat starting with an idea and a couple of years later holding a published book in your hands. Also remember that editors, agents, bookstore owners and managers, everyone in the business all the way through to the most important person, the reader, is in it because they enjoy books.

But being a writer isn't easy. There is a large degree of craftsmanship required to write a novel. It's not magic; it's hard work combined with the ability to constantly accept being critiqued and to critique one's self.

Publishing is a business. Like any other job, there are good aspects to it and bad ones. Like any other job, experience and business savvy count. And like any other art form, passion and desire also count.

I think writers become authors through many paths but there are two major ones. Some come from the craft side of the house. Others from the art side. A few geniuses have both to begin with. If you're the latter, you probably don't need this book. But most of us fall into one of the first two categories. That's the first self-appraisal you have to make: right now am I more of an artist when I write or a craftsman? Once you figure that out, the next several years of your life should be dedicated to doing better what you already do well and learning to do the other half which you know little about.

I started consciously as a craftsman and subconsciously as an artist. I focused a lot of my early energy into techniques and plotting and the business end of writing. As I progressed I realized I was missing something. How did I realize that? Very simple—because I wasn't where I wanted to be and I wasn't satisfied with what I was writing. Once I realized this, I had to sit down and do some hard soul-searching. What *wasn't* I doing? What was I missing? And to do that introspection, I had to drop many preconceived notions. I had to accept that I was lacking in the 'art' side of the writing house. I subsequently put as much energy into drawing that out of me as I had the craft.

That's an advantage to this book. It was written over the course of my writing career so you are going to get information written when I was tightly focused on craft, and you are also going to get information when I was tightly focused on the art of writing. Most writing books give you one or the other—here you get the whole deal.

Another advantage to this book is that I have both succeeded and failed as a writer. My first series of books under my own name stopped at book 6. I was not offered a contract for book 7, even though I pitched an idea to keep the series going. In the publisher's eyes, that series had failed and therefore I had failed. However, by the time I was pitching that book 7 under my own name, I was published under two other names, one of which was starting to hit some bestseller lists. So I've also succeeded as a writer. Thus I speak from personal knowledge when I say "Don't do this" and "Do this."

The bottom line is the book. I love books. I love reading them and I love writing them. So if you love books, the pages that follow are a glimpse behind the mysterious curtain of how they are born in the crucible of passion and idea, then written, and published.

This book will take you step by step on the journey from original idea to the book in the reader's hand.

The Fiction Writer's Toolkit

1

Welcome to the Novelist's World

Writing can verge from being a burning passion to a mild interest for different people, but the desire to put words on paper is lurking in almost every person who has ever walked into a bookstore and opened a book. If you've ever had those fateful words: "I've always wanted to write a book" scamper across your mind, then the following pages are a guideline to do just that. Or, if you are simply interested in the inner workings of the three critical components that produce a book for the reader—the author, the publisher and the bookstore—then the following pages are a window into that world.

If you desire to write a novel because you want to have a bestseller and make a bundle of money, my advice for you is to play the lottery; it will take much less time and your odds will be about the same, if not better, and I can guarantee that the work involved will be much less. An agent I know reviews approximately 150 submissions a week, every week of the year. That's about 7,800 submissions a year. Out of all those, he accepts as clients approximately four to six a year. And he isn't a publisher—some of the clients he signs up don't make it to publication. The Authors Guild estimates that even among those writers accepted for publication, less than ten percent earn enough to make their living at writing.

I recently read an interview with Michael Crichton where he said that when he was deciding between entering the writing world or going to medical school, he was dismayed to learn that only two hundred people in America make their living writing novels; then he went to medical school. I think the number is higher than that, but not by much. Stephen Coonts made the interesting point that simply based on numbers, in any given year, your odds are higher of becoming elected to the US Senate than becoming a New York Times Best-selling Author.

At a writing workshop I attended, an editor for a major New York publisher told the novice writers in the audience that writers rate only above migrant workers in pay scale and, when the audience laughed, he told them he wasn't joking. With the shrinking size of the mid-list, those words are becoming more and more true.

With those negative, but realistic, facts out of the way, let's turn to the positive. You write for *you*. You write because you have a story in you that have to come out. This is the core of the art of writing. Pearl Buck said:

"The truly creative mind in any field is no more than this: a human creature born abnormally, inhumanly sensitive. To him a touch is a blow, a sound is a noise, a misfortune is a tragedy, a joy is an ecstasy, a friend is a lover, a lover is a god, and failure is death. Add to this cruelly delicate organism the overpowering necessity to create, create, create—so that without the creating of music or poetry or books or buildings or something of meaning, his very breath is cut off from him. He must create, must pour out his creation. By some strange, unknown, inward urgency, he is not really alive unless he is creating."

I believe passion either is or isn't present. This passion and desire cannot be taught but it can be unearthed. It cannot be given, like a relay baton, from one person to another. I believe it to be *the single most important factor* and I discuss it in parts of this book. However, I do believe that *too much* discussion on the topic of creativity can actually stifle the drive in some people. They start thinking that they have to do and think exactly like everyone else in order to succeed and that is not true. That is why I say that there are no absolutes, no hard and fast rules in writing. Follow *your* path.

I have listened to many writers speak and while much of what they say is the same, there is often something that is very different. Usually that different thing is part of their creative core, the way they approach their writing. However, on a certain level, I think most creative people operate in a similar manner. I write about this in Chapter 1: Internal Characteristics of a Writer.

In this book, when I discuss how to write a novel, I talk a lot about the craft of novel writing. The art is woven into the craft with deeper insights. This aspect is something that took me many years and much discussion and thought and learning to begin to understand. There are some people who start with the art and then have to learn the craft. Both parts are essential and the line between them is a thin one, transparent at times. The best writers merge them together to the point where this is no line.

For me, the craft is the intellectual aspect of writing. The art is the emotional aspect. A great writer engages both the reader's thoughts and emotions, thus being both a good craftsmen and a good artist.

One of the paradoxes of writing and something to keep in mind when going through this book: I am going to present techniques, ideas and formats that are the "accepted" way of doing things; yet the "accepted" way makes you the same as everyone else who can read a writing book and follow instructions, and your work has to stand out from everyone else's. So how do you do that? How do you do things the "right" way yet be different?

Everything mentioned in this book is a template; do not allow anything to stifle *your* creativity. Remember the paradox. The best analogy I can come up with is that if you were a painter I am telling you about the paint and the canvas and lighting and perspective, and how to sell your work to a gallery, etc. etc. but ultimately you are the one who has to decide *what* you are going to paint and *how* to paint it.

Another thing is to understand the techniques and methods, and then use your brilliance to figure out a way to change the technique or method to overcome problems and roadblocks. To be original—an artist—with something that's already been done. Also to mix techniques and methods in innovative ways.

Remember, *most* "writers" don't do things the "right" way. I listed daunting numbers above but simply by reading this far you've lifted yourself out of the pack of "writers". I am constantly surprised at the number of people who want to write novels but don't bother to learn the basics. Or even more amazing, the people who want to be a writer but don't read.

What are the basics? The first one is write a lot. The second, and it actually comes before the first, is be a voracious reader. The third is learn the proper way to do business things in the world of publishing such as the right format for a submission, how to prepare a manuscript, how to write in the correct perspective, use proper style and syntax, do chapter breaks, etc. etc. etc.

The majority of people who want to be published novelists don't want to learn anything because they already think they know all they need to know. If you are reading this, then you have already accepted that you don't know all you need to know and therefore you are truly well ahead of the pack.

The purpose of this book is to expose you to the tools and methods to express your creativity, and to increase your odds of rising above those other writers languishing on the slush pile. I do believe the tools that are used in the craft of writing can be taught. As I mentioned above, the one tool that I don't believe you can "teach" is the passion and the creativity, the force that drives

3

all the tools enclosed within this book. However, we can discuss it and you can gain insights into the creative force behind writing and the artistry that produces stories that draw in the reader.

Beyond that passion and personal insight, though, in most cases, a lot of published writing is *not* a special gift or a mystical talent. It requires hard work and can be learned, just like any other skill. I liken it to bricklaying; you learn one brick at a time and you get better the more bricks you lay. And you start by building a house, not a palace. More on that later.

I am somewhere between the house and the palace stage. I've had people come up to me at writing conferences and say that I incorrectly used one of the tools listed in this book and I sometimes agree with them. If I could use every tool in this book perfectly I wouldn't be taking my time to write it; I'd be too busy lying on the beach in Hawaii waiting for the royalty checks from my mega-bestseller to come in. Actually, that's not true because I write more for the enjoyment of creating than making a buck. I'll talk about this more in the business end. Also, as time has gone by, I am doing more of what I say in this book than ever before and becoming a better writer because of it.

Why should you read this book rather than one of the many others books on the market about writing? You shouldn't read this instead; you should read this in *addition* to those other works. The advantage of this book is that my perspective is much closer to yours, the beginning writer, than, say, the perspective of a best-selling author, although they all started where you are. I began writing this book shortly after my first novel was accepted for publication in 1990 and have been adding to and modifying it ever since. Thus this book presents a spectrum of my experience, not just my current experience. In here you will find me writing in present tense about things that in real time happened years ago, but I've kept many of those passages because they offer insight from varying levels of my writing experience and thus give other writers at various levels more opportunities to connect their experiences with mine.

I think it is an advantage for you, the "new" writer (I say new only in terms of being published; you may have been writing for decades.) to read a book written by someone who shares your view.

I believe it is important for me to say more about writing as a career. Quite honestly, when I participate in writers' groups, if there are ten people in the room and we all read our work, I recognize that sometimes one or two of the people there can "write" better than I can. By that I mean they can put words and sentences and paragraphs together much better than I can. In many cases they can also get across their thoughts and feelings better than I can. Yet somehow I am the "author" and they aren't. Why?

There are several reasons. One is that there is so much more to a book than simply writing words; there is a story that must grow and come to life and interest the reader. And, also, because besides being an art, writing is both a **craft** and a **business**.

If I wanted to be an architect I should not be satisfied that I only had grand visions of what the design for my buildings should be. Nor would anyone be impressed with my visions if I couldn't put them into the proper format. Nor would anyone be interested if my design was so impractical that it couldn't be built. I would have to learn the craft of design and also the business of building and then apply my vision to that. I would also need to understand how the people who actually build the building operate, and interact with them in a professional and knowledgeable manner. And, perhaps most importantly and most often forgotten, I would not have any success if no one wanted to buy my designs.

The majority of writers fail because they may have the innate ability and drive, but no direction or focus. That is another purpose of this book: to allow you to direct your vision into a mode and medium that others will want to buy and read.

Colleges abound in creative writing courses. "Write what you feel," I was told in one fiction-writing course I enrolled in. Fine. In fact the more I write, the more I realize that is an excellent concept. But beyond those excellent words, practically nothing was taught. The class consisted mostly of critiquing, but even the critiquing didn't seem to have a *positive* purpose. Too many flaws were unearthed without suggestions for fixing the flaws. Critiquing serves a critical function in the writing process (pun intended), but it should be directed in a positive way with possible solutions offered. You not only have to write what you feel, but you have to do it well enough so that the reader can feel the same thing.

I've talked to and taught many creative writing students and they all seem to want to scream something along the lines of the following at their instructor: *"Don't just tell me what not to do, tell me why I shouldn't do it and give me some ideas for ways to improve my work. At the same time allow me to write what I want and don't impose your feelings and prejudices on my content. And maybe, just maybe, you could also teach me something positive before you ask me to write and start critiquing me."*

But let's take the architecture theme a little further. Would a professor look at an architecture student and say: "I'm not going to teach you anything about blueprints, building design or materials or anything else that has to do with the job. Just go ahead and design your building according to what you *feel* it ought to be and when it collapses, I'll tell you why." How many students would he have?

All the above is not to put down creative writing courses or to add my two-cents to the chasm between the "literary" field and the "genre" field. I think the two have much to learn from each other and the line separating them is an artificial one. You must write what you feel or it will be flat and false (*and* there would be no reason to write it), but you must remember that to make another person feel what you want to impart through the sole medium of the printed word is a very difficult task and requires discipline and conscious awareness of technique.

Creative writing courses tend to emphasize books focused on characters, what most people call literary writing. The only difficulty with that, quite frankly, is that in order to sell a character-oriented book, you must pretty much be a genius at writing. Above I said that "most" writing could be learned. I think the genius that produces books that are almost entirely about people is very difficult to learn. There are only so many Faulkner's and Fitzgerald's and Anne Tyler's and Clyde Edgerton's every generation. That is not to say those people didn't work very hard at crafting their style, but there is a certain amount of something they have style-wise that is very hard to define and capture.

However, if you walk into a bookstore, you will find that well over ninety percent of the fiction that lines the shelf is not character oriented, it's plot oriented. (A caveat here. Although a story may be plot oriented it should be character driven. I will explain this apparent paradox later in the book, but it's taken me almost fifteen manuscripts to work out so let's take it slowly.)

By plot-oriented that I mean the story line is the core of the novel. Think about why people read fiction: primarily for entertainment. I have listened to and read extremely well written words in writers' groups; material that made tears come to my eyes. Coming of age stories; personal crisis stories; moral dilemma stories; etc. etc. But I also knew the odds against those stories selling was tremendous. Most people *live* those things. They only want to read about it if it is *superlatively* written. However, they will read a *well*-written story if it is about something they don't know much about or haven't directly experienced. Hence the popularity of Stephen King, Tom Clancy, Michael Crichton and all those other "genre" authors.

However, also notice how well drawn out the characters are in most of those books. Just because a plot initiates a story, that does not mean you throw the characters out. In fact, once the plot initiates, the characters come alive and dictate most of the course of the story. The opposite can be true also—characters can initiate and the plot follows them. To me, the key about the art side of writing is more psychological than literary. I think insight into the human condition, into people, is critical for the writer. As important is the ability to make this applicable to a broad spectrum of readers; too often, writers who focus on character, focus on themselves and situations they know, and are unable to broaden it to the 'human condition' and not just their condition.

I just judged a contest on submissions and almost every story idea was very personal and character-oriented. I got to the point where I longed for someone to say: "Hey, I've got this great western, or sci-fi story, or any genre."

I am not trying to dissuade you from writing about whatever it is you feel you need to write about. I am simply pointing out reality. I believe for most of us it is better to start at the simplest level and work our way up, rather than try to start at the top. I will talk more about this in Chapter 3: What To Write, because, based on what I have seen year after year in the form of submissions, most people pour their souls into personal projects before they have learned the skills necessary to write that type of story and also before they understand the craft and business of writing. I am sure that the man who built the Brooklyn Bridge did not start with that project. He built many smaller bridges first over the years before he created his masterpiece.

I didn't long for a genre story because I don't like personal or character-oriented stories—quite the opposite, those are my favorite books. The problem was that most of these people weren't quite sure what it was they were doing. They weren't skilled enough to focus their energies on such stories.

Remember something about the art of writing: **It is the only art form that is not sensual.** You can see the colors and strokes that make a painting, feel a sculpture, and hear music. The manner in which each individual piece in those fields impacts on the senses is different. But every writer uses the same letters on a piece of paper. You have twenty-six letters that combine to form words, which are the building blocks of your sentences and paragraphs. And most of the time you are stuck with the words of the language, although that is not necessarily true for those of you truly enterprising persons. Everyone has the same words, and when I write that word and you write it, that word goes into the senses of the reader in the same way. It's how we weave them together that impacts in the conscious and subconscious mind of the reader that makes all the difference in the world.

A book comes alive in the reader's mind. You use the sole medium of the printed word to get the story from your mind to the reader's. To me, it is the wonder of writing to create something out of nothing. Every book started with just an idea in someone's head. Isn't that a fantastic concept?

Throughout these pages, I speak not only from my personal experience, but from the experience of other authors, agents, readers, teachers and editors I have met and talked to; from reading interviews with very successful writers; and from intense study of the field of writing. I say this because I believe you can and should learn as much as possible from every source you latch on to. Take what you need and leave the rest.

I listed the grim statistics of getting published on the preceding pages. But I tell you one thing that I very firmly believe: If you are willing to put in the effort and the time and become open-minded enough to recognize and understand the realities of the writing and publishing business, you will put yourself far ahead of those who believe that there is some mystical force at work. I have seen numerous cover letters where the prospective author has written something along the lines of "I hope I am lucky enough to be selected for publication." Luck comes to those who put in the sweat and blood and time.

For some strange reason, fledgling novelists seem to think they should be able to bat a 1.000; that their first manuscript should be accepted and their career started. The reality is that even among published authors, the acceptance rate is usually nowhere near the perfect mark.

Screenwriters are often hired on the basis of what is called a 'spec screenplay'. Spec stands for speculation which means they write the screenplay on their own time, without anyone paying for it. Then they send it around, not so much to get *that* screenplay optioned or made, but rather to let people who read it know what their abilities are and perhaps hire them for another project. An unpublished novelist is writing on spec, but also understand that that first novel is rarely the one that is purchased. It is an investment in time to learn the art and craft.

Too often I see writers hold on to their first manuscript too tightly, spending so much time rewriting it, that they could have written two or three new, and better, manuscripts during that time period. In part III of this book, the first thing I tell writers to do after finishing their first manuscript, *before* trying to market it, is start writing the second manuscript. At the Jackson Hole Writer's Conference I was on a panel with Sue Grafton and this was a point she emphasized: too many people were holding on to their first manuscripts and they needed to let go and move on.

Some more words about making a living at writing. I just recently cut out a newspaper article about a writing conference where the distinguished panel was going to discuss "real" writing which the article defined as "writing that springs from within, as opposed to writing to make money." I've run into that sort of thinking quite often. Dean Koontz's book on writing has an entire chapter dealing with this issue. Suffice it to say this: the more money you make writing, the more time you can devote to it, the better writer you become, and ultimately, most importantly, the more people that read your writing.

On the other hand, if you are quite happy to write something of great import only to you or a select group of people, then most certainly do so. Ultimately, *you* are the one that has to be satisfied with what you write. The bottom line, in my opinion, is there does not need to be an "opposed" in the sentence in the above paragraph. It should be an "and".

I take neither side of the genre vs. commercial writing because I don't believe there are two sides. Jean Auel, the author of <u>The Clan Of The Cave Bear</u> series had an interesting comment to make. When her first novel came out it was very well received critically. However, once it became a bestseller she noted that the same critics were now turning against her because she no longer had simply a literary success. It was now a commercial success and those same minds couldn't seem to accept that the two were compatible. I believe the two are compatible and you should approach writing with an open mind.

One of my favorite novels of all time is <u>Lonesome Dove</u>. Is that a western? Would seem to be, wouldn't it? It also sold extremely well and continues to sell. It was made into a TV miniseries. But it also won the Pulitzer Prize. So it's literature right? It's a book, a damn good one. Let's not get too caught up in stereotypes.

In this book I do sometimes make a distinction between genre and literary writing in terms of definition for discussion purposes, particularly when we discuss marketing. It is an arbitrary line and one that you can easily find hundreds of examples that don't fit either, so remember it is just for discussion purposes. I define genre writing as those stories that would be shelved in a specific place in a book store that has a sign above it such as science fiction, romance, fantasy, mystery, thriller, men's adventure, western, etc. I define literary works as those that would not fit in any of those categories and whose focus is primarily on the characters in the story.

However, to muddy up an already unclear picture, look at the top-selling authors in many genre fields. They are such good writers that they could probably write about changing the oil in their car and you'd want to read it. They make their story come alive and the people live and breathe, even if the world they are in is one of mystery or fantasy or science fiction. That is the goal regardless of type of book.

There is an interesting attitude I run into quite often at both writers' workshops and university writing programs. There always seems to be one person who says: "Look at all the crap on the shelves in bookstores. I can't believe that such junk gets published. I certainly can write a better book than that."

My first question would be: "Have you written a manuscript?"

If the answer were yes, my second would be: "Have you sold a manuscript to a publisher?"

I agree that there are some works on the shelves (I'm sure some would include mine in this category) that is "crap." But until I designed and built my own skyscraper, I wouldn't put down the architect who has built one, because I simply don't know what is involved until I do it.

9

Genre fiction *is* difficult to write, contrary to what many say. If it wasn't, a lot of people, to include many of those who put it down, would be doing it and making money. Publishing is not a kind business and very, very, very few people make it. To put together a good mystery or a good thriller is much more difficult than it appears at first glance.

Near the end of this book, I have a section on screenplays, a field I ventured into after seven years of full-time novel writing. I was like many people, watching movies and seeing gaping holes in the plot and going: "My God, how could they have written that?"

And then I started writing screenplays and suddenly I began to understand why movies come out the way they do. And I realized that seemingly simple movies are very difficult to write. Get it out of your head that the people who worked on the movie simply were stupid and didn't see the "holes" that you see. What I suggest doing is finding *why* that hole is there? Why did they have to do it? Because it was a conscious trade-off. If they had fixed *that* hole, what other part of the movie would have fallen apart?

There are places in this world for everyone. This book is for the person who wants to be a published novelist. If you want to take a different path, say getting an MFA and teaching creative writing, then you might disagree with some of what I say in here although I hope not. Please understand that I don't disagree with what you say. I have great respect for those who pursue other paths with different goals. They know and have experienced many things that I have no clue about. They also have knowledge and experience that I can use to become a better writer.

I cut an article out of the Tennessean a few years back written by the book editor for the paper, Robert Wyatt. The title was: <u>Publication is no sign of real merit</u>. His point was basically that getting published, like many other things in life, is as much a result of chance as skill. And he is correct to a certain extent. But, again, I do believe that luck comes to those who increase the odds through hard work and dedication. I guarantee you one thing—you will never get a novel published if you don't write a manuscript and market it. Sounds simple. It isn't.

If you didn't want someone else to read your writing, then I don't think you would be reading these words, and the best way to get someone else to read your writing is to learn how to write as best you can *and* to understand the business end of writing.

How should you use this book? Read it through from start to finish. I had to decide on an order, and I decided to put the writing before the business section, but I could have just as easily, and maybe should have, put the business section first. You *must* understand the business end of writing if you wish to be published.

Also, I make many links between writing your book and marketing it. There is quite a bit of overlap. The first thing you have to lock down when you start your novel is your one sentence original idea. The first sentence of your cover letter when you do your submission is most likely that same original idea. What your editor will use to pitch your manuscript to his or her publisher is your one sentence original idea. What will go on the jacket flap of your novel is your one sentence original idea. It all ties together.

Just this morning I cranked up my old computer (pre-laptop, pre-hard-drive, original, 1984 model, 512K Macintosh) and went searching through my old single-sided 400k disks. I found the original copy of the first manuscript I ever wrote. I pulled up Chapter 1 (I had to reconfigure it to a different program since I hadn't used the old one in years) and read my opening page. I just about died. It was **terrible. Awful. Embarrassing.** But if I had never written that fifteen years ago, I would never have gotten to where I am now. You have to start somewhere.

Writing is an art in that you are communicating your ideas/thoughts/emotions to others. There are two vital components involved, which we will talk about in the following chapters on how to write. The first is the idea or thought (the story). The second is the communication mode (the writing itself or style).

1. INTERNAL CHARACTERISTICS OF A WRITER

If you wanted to become a nuclear engineer or a psychologist, you would go to college and achieve the appropriate major in four years. Then you would specialize and go to graduate school for a number of years. Then you would have a work practicum where you would actually learn your job by doing it. In many cases, during the practicum, you pay for the opportunity to work for someone else. When I was working on my Masters degree in education, I was less than thrilled with the practical aspects of student teaching, whereby I would have to pay tuition to the university so I could go to a local school and teach, something the actual teacher was getting paid for, but that's the way the system worked if I wanted to become certified.

Nevertheless, many people want to be become a published author by sitting down and writing a single manuscript and selling it. In fact, I've run into many who want to pitch their idea, get the publisher to give them a contract and *then* write it. It doesn't work that way. Writing is no different from any other profession. It's a simple rule, but one that every one wants to ignore: the more you write, the better you will become. Practically every author I've ever talked to, or listened to, or read in an interview, says the same thing. I just saw

11

Stephen King on C-Span the other day and he also said it: the most important thing to do to become an author is to **write a lot**.

One professor I listened to said you needed to write a million words before expecting to get published. I'm currently around word five million and still learning so much.

Referring back to where I talked about those who want to make a bundle of money writing; there are also those who pin all their hopes and dreams of being published upon their first manuscript. And when that manuscript isn't published, their writing 'career' is over.

Let's look at the positive side: I mentioned the odds are strongly against getting published. But simply by taking the time and the effort to read this book, you are increasing your odds. By continuing to write beyond your first manuscript, you vastly increase your odds. Many writers gush over the amount of money John Grisham made for <u>The Firm</u> but they forget that <u>A Time To Kill</u> was published years previously to lackluster sales and failed. What is important to note about that was Grisham realized he hadn't done something right and worked hard to change.

From talking with other published writers, I have found it is common that somewhere between manuscript numbers three and six, comes the breakthrough to being published. How many people are willing to do that much work? Not many, which is why not many succeed. On top of that, there is the fact that publishers do not want to make a one-time investment in a writer. When a publisher puts out a book, they are backing that writer's name and normally want to have more than one book in the pipeline. Multiple book contracts are very common; with their inherent advantages and disadvantages which will be discussed in the business section.

Not only is it hard to get published, it is also hard to be successful when you are published. Nine out of ten first novelists fail. I've failed after six novels under one name. I "failed" after two books under another name. Failure comes because of a number of reasons but the sign of it is common—enough books don't sell. I discuss this in the business section.

If you wanted to become a symphony musician, you wouldn't expect to get there the first year after you pick up an instrument. It takes a lot of time and practice and the best practice for a writer is writing. And for novel writing, it's usually writing novels, although there are some very successful novelists who honed their craft in short stories or magazines or newspapers.

Read interviews with people who are successful in the arts and entertainment industries (or pretty much any profession) and you will find a common theme (with a few exceptions of course): a lot of years put in before the big "break" came. I've read of and heard actors and comedians talk about spending decades working in the trenches before they became famous. People seem to think that writers are different and, while in some highly publicized cases they are, most published writers have spent many years slugging away before even their first novel was published. At the time I am reviewing this chapter, the number two, soon to be number one, bestseller on the NY Times list is a first novel. The author received a two million dollar advance. So much for my theory, you say. Yes, except for the fact that that particular author spent *thirty years* in Hollywood writing for shows, honing his craft. I wish him well with his advance and his success; he earned it. Sue Grafton spent years writing for TV before she attempted her first novel. And it took getting to her G book to hit the bestseller list.

Simple perseverance counts for a lot. I think many people with talent lack the drive and fall out of the picture and people with maybe not as much talent but more drive take their place. I've gone through some hard times in my writing career and I expect more in the future. I've gone through times where a "normal" person would have folded up shop and gotten a "real" job. I haven't yet but others with more talent have. What about you?

There is a noted exception to this rule and that is celebrities who get six figure advances for books. I know authors who are incensed over "so and so" who is a famous whatever getting a book deal. The issue there, though, is that most of those people put the time and effort into becoming well known for whatever they are well known for. And the name on a book jacket sells. It's part of the business. Few people are handed success. If someone worked for it in another field and tried to transfer it to the field of writing, then they are taking a risk. There are numerous books by celebrities that have bombed, and also many that have succeeded.

Something else to consider about those big advances—they can also turn into a big failure. If you get a $10,000 advance and fail, no one notices much. If you get a quarter million dollars and don't earn out your advance and fail, you can be sure everyone in the industry takes notice. Hard as it is to believe in this day of 'overnight' successes, but most writers aren't. Most earn their way and pay their dues with many manuscripts and many years of learning and studying.

The 'job' of being a writer is rather interesting if you consider it. It is one where whether you get hired or not totally relies on the product—the manuscript—and not at all on who you are, what you look like, etc. When you send submissions out, you are sending the end result, not the process, and it is judged as such.

Let's get back to where I talked about people in other professions doing a work practicum. Besides writing novels and reading, the other advice I would give would be to attend conferences and workshops. I address this near the end of this book, but it is a worthwhile investment of your time and money to go to a workshop/conference or two.

The other day a local college student interviewed me and she asked me what she could do to help become a writer. I replied with my usual "Write a lot," then thought for a second, looking at this nineteen year old woman. Then I said: "Live a lot. Experience life, because that is what you are eventually going to be writing about."

Think about the lifestyle of an author, the lifestyle you are hoping to achieve. Most people want the end result: a published novel in the bookstore, but they don't pay much attention to the life that produces that end result. A writer's life is one of paradoxes. You have to be interested in people, yet you work in one of the loneliest jobs there is. You need inspiration and passion, yet also possess the self-discipline to trudge through writing 400 pages of a manuscript. In other words you have to have a split personality and be slightly nuts.

I very much suggest studying the lives of writers. Read interviews with authors and see what they say. Go to conferences and talk to them. Listen to them talk about several things: how they became authors, how they live, how they feel about writing, how they write. Many worked very strange jobs before getting published. Almost all struggled and spent many years of suffering before they succeeded. I say suffering in terms of financial or career terms, not in terms of the writing itself. Most writers enjoy writing.

I know I sound somewhat mercenary at times with my constant reference to the business end of writing, but please remember I would not be writing for a living if I didn't get a thrill from the process of literally creating something out of nothing. I was making a heck of a lot better living in my previous career, but I love this job and hope to do it for the rest of my life.

So what do you need? Briefly you should have a large degree of all of the following:

PATIENCE AND SELF-DISCIPLINE It takes me on average about four to six months to produce a finished manuscript. And that's working full time. When writing, I usually work seven days a week, anywhere from eight to fourteen hours a day. It's hard for me to say how many hours a day I work because I am almost always 'working'. If I'm not sitting in front of my computer, I'm in the library researching or watching the news for interesting facts or simply thinking about my story, playing it out in my mind, watching my characters come alive. I have many of my best plot ideas when driving or riding my bike. Sometimes I wake up in the middle of the night with an idea, which is why I have my micro cassette recorder next to my bed ready for instant use. Just this morning while taking a shower I had a breakthrough and reworked a story concept I was pitching to a publisher.

But it *is* 99% perspiration and 1% inspiration. If you write only when excited or motivated then you'll never finish. You have to write even when it's the last thing you want to do. Just put something down. You can always edit it later or throw it out (you'll do a lot of throwing out and it hurts but it's the sign of a mature writer). I eventually average 500 to 550 pages of manuscript to produce 400 good pages in a final draft. To sweat over that many pages and then "lose" them hurts but not as much as getting the manuscript rejected. The longer I've written, the *more* I've become a fan of rewriting and editing. And now, years after I wrote the previous sentence, the more I've become a fan of outlining and doing a lot of work before I write the first sentence of my manuscript. This is a trend among several authors I've talked. Both Terry Brooks and Elizabeth George got back lengthy editorial letters on the first book they sold. They determined then and there to make sure that future manuscripts would not require such rewriting. And they didn't. They learned to know what they were doing before they did it.

Try to give yourself a goal to work for. For several years I wrote a minimum number of pages each day: at first five, then ten. Then I wrote six hours a day. When I say write, I mean I sat at my keyboard for six hours minimum every day. While that doesn't sound like much, it actually translated into a considerable amount of work. That doesn't count the hours I spent on marketing, correspondence, teaching, book signings, working on outlines, etc. etc. I actually used a timer like a stopwatch that I punched into when I started typing and I punched out of when I leave the keyboard, even to just go check the mail. While that may seem extreme to many people, it is what worked for me at the time. Now I have gone back to trying to do a minimum of 40 to 60 pages a week, but even that is flexible. Sometimes more, sometimes less.

The bottom line is that I have developed an inner "writing clock" that works in terms of weeks and months that lets me know how much I have to produce and how quickly. It varies its pace depending on the project at hand and it took years of experience to develop this inner clock. I force myself to put the time and effort in, even when I don't feel like it.

It might sound strange, but the longer I have been doing this for a living, the harder I work. My work habits have gotten better, not worse. I produce more pages of better quality per week now than ever before. While a large degree of that is due to learning to be more efficient, some of it is also due to increasing awareness on my part of the realities of this business and an intense desire to stay in it.

Being your own boss has its inherent share of problems besides the benefits. For a while I figured if someone going to work in a factory has to punch in on a clock, why don't I? This is something that you have to suit to your personality. Some authors use a system of positive reinforcement. For me, keeping my inner writing clock in balance means I can actually then relax and not feel guilty about not being at the keyboard. A big problem about working for yourself is that you sometimes feel that you should always be working (since you always can.) and I need to have a system where I can take some time off and not feel guilty. For the past six years I have not taken what I would call a true vacation yet. I recently went on a road trip but took along my camera and looked at sights for the book I am now writing. I feel that is the price I have to pay to continue to work and survive in this field at the present time. Maybe that will change in the future, but right now it is a price I am willing to pay.

Experiment and find something that works for you in day-to-day writing. Maybe it will only be for one hour every morning before everyone else gets up—keep doing it. You'll be amazed how much you can get done if you stick with it.

Scott Turow wrote <u>Presumed Innocent</u> on the train to and from work in Chicago. So don't let circumstances stand in your way.

All the thinking, talking, going to writer's conferences, classes, etc. are not going to do you any good if you don't do one basic thing: WRITE.

For many, finding undistracted time may be their greatest challenge to being able to writing. The demands of job, family, school, whatever, can be overwhelming. And it is not so much that you can't find the time, it's that you can't find quality time. Trying to write after working ten hours at a very mentally demanding job may be next to impossible to do, but some people manage to do it.

You have to understand yourself and how you function. How many hours in the day do you have of 'good' mental time? When your brain is working at its peak? Because even on 'bad' writing days, your mind has to be working at its peak performance.

Unfortunately, there is no apprenticeship system in writing; no way you can make a living at it, while at the same time learn the craft. The "break point" where you can be published and get into the business is very high and is why most people fail. There are some who do an apprenticeship writing for magazines or newspapers. There are some genres where this works particularly well, such as the crime reporter who ends up writing mysteries, but in most cases I know of, such people became reporters because that's what they wanted to do, not as a stepping-stone to becoming a novelist.

When I taught martial arts, I always found that the majority of the new students quit right after the first month. They came in and wanted to become Bruce Lee rolled into Chuck Norris all within a couple of weeks. When they realized it would take years of boring, repetitive, very hard work, the majority gave up. It doesn't take any special skill to become a black belt; just a lot of time and effort to develop the special skills. The same is true of writing. If you are willing to do the work, you will put yourself ahead of the pack. You must have a long-term perspective on it. When I discuss the publishing business in the latter part of this book, I use one word to describe it: SLOW. Therefore, that requires that you, the writer, have patience.

I think a hard part of being a writer is also knowing what exactly 'work' is. For me it was hard to accept that kicking back and reading a novel was work and I wasn't being a slacker. Sitting in a coffee shop and talking with someone is work. Living is work for a writer in that you can only write what you know, so therefore experience is a key part of the creative process.

THE ABILITY TO ORGANIZE As those pages pile up, you'll find yourself weeks, months, maybe years away from having written that opening chapter. That's where your organizing skills come in. You have to keep track of your characters, your locales, and the action, to make sure it all fits. I use a spreadsheet that I call a story grid when I write to keep track of all that. (Appendix 5). This spreadsheet is not an outline, but rather something I fill in as I write, to help me keep track of what has been done. It helps when you need to go back and look up a specific part or change something.

From left to right, the story grid has:

1. The chapter number.
2. The start page number for that chapter.
3. The end page number for that chapter.
4. The date the action takes place on.
5. The local time.
6. The Zulu or Greenwich Mean Time equivalent of the local time—this is to keep my story in proper time sequence order as it goes to various spots around the world in different time zones.
7. The location of the action.
8. A brief description of the action so I can easily find it.

I also keep numerous indexed binders with all my research material handy. I spend a considerable amount of time organizing my research material so I can find what I'm looking for. Details can drive a story, and the more details you have accessible in terms of research, the more options you have in your plot.

When I discuss how to write later, you will see where I refer to looping and tightening your subplots. The ability to organize is extremely important in keeping your story tight and fast moving.

It is an interesting that something which takes me a year to produce can be "consumed" in less than a few hours. I don't even remember some of the things I wrote in my first few manuscripts, things that my readers remember very well. Since I have a series, I need to be very conscious of what I've done so far and organization is critical in doing this.

AN ACTIVE IMAGINATION A novel is a living, active world you invent. Imagination is essential.

In some ways a novel is like a chess game in that you have to be able to think half-a-dozen to a dozen steps ahead for all of your pieces (characters) while at the same time considering what the other guy might be doing (the limitations of your scenario and the mode/perspective chosen to present the story). You have to pick the successful moves and the correct strategic direction given a very large number of variables. But you are also limited by the personality of the characters you've invented—they have to act within the 'character' you have given them, much like each chess piece is capable of only a certain type of move. It is your imagination that allows you to thread the proper path. And in most cases, there are numerous "all right" paths, but one stands out above the others as the "best" path and finding the "best" one is critical.

THE MIND Yeah, you do sort of need one to be a writer, contrary to some people's opinion that know me. I'd like to say a little bit more about the mind for two reasons: one is that ultimately it is the primary tool you use when writing. Second, to write good characters, you need to understand the mind because it is the driving force behind your characters' actions.

As a "machine" the brain is very inefficient. Physiological psychologists estimate that we use less than ten percent of our brain's capabilities. (Rent the Albert Brooks movie Defending Your Life and see how he uses this in his story.) In many ways, that is what makes writing fiction so hard and draining: you are trying to expand the portion of your mind that you normally use in order to be able to touch the portion that most other people use. A little bit of understanding of that other 90 or so percent is useful. It is commonly called the subconscious and plays a very large role in determining our character (key buzz word). Whether you agree with people such as Freud and Jung, it is useful to know a little bit about their theories. A fully rounded character has a complete brain and while they may only consciously be using ten percent, that other ninety percent affects their actions.

As a writer you will start having dreams about your story and your characters. That is your mind working even when you consciously aren't. You will also run into "writer's block" which I believe, when real, is your subconscious telling you to hold until you realize in your conscious mind something important with regard to the story. This is where the "write what you feel" school of creative writing comes in. I believe what they are focusing on is this very thing: the power of the subconscious (90% vs. 10%). It is more than feeling though; it is a large part of your brain and the better you can get in touch with it and use it, the better your writing will be.

This is something that is hard to discuss—writing by feel. People often ask about getting a book doctor or editor to read their work, but I think a writer is the best editor of their own work if they can be objective with it. Everything that an editor or agent has pointed out that might be flawed about a manuscript I sent, I 'knew' in my gut wasn't quite right before I sent it out. That's not to say other readers can't help you, but a novel is ultimately the author's responsibility.

There are many experiences a writer should have in order to understand both their own mind and the minds of other people. You have to remember that you are not the template for the rest of humanity. Hard as it may be for some to believe, there are differences between people.

I've sometimes said the best thing about a writers' group is not necessarily the critiquing or networking, but rather watching the different 'characters' in the group and trying to figure out what is motivating them to act the way they do.

If you don't understand yourself both mentally and emotionally, you might have a hard time understanding others. Therapy can be a very useful tool for a writer to dig into their own mind to figure out where they are coming from.

After listening to many authors speak of their creative processes I realize they are talking on two levels. There's what they are saying and there is what they are meaning. The saying part often varies, but they almost always mean the same thing. For example, there is the issue of outlining. I know writers who swear by outlining and others who say they don't outline at all, they just write. However, I've also found those who don't outline tend to do a lot of rewriting, thus the first draft of their manuscript might be considered a very detailed outline. Those writers who do a lot of outlining tend to not want to do much rewriting. But in the final analysis, although the two methods seem very different, they are actually the same in creative essence.

Also remember that there are two sides to the brain. The right side is your creative part while the left is more analytical and logical—this is where the editor part of you resides. Sometimes you have to silence that editor while creating or else nothing will get done.

CONTENTMENT & DESIRE I started this book by saying wanting to make a million dollars isn't the best motivation to write a novel. But you do need some tangible reasons. In a perfect world I suppose we could accomplish all the things we would like without having any external stimulus. But this isn't a perfect world. I find putting my back against the wall helps. I wrote my first two novels living in Korea. I studied and taught martial arts six hours a day and went nuts the rest of the time. I wrote to keep my sanity. Then after getting published, I wrote to make money to live on. I had job offers where I could be financially secure, but I didn't take them. I wrote, and continue to write, because I have to both internally and externally.

No one wants to talk about money. I remember watching the movie <u>White Palace</u>. In it the character Susan Sarandon plays is having a relationship with a younger man and she goes with him to his apartment for the first time. She's very impressed with it and asks him how much he pays a month. He's non-plussed and hems and haws. She looks at him and says something to the effect of: "We can sleep together and make love, but you won't tell me how much you pay for your apartment?" (I think her language wasn't as mild, though.) That comment struck me because it's so true of our society. Talking about money is more taboo it seems than talking about sex. I find this particularly interesting when we consider the academic side of writing. I was sitting in a writer's group that I helped form and we had invited a professor who edited the local university's literary publication to talk to us about the magazine. He started out by making the comment that: "If you think you can make a living writing, forget about it."

Well, you can make money writing. I've done it now for almost fifteen years. I've heard some authors and freelancers say never give away anything you've written for free, even if just to see it in print, and I tend to agree. If someone isn't willing to pay for it, then work harder to make it good enough so someone will. Quite honestly, publishers will not be impressed with your credentials of getting published in publications that they never really heard of and didn't pay you anything other than to give you three free copies. I'm not saying absolutely don't do that, but if you do, realize it is only a step and you need to move beyond. Don't get stuck there. This is especially true these days with the growth of the Internet. There's plenty of places you can 'post' your writing, but that hasn't yet replaced getting published (I discuss e-books near the end of this book in Chapter 37).

I am not saying write simply for the money, but if you don't factor money into the writing equation somewhere, and take it as a serious factor, you will fail, because eventually you will have to get a "real" job. Money cannot only be a source of motivation, but it is the basis for making a living at writing, which is very hard to do. It's a vicious equation: to become a better writer, you must write—to write you must have time to write—to have time to write it most certainly helps to make some money at it.

OK, now that I've gotten the mercenary side of the business out of the way, go back to Pearl Buck's quote: the root of your desire must be a passion to tell a story. Some people tend to look down upon telling a story in a format such as science fiction or mystery or action/adventure. But if that's your passion and your story, then tell it and don't worry what anyone thinks. I think there is one bottom line on how good a writer is: how many people read his/her book. That's called "commercial" writing and sneered at in certain quarters, but if no one wants to read what a person writes then maybe he or she just isn't writing that well. Think about it.

I sat on a panel at a conference and they asked each of us what we liked and disliked about writing for a living. The answers were interesting. I think an author needs the paradoxical combination of being able to be content and discontent at the same time. Because publishing is such a slow business and positive feedback so rare, you have to be reasonably content for long periods of time by yourself. At the same time you have to motivate yourself to write the manuscript, to do all the dirty work that needs to be done, to pursue long-range goals.

SETTING OBJECTIVES I've talked about what you need. Now let me mention something we could all do without: procrastination. If you're like me, when you were in school, that term paper never really needed to be done until the night before it was due. I remember at West Point the radio station would have a contest the night before the big Social Sciences paper was due. They would have call-ins with the award going to the person who could claim they were starting their paper the latest.

In fact, for me, the one time I did a paper early—in fact so early that I was able to get feedback without a grade—the instructor gave me some basic pointers which I incorporated, then turned in the paper—again early, this time for a grade. I got an F. So much for positive reinforcement.

My main theme is that to become a writer you must write. You can be the greatest marketing specialist in the world, but if you don't have a product to market, you're not going to get published. I am very big on understanding the business aspects of publishing and marketing your work correctly, but I have seen people (including myself at times) forget one very important rule: you have to have a good product. Putting ninety percent of your effort into trying to sell your work when it is simply not good enough, is a waste of time. Put that effort into writing another manuscript that is good enough.

The best way I've found to overcome procrastination is to set objectives, both short and long range. I set a daily objective of a minimum number of pages to write or a certain number of hours a day at the keyboard. If I'm researching, I give myself a goal of perhaps a book a night to be looked through and summarized.

I also set long-term objectives. I print out a calendar about once a week with the next twelve months on it. I block out every known appointment, such as book signings and classes to teach. I then break it down by writing projects. I block out weeks and months to write or outline or edit a certain book. I set weekly writing goals (which break down into my daily goals). I post that long-term calendar on the left side of the board, which is on an easel in front of my desk. The right side of the board is a dry erase board. On that I list everything I have to do that day (to include hours of writing, phone calls to be made, things to be mailed, etc., etc.,). As I accomplish each, I wipe them off the board. At the end of the day, if something is left up there, not only have I not accomplished what I should have, it's still up there for the next day. Since I am my own boss, it is very easy to slip up, but with my time objectives sitting there on my bulletin board, less than four feet from my nose, it becomes a little harder.

If you feel such cold objectives interfere with your creativity, you might be right. But a novel is a hell of a long way to go simply burning the fuel of passion. One common fault that many suffer from is starting a novel, getting about a quarter of the way in, then dropping it to move on to something "better", and starting a new novel. I know in everything I've worked on, about a hundred and fifty pages in, my mind has already started to move on to a new project and I'm somewhat bored with what I am working on. That's where discipline and a schedule come in. If my next project isn't due to start for three more months, then I have to work those three months on my present project in order to earn the right to start the new one.

WRITER'S BLOCK I put this section right after procrastination because you have to decide whether your creative juices have run dry or you are committing the sin of procrastination. On the whole, I have to honestly say most often when I grind to a halt, I am doing the latter.

Ways to overcome the "block":

1. Have a good outline. Since you've already poured a lot of creativity into your outline, you can usually keep going.

2. As the commercial says: Just do it. Just write. It might be awful but at least it's something other than a blank page.

3. Work on something else for a while. Looking up at my work board, right now I have:

   a. One manuscript on the market at a publisher.
   b. One partial manuscript/concept on the market at four different publishers.
   c. One partial manuscript/concept at an agent, looking for representation.
   d. A screenplay getting read by a producer for rewrite.
   e. Two concepts for third books to follow two two-book contracts with major publishers that need to be outlined in time for a new contract.
   f. Two new ideas that I'm researching and beginning to outline.
   g. Two manuscripts getting edited at publishing houses and due back in the next month for more work.

As you can tell, I have so much else going on that I value the time I can spend focused on simply writing. But if I do get a block, I have plenty of other things to work on, including this book. It has been written over a fifteen-year span now going from about twenty manuscript pages on the first draft to over three hundred and fifty.

4. If you are sure that you need to pause to rethink where your novel is heading, give what you do have to someone to read to get some feedback. Talk to other people. Clear you head. Free associate. Turn everything in your novel around and look at it from another perspective. Do some more research. Scream. Pound your forehead into your keyboard. Then write.

<u>OPEN-MINDEDNESS</u> You could also call this "willingness to change." This is not only important when starting out, but it is perhaps even more important after first getting published. You should be willing to learn from any source to improve your writing.

Before you can be willing to change though, you have to be willing to say the three hardest words in the human language for most people: "I was wrong." This should be followed with: "Maybe I'm not doing this the best possible way. Maybe I can learn from someone else."

One thing I see too much of is writers who want validation instead of help. They want to be told how great their manuscript is and have a publisher put the check in the mail. They don't want to hear what's wrong and what more work needs to be done. I find this very strange in the environment of conferences and classes, where the entire purpose is not validation but to become better writers.

After three books published, I took some graduate literature courses at the local college. It was a very worthwhile experience and expanded my horizons. In fact, the longer I write, the more I appreciate the literary side of the house. I think many genre writers get too caught up in the "formula" of their genre and trap themselves, becoming unable to write anything different. In the same manner, if you have a background in literature, don't turn your nose up at information that seems too "common" or genre oriented.

I read a book on screenplays and learned some things about writing that I can incorporate not only into my work on screenplays, but also my novels. I found the way a screenplay is broken down interesting and I use it later in this book to help you get the big picture on how a novel works.

I recently watched the visiting writer at a local college come into our writer's group to do a reading. She walked in, did her reading, took her applause, and then walked out. I guess she was simply too good of a writer to waste her time listening to the other people in the group read or discuss writing. She didn't bother to find out whom she had just read to and because of that she lost the opportunity to network with several published authors who might have helped *her* in her attempts to publish her next novel.

That's another lesson I've learned—you never know who you're dealing with so be courteous and open to all you meet. No matter what your mind-set, listen to others and what they have to say about writing even if you disagree with them. You might find yourself agreeing a year or two later. In this book, you might find me appearing to be somewhat schizophrenic, taking several different perspectives, some of them seemingly opposed to each other, but remember, I began writing this in 1990 and have been adding to it ever since, so in these pages you see some of my own evolution as a writer. I do have to say that for mainly ego reasons, I was very touchy when first starting out at what I perceived to be "snubs" from the literary community toward genre writing. Now I see that attitude to be naive and wrong. You have to decide what *you* want to do and pursue it, regardless of what others say or believe. Another thing I have learned, which I discuss in the chapter on reviews (30), is that it is guaranteed that someone, somewhere, will not like what you've written after you get published. It's also guaranteed that some of those people feel a burning desire to inform you of those dislikes.

The biggest change I have made over the years is to change my perspective on plotting and characters. I will discuss this in detail further in this book but for my first dozen manuscripts or so I believed that the plot drove the story. Now I try to let the characters drive the story. In order to make that change, though, I had to admit that what I was doing was not the best way to work and be willing to look at points of view diametrically opposed to my own

You can't ever get better if you don't first admit you're not doing it the best possible way. When I taught a writing correspondence course, I would have to say that 80-90% of the students were unwilling to change anything based on the feedback I was giving them. The first question this raises is why they even took the course in the first place? The answer I mentioned above—they wanted validation. The few who did change, who did the hard work and reworked their material, and put the time into thinking about the questions I would pose—they made great strides as writers.

This open-mindedness also comes into play in the business side of the house. Too often, new writers want to do things *their* way and expect editors, agents—the entire publishing community—to change and see everything the same way as they do. Frankly, that isn't going to happen. There are many things wrong in the business, but there are also many things right. And just because *you* might not see the reason why certain things are the way they are, that doesn't make them wrong. I have had some very simple lessons beat into my head by my agent or editors that seem so basic now, but I just didn't get when I started out.

Remember, also, that change takes stages. First one has to accept that there is a need for change. Then you have to intellectually accept the change, which isn't total acceptance. After a while of living with the mental acceptance, you will gradually have emotional acceptance of the change, which is total acceptance. That is why it takes years and years to change, if one ever does.

I also constantly have to reinforce to writers the fact that the reader does not know what the writer knows. That a writer must be able to get out of their own head and into the head of a reader who is starting from page one.

If you start your manuscript with fifty pages of expository material, knowing that your great hook is on page 51, realize one thing—the reader doesn't know the great hook is on page 51 and very few will both to wade through that much background information without knowing *why* it is important or that the hook is coming.

THE WRITING ROUTINE It seems like people always want to know what a writer's "routine" is. I always get that question when I teach and I always have a hard time answering it. I have the same sort of answer when people ask about some of the material in the next chapter: I will use and do whatever it takes to get a manuscript done. If I have to outline on an easel pad, I do it. If I have to write in chalk on the side of an apartment building, I'll do it. If I have to call the homicide squad to ask a stupid question, I'll try to get someone else to do it, and when they won't, do it myself.

Each individual has to discover what works, but the operative word in this sentence is *work*. Don't lock yourself in—find what works, and if it stops working, find something else.

One interesting thing I have found is that the entire creative process has many paths but they all seem to parallel each other. I listened to a panel with Terry Brooks, Elizabeth George, Bryce Courtenay and Dan Millman one time as each talked about their own unique process of writing a novel. And on the surface it appeared that all were very different in their approach, but underlying what they were saying, I could see that they all did essentially the same things, just differently. Confusing? For example, Terry Brooks is a big fan of outlining and hates rewriting. But Bryce Courtenay doesn't outline, he just starts writing and then spends a lot of time rewriting. But in essence, Bryce Courtenay's first draft of the manuscript is equal to Terry Brooks polished outline. The same thought processes and amount of work go into it.

PASSION: This is what *you* feel about what you are writing about. I talk about intent a little further on—what you want the reader to feel from the book. You also have to consider how *you* feel about what you are writing, because consciously or subconsciously, it will come through in your writing.

Your passion could be to tell an interesting and entertaining story. It could be to write a novel about what love means to you. Sometimes when I am trying to get a writer to get back to their original idea, I ask them what is most important about their book to them? What do they feel the most about? This is the core of the book.

I refer to this throughout this book, but one thing I believe is that if you are a writer, no one can stop you from writing.

This brings up the difficult subject of rewriting and changing. I've seen writers totally change their manuscript based on the off-hand comment of an editor/agent/writing instructor. Sometimes the change is for the better, but sometimes it tears the guts out of the book. I think a writer has to be true to himself or herself first. But the writer also must be objective enough to get out of their own head and see if what they have written works. To have these two capabilities reside inside of one person is a paradox and why it is difficult for most people to do this successfully.

2. THINGS YOU MIGHT NEED.

Like any other profession, there are tools the writer uses. Here are some you need to consider:

A computer/word processor. Tolstoy's wife copied six drafts of <u>War And Peace</u> in freehand for him as he wrote it. Since most of us aren't as lucky to have such an understanding spouse/friend, a word processor is almost indispensable. My hat is off to those legions of writers who produced their works before the day of electronic 'cut' and 'paste'. The prices have come down considerably over the last several years. I recently bought a computer with hard drive that cost less than half of what the same make computer (with no hard drive) cost me eight years ago. You don't need anything fancy, just something that will work and crunch words.

(Note: If you can't afford one or it just isn't practical, in many places you can get access to a computer at a local university or library.)

If you are going to get a computer, I suggest getting a laptop. They work the exact same way as a regular desktop, but they give you much more flexibility. You can take it to the library to do research; you can take it on trips, in to the job, or work while you commute. I just purchased an adapter for my laptop that plugs into the cigarette lighter in my car, which allows me to charge my battery while on the road which increases my working capability. I haven't yet learned the trick of writing while driving and am not sure

I will attempt that feat. But I have been known to tap out some thoughts and ideas at rest areas.

I used to do quite a few "book signings" at military post exchanges throughout the country. This consisted of sitting in front of the PX for twelve hours at a time trying to sell my books. I spent a lot of that time at the keyboard of my laptop, tackling two jobs at the same time. I carry an extension cord as part of my standard equipment in my briefcase so that I can plug in.

The bottom line is that you need a word processor. There are what I would call "upgraded" typewriters on the market now that do that function without the expense of a computer. Those are fine. Basically the machine you use should have the ability to store your words and allow you to rework them through editing and cutting and pasting electronically. In fact, most computers nowadays are much more powerful than what you need, capable of making phone calls, balancing your household budget, finding you a life partner on the Internet, doing the laundry and a whole list of other tasks— and all you need is something with a keyboard that will allow you to save what you write.

Always, always, always, and always, back up your work. And do it often. Nothing is more agonizing than to lose pages you have just written because of a mechanical malfunction or a power loss. I was in an interesting position writing my first couple of manuscripts in Korea. The power there would cut out at the strangest times and I learned to hit the keys for save almost automatically at the end of pretty much every paragraph. An interesting aspect of that is that when you rewrite immediately what you've lost, it is always somewhat different.

I keep the latest copy of what I'm writing on my hard drive and back it up on disk every day. Every week I back up the back up onto another disk, which I leave in my car. You never know, my home may catch on fire and the computer and home back up disk be destroyed. Paranoid? Slightly, but I know there's someone out there who lost everything when they thought it was backed up.

Can't I simply write on legal paper with a pencil? Someone might ask. Certainly. If that's the way you write best. I just read an interview with Joyce Carol Oates and she does her first draft with pen and paper. I've heard that some authors dictate their stories onto a micro cassette recorder and then transcribe it. Whatever works best for you. I'm just suggesting a word processor as the easiest way for most people. I met someone at a writer's conference who wrote his manuscripts out in longhand and then gave them to a typist to do up. He bemoaned the fact that he couldn't afford to buy a computer. I had to point out to him that the amount of money he paid the typist for one manuscript would go halfway to the purchase price of a computer.

Computers have advanced quicker than I have. I remember having to save each chapter as a separate document because that was all my computer could handle. Made it very difficult when editing and printing. Now I can save an entire manuscript as one document, which certainly makes things easier. I can even open two manuscripts at the same time on a 17" monitor and compare them side-by-side.

A printer. Spend the extra money for a laserwriter or inkjet printer. You need letter quality. Many publishers won't even look at dot matrix. If you've ever tried reading a manuscript printed on dot matrix you'll understand why. Laser printers used to be expensive when they first came out. My first one cost more than my computer. The cartridges are also expensive, but ultimately cost less per page than buying ribbons for a dot matrix. Also, you should recharge laser cartridges, which saves you quite a bit of money over buying new ones and also is good for the environment. I've recharged my own on occasion but found it to be quite a messy process, involving much inhaling of toner, which I don't believe, was particularly good for my personal environment. There are companies that do it, and, although for the work involved they charge quite a bit, it's still cheaper than a new one.

I just upgraded for the third time to a multi-function machine and find it useful in not only laser printing but getting paper faxes which can become important when you start dealing with changes to a manuscript.

On my first manuscript, written in Korea, I couldn't find ribbons for my original dot matrix ImageWriter printer anywhere (see- I was breaking one of my own suggestions there. But how do you think I learned that lesson reference dot matrix?). I went everywhere, even visiting dark alleys with my Taekwondo Master where he'd talk to shady characters in the black market trying to track down the elusive item but to no avail. I ended up buying ink and a pad and reinking my cartridges by hand, using a pencil to turn the ribbon and pressing it down onto the pad. It took a long time and my hands were sore for days but it worked.

In the same manner, the keyboard of my computer broke down while I was in Korea and again I was left without being able to get a replacement or getting it repaired. The "x" and "c" keys wouldn't work. I think the little squirrels that carried the x and c nuts from the keyboard to the do-hickey in the big brain of the computer were on strike or had run off with native Korean squirrels—but anywho—So what I did was electronically cut out the letters "cCx" from an old document and stored them in that grouping. Then any time I had to use any of those three letters, I would hit the two key command for paste. If I wanted a "c" I would then backspace twice and continue on. I got to be almost as fast getting a pasted "c" on screen as if the key actually worked. Unfortunately, I didn't have a capital X anywhere in any of my old documents so I avoided them as much as possible (not hard to do) and when I absolutely had to use one, I enlarged the font size of the small X until it looked like a capital X.

I tell these stories to remind you to never let equipment stand in the way of your writing. Lincoln once wrote a pretty nice piece of prose on the back of an envelope on the way to a place called Gettysburg. Of course—as we will discuss in the second half of this book—if he had tried submitting it in that format to a major New York publisher or agent he wouldn't have made it off the slush pile. Well, actually, Lincoln, as President, would have. You and I wouldn't have.

<u>A place to write</u>. This is very individualistic. I like quiet most of the time. You will also need plenty of room to lay out pages and research along with a bulletin board to keep that list of characters and key information posted where you can constantly refer to it.

My work area has expanded over the years. Currently I have a large wrap-around desk with over nine feet of length, a large four space file cabinet, two window sills full of books, five steel shelves holding various materials, two ceiling high bookcases, several vertical files, two cork bulletin boards, a dry-erase board, etc. etc. The bottom line is that I need plenty of area and I like to keep my work as organized as possible.

Some people like to grab pencil and notepad and curl up in bed. Others climb a mountain and like to write on the peak. Again, whatever works best and is within your realm of possibilities. I'm writing this paragraph sitting behind two card tables at a book signing I'm doing at the main mall post exchange at Fort Rucker, Alabama. As you can tell, I don't exactly have a line of people waiting to buy books, but I'm using the time to my advantage and not worrying that I'm not sitting at home behind my desk.

<u>THE FOLLOWING ARE TOOLS THAT MIGHT HELP YOU IN YOUR DAY-TO-DAY WRITING:</u>

<u>A master character list</u> with descriptions and history of each person in your book. Every time you use a name, write it down and give a brief description, even if you think it is a character you will never use again in the manuscript. I don't know how many times I've had to go searching back, looking for the name of that minor character that I used somewhere in the first hundred pages and who suddenly, unexpectedly, reappears in chapter 23. It helps

considerably to have this character work done *prior* to starting the novel—more on this in the chapter on characters (10).

I've also used the same name for different characters in the course of a manuscript, which is another good reason to keep track.

In a similar way, write down any 'fact' you make up or use so you can keep track of it.

<u>Maps of locales</u>. If you can't stay oriented, your reader can't either. When I read <u>Lonesome Dove</u>, I had my atlas at my side and followed the herd from the Mexico-Texas border all the way up north to Montana. As an author, you have to do the same thing. I own—let's see as I look about—at least eight different maps/atlases within handy reach, including:

-The Rand McNally Universal World Atlas
-The Times Atlas of World History
-The Universal World Atlas
-Rand McNally Road Atlas of the US
-Rand McNally Road Atlas of Europe
-The Atlas of Earth Mysteries
-The Atlas of the Second World War
-The West Point Atlas of American Wars
-A Michelin map of "Africa: Central and South; Madagascar." (This is specific for a certain book I'm currently working on)
-A Xeroxed copy of a geographic map of a section of the Rocky Mountains. (again for a specific project).

I just bought a $200 atlas at my local bookstore because I have found maps to be critical to my stories. I always end up having to look up very strange and rare places. Know where Ngorongoro Crater is? I'm using it in my next book and I didn't know where it was either until I tracked it down in an atlas.

Not only do these atlases and maps give me locales, they give histories and facts about the locales that often become essential to the story. When I get down and dirty in some action scenes I use topographic maps to give me a feel for terrain. Maps are also useful in determining distances—remember people do take time to travel—unless of course you're writing science fiction in which case—well, make sure your rules work and remain consistent within the covers of the book when your spaceship hits warp drive.

There are certain genres where maps are very important. If you've ever read <u>The Lord of the Rings</u> you know where the Shire is in relation to Mordor. And if you write historical fiction people might want to know what the political boundaries of the time were.

Also, and I shudder to mention this, there are people who don't exactly know where, let's say, Madagascar, is.

When I was in Special Forces before we went to another country we did what we called an "area study". We spent time learning everything we could about the place: topography, weather, customs, languages, religions, etc. etc. As a writer I do the same thing when I write about someplace.

Diagrams of important places- i.e. houses, the rooms, etc. Again, to keep you oriented. If you can't stay oriented, your reader certainly won't be able to. If your main character turns left into the bedroom for the first 15 chapters and you make a mistake and have her turning right in chapter 16, there is no doubt but that it will be noticed. One thing about a book—the reader can always turn back and check your information.

A dictionary. And yes, I have seen cover letters with words misspelled. One thing I have learned over the last several years is that although I may think I know what a word means, occasionally I am wrong. Sometimes it pays to look it up and know exactly what you are saying.

A friend of mine walked out to her sporty convertible outside a store and found a note stuck on her windshield. Some guy who had been eyeing her in the store had left it. She opened it up and read:

"Let's meat." and then listed his phone number.

Needless to say they didn't meat. Spelling is important.

Story grid (Appendix 5). This keeps you oriented and allows you to go back and find certain passages quicker than having to reread the entire manuscript. For the type of stories I write, it is extremely important to be able to keep track of location, time, characters and action.

Take a look at the Appendix. From left to right across the top I have the chapter, the starting page number, the ending page number, the date and day of the week (which can be quite important.), the location of the action, the local time, the Zulu time, and a brief description of what happens.

Zulu time is Greenwich Mean Time. Remember that while it noon in Washington it is nighttime in Tokyo and you can't fly between the two in 30 minutes (unless you're writing science fiction, of course).

Different time zones can become critical to some types of stories. Quick quiz: What is the only place on Earth that has no time zone?

Answer: Antarctica.

Quiz: What place on Earth is on a half hour time zone?

Answer: Central Australia.

When I deployed overseas in Special Forces we wore two watches, one on each wrist. One had the local time wherever we were and the other was set to Zulu time. The latter was the time we used to coordinate all messages, resupplies, operations, etc. with higher headquarters, which was usually in a different time zone than we were.

I know this story grid doesn't seem like the most artistic thing in the world, but I find it very important. While writing is a creative task, I find writing a novel also requires quite a bit of organizational ability and sometimes it is difficult to find the two traits in the same person. Once you start your story—and I will go into this in more detail later on—the story takes on a life of its own and in a paradoxical manner, your creativity is limited by your creation growing on its own.

The story grid is not an outline. It is filled in as the manuscript is written to allow me to keep track of what I've already done. I find it to be particularly helpful when rewriting. As you will see when we get to subplots, when you change one aspect of a novel, it tends to change things in other places. It's easier to realize and find these other places using the story grid.

Summaries of important information. I summarize research articles and books, writing the important information (along with source and page numbers.) down in bullets on one page that I can quickly scan. Sometimes when my story stalls out, I look through the "bullet" pages of information and am reminded of some piece of information that allows me to rejuvenate the story line. Remember that class on research that you had in school so many years ago? The same applies to writing fiction.

I keep saying the details drive a story, and the more information you have, the more details you have. Large sections of some of my books are based on facts that readers think are fiction.

Newspaper/magazine articles. I can take any newspaper and come up with two or three book ideas from the front page. Newspapers and magazines can give you great background information. What I particularly like about articles is that they do a lot of the research for you, summarizing information. I index excerpts and place them in three ring binders for handy reference. It might be very fresh in your mind today when you read that article but five months from now when you're in the middle of writing chapter 27 you'll be lucky if you can even remember reading the article, never mind what was in it—writing a novel is a <u>long</u> process.

Videotapes. When I was writing about Ayers Rock in Australia (<u>The Rock</u>, Dell paperback 1995) I was in the position of writing about a place I'd never been to. I did not have the funds or the time to fly to Australia to research an idea that I had not sold, so I did the next best thing. I rented travel videos and toured the country via my TV. I was able to sit at my desk and describe scenes as I watched them.

Of course I didn't have the actual feel of the place, but I could gain some of that by researching travel accounts of people who *had* been there. Ask around—you'd be amazed at the people in your neighborhood who've gone to the strangest places or have had the weirdest experiences.

In the same manner, I just watched a video on the search for Atlantis and was able to see some of the potential locales for another one of my manuscripts. You can learn about firearms, medical procedures, bungee jumping, hang gliding, etc. etc. all from videos. Naturally it is best to actually go to the locales and do the action yourself so you can write about it validly, but when that isn't possible, this can be the next best thing.

The Discovery Channel constantly amazes me. Often I have it on while I am working and I always keep a blank tape handy to pop in when something interesting comes on. It's kind of neat to be writing a book that has the Great Pyramid in it, and while writing, a two hour special on the Great Pyramid comes on TV. In the same manner, if you want to know about life on board an aircraft carrier, paddling up the Amazon, etc., sooner or later, it comes on TV.

In fact, videos can give you information that you can't get any other way. I wrote a manuscript that had the Golden Gate Bridge figuring prominently in the story. I bought a video and the making of the bridge and was able to see things that there was no other way to see.

Xeroxed pages from encyclopedias or other reference sources. Sometimes you might need to get technical and it helps if you have the information handy.

An indexed binder with most of the above information in it so you can find it when needed. Having stacks of information that aren't organized does you little good.

Access to a copying machine. At a nickel a page, times 400 pages in a manuscript, it can get quite expensive making copies of your work. You can also become a great irritant to a friend who gives you access to their copier—another advantage of laser printers is that I can print out multiple copies of manuscripts without having to go to a copying machine, usually for about the same amount of money.

Stationery? I sat in on a class on freelance magazine writing and the instructor insisted that everyone, even brand new writers, go out and order up stationery with the word "Writer" somewhere on it to impress editors they submitted their work to that they were professional. While that may be true for freelancing articles, it is not so for the novel market. If you have no publishing credentials, getting a fancy letterhead with your name on it and the word writer or author somewhere is not particularly helpful and in some cases that I've seen, looks rather silly. I used to use "Member of the Author's Guild" on my letterhead for one reason: You can't be a member of the Guild until you've been published, which means something to the person looking at my correspondence. Then I used "Author. Member of the Special Forces Association," since I parted ways with the Guild. Now I just have my name, address and phone number and my logo.

In brief, I suggest not worrying about stationery until writing truly is your business.

A micro cassette recorder can be helpful to put thoughts down when driving or you're in a position where you can't write. I also place mine by the side of my bed at night and when I wake at three in the morning with that brilliant idea, I mutter it into the recorder and play it back in the morning when my cognitive functioning is somewhat better.

I occasionally use a **large easel pad** when I work. I put my outline on it and fill it in as I write. The large page allows me to put quite a bit more down than a regular notepad. I use this because I am visually oriented when I think of a story. I can scrawl notes all over the large space and refer back to it more easily than if I had twenty smaller sheets of 8.5" by 11" paper.

At the present moment, the easel pad is flat on my desk, with the outline of the end of a book scrawled across in it in numerous notes along with various reminders of editing to be done and phone numbers from calls I received while I was working.

A lot of books. This sounds superfluous, but to be a good writer you have to be well read. Not only that, but as you will see when we get to the research chapter, often other fiction novels can be good sources for not only facts, but techniques of writing that you will find helpful. Whatever problem you run into, the odds are some writer in the past ran into the same problem—how did they solve it? Then, being the brilliant person you are, you have to figure out a better way.

3. WHAT TO WRITE?

Mark Twain said, "Write what you know." I would add four things to that:
1. I might rephrase it to say: "Write what you know *and feel something about.*"
2. You will most likely write something in the same area you like to read in.

3. Understand that some of what you know and feel something about, other people might not be particularly interested in, especially if they know the same thing. Unless, of course, it is written in a superlative manner.

4. You can also write about *what you want to know*. Elizabeth George writes best-selling mysteries based in England and she lives in California. I write about myths and legends because they interest me and I'm willing to do the research to learn more. I believe that if I can find material that interests me, it should interest some readers.

Usually your background will dictate what your story is about. That's not to say that since you haven't ever gone into space that you can't write science fiction, but it does mean that you know something about the physics of space flight if that is going to be in your manuscript. As you will see later, when it comes to marketing your manuscript you are also marketing yourself. Think about when you read the book jacket for a writer you never heard of. If they've written a thriller that's set in Antarctica and in the bio it says they spent three years studying ice formations in Antarctica you're going to give the author more credit.

I think it is even easier than that: you will most likely write whatever it is you enjoy reading. The best preparation for becoming a writer of mysteries is to have read a lot of mysteries.

Some words of advice here: start with something simple. Don't try to write the Great American Novel on your first try. I am constantly learning more about writing and am polishing my skills every time I write and it's nice to be able to learn and make a buck at it too. As I learn more, I can write more difficult plots and characters.

And now some words of caution. I've said you should write what you know and you should keep it as simple as possible, but be careful. A common problem with new writers is thinking that *their* life story will be extremely interesting to the reading world. This is my third addition to Mark Twain's saying. There is nothing inherently wrong with writing about yourself, but be realistic about the possibilities of someone else wanting to read it.

Writing about something you care about very deeply has the advantage of adding passion to your prose. It also has the disadvantage that some writers can't separate themselves enough from what they write to adequately judge its content or style. I have watched writers waste *years* on the same manuscript, trying to polish the editing, doing rewrites on various subplots, etc. when they were not willing to accept a fundamental problem with their story: the basic idea wasn't that interesting.

I have seen many writers become too emotionally attached to bad ideas. Remember I mentioned earlier that open-mindedness is a very important trait for writers. I have an entire chapter later in this book devoted to the reader (22). The reason for that? Because too many writers get tunnel vision and fail to objectively evaluate their own work in terms of someone who has no emotional attachment and is seeing it for the first time. Just because you feel something, that doesn't mean you can get the reader to feel the same thing.

There is a problem every writer faces when approaching his or her first manuscript: You are trying to do something new. Most wise people when trying to do something new use the KISS technique—keep it simple. You are trying to juggle two glass balls: the story and the writing. The simpler you make the story, the more attention you can give to the writing.

That sounds rather simplistic, but I have seen many writers get in over their heads by trying to write a very complex first novel and the writing suffers as they wrestle with the story. Most first novelists can do one or the other well, but very few can do both well. Since you must write well, give yourself a break on the story. When I was still unpublished and got hooked up with an agent, his first (and only) comment to me was to simplify the plot of the manuscript he had looked at. I had too much going on and was not a skilled enough writer to keep it all going. I did as he suggested and that book was the first one we sold.

In fact, I've come full circle. I've written a couple of series of books that have done well but are very complicated, with complex story-lines involving a large cast of characters and generally rewriting the entire history of mankind. Talk about difficult. I've also written some thrillers that were quite complicated. The next book I write that's not under contract is going to be a very simple idea and story line where I can focus on giving my characters the depth I used to devote to the plot.

Another problem: perfectionism. Some people think that the writing has to be perfect. They spend an inordinate amount of time on editing and rewriting. Sometimes, you just have to accept it's either good enough, or that the horse is dead and can't be brought back to life.

I am going to go on here on my soapbox a little bit longer. I just finished looking at a couple of dozen "novel submissions" for a contest I am judging. I have yet to see one that was not about "love, death, divorce, child abuse, broken hearts, etc. etc." Nobody said, "hey, I've got a great science fiction story here." Or a horror story. Or a thriller. There's nothing wrong about writing about love, death, etc. but none of the writers were up to the task.

Now, here's exercise number one. Go to the bookstore. Look around. What is the largest section? From the bookstores I frequent, the answer is: Computers. Second largest? Self-help. Ah—what is self-help about? "Love, death, addiction, child abuse, broken hearts, etc. etc." And last I checked it is non-fiction.

Remember why people read fiction: most of the time we read to escape "death, abuse, addiction, broken hearts, etc. etc." We read primarily to be entertained. Yet, here are all these aspiring writers trying to write what I call The Great American Novel. How many of these types of books are on the bookshelves? Maybe 10 to 20 percent of the hardcover new releases. Less than 10% of the paperback original releases. You figure it out.

I am really starting to believe that this is the number one problem most new novelists have: they pick very difficult subject matter for their story. The craft of writing is difficult enough. The more difficult the topic is, the better the writing has to be.

The bottom line is that you need to have an original thought/idea that will spark you and others.

4. THE ORIGINAL IDEA

The original idea is the foundation of your novel. When I say idea, I don't necessarily mean the theme, although it could be. Or the most important incident, although it could be. It can be a setting. It could be a scene. It could be a character.

It is simply the first idea you had that was the seed of your novel. All else can change, but the idea can't. It might be a place; a person; an event; a moral; whatever. But you did have it before you began writing and you *must* remember it as you write. If you don't, your story and style will suffer terribly. You should be able to tell your idea in one sentence. And repeat it to yourself every morning when you wake up and prior to writing. Knowing it will keep you on track.

A TEST: Write down the original idea for your book in *one* sentence.

If you can't do it, then you need to backtrack through your thought processes and find it, because you had to have had it. Everything starts from something. Idea is not story, something I'll talk about in detail later. The original idea is the one thing in your manuscript that cannot change.

So, the above isn't very clear? OK. In one of my early novels, the original idea was an action: *What if Special Forces soldiers had to destroy an enemy pipeline?* That's it for Dragon Sim-13. Not very elaborate, you say. True. Not exactly a great moral theme. Right. But with that original idea there was a lot I could do and eventually had to do. I had to change the target country after the first draft. But that was OK because I still had the original idea. I had to change characters, but that was fine too, because it didn't change my original idea. I had to change the reason why they were attacking a pipeline, but again, OK-dokey because—you got it—the original idea was the same.

The author I mentioned earlier who received the two million dollar advance for his first novel said it all began with an idea: What if a man sitting in a Paris Cafe sees someone who had played a significant role in his earlier life but he hadn't seen in 20 years?

Think of all the possibilities that simple idea allows, but also think of the start point it gives you. He doesn't say who it was the man sees; he doesn't even say why the man is in Paris in the first place; heck, he doesn't even say who the man is—is he a spy? A tourist?

You will have plenty of latitude after you come up with your original idea; in fact, I always find the finished manuscript turns out to be different from what I had originally envisioned, but one thing is always true: that original idea is still there at the end.

For my first original idea, I made it as simple as possible for me to write the story because when I was in the Special Forces my A-Team *had* run a similar mission on a pipeline. Since I had a good idea what would happen in the story, I could concentrate on the actual writing of the novel. And it needed every bit of concentration and even then was barely readable.

I've sat in graduate literature classes and heard students say: "The author had to have a moral point in mind when they wrote that book." I agree, but sometimes it is not at the forefront of the story. Many authors write simply to tell a story started by that original idea, which indeed might be a moral point, but sometimes is a story that they wanted to tell and the theme developed subsequently.

A moral or theme does always appear in a book by the time it is done. Go back to what I said about the subconscious. No matter what expectations or thoughts an author has when they start writing, a lot more appears in the manuscript than they consciously expected.

After you have that original idea, you should spend a lot of time wrestling with it and develop some feelings and thoughts about it. I try to look at my main characters and determine what will happen to them emotionally, physically and spiritually as they go through the story. Who are they at the beginning of the story and who are they at the end?

This is an example of being aware of what you are doing. I said above that not all authors have a conscious theme when they write a novel, but experience has taught me that it is better to have your theme in your conscious mind before you start writing. It might not be your original idea, but it will definitely affect your characters and story.

The reason it is important to have a theme in mind is because people want to care about what they read and the characters. If there is some moral or emotional relevance to the story they read, they will become more involved in the story and enjoy it more. Even if the reader doesn't consciously see it either.

Using "What if" can be very helpful to clarify your original idea, and also—as we will see later—when you try to write your cover letter and synopsis for submission.

"What if a housewife realizes her life is empty and decides to change it?" Not very specific you might argue, but the specifics will come out later. You have the original idea that will allow you to drive from a start to a finish.

John Saul at the Maui Writer's Retreat runs a seminar called "What if?" where he has writers put their one sentence up on butcher paper and analyzes it. He makes sure every word in the sentence means something. For example:

What if Mary has to stop a band of terrorists?

How could this be improved? What does Mary mean? How about 'a housewife'? Stop a band of terrorists from what? How about 'assassinating the president'? This gives us: What if a housewife has to stop a band of terrorists from assassinating the President?

The second what if is better than the first one.

Sometimes the original idea could even be a way to tell a story, rather than the story itself. Telling the same story from two different perspectives, usually presents two different stories. For example, an original idea is "What if a person with limited mental capacity interacts with the world?" In the film A Dangerous Woman (films work the same way) shows normal, everyday life with the main character being a woman who always tells the truth. Boy, you want to talk about someone who is dangerous. Think about it. The film is an excellent portrayal of our society, but the original idea was the different perspective. What was Forrest Gump about? It had the same basic what if. Wasn't it the main character's perspective that made the story, rather than the actual events?

Whenever I watch a film or video I try to figure out what the original idea the first screenwriter had. For example, in the movie True Romance written by Quentin Torrentino, there is a scene at the end where there are four groups of people in a room all pointing guns at each other in a classic Mexican stand-off. Rewatching the film, I can see the entire movie driving to that one climactic scene in the mind of the writer. In an interview, Torrentino said that scene was the original idea. He didn't know who the people with the guns were; where the room was; why they were in the room; whether it was the beginning, end or middle of the movie; what the result of this stand-off would be; etc. etc. He just had this vision to start with.

Again, idea is not story. We will get to that.

I said that the original idea is not necessarily the theme of the book. It can be, but the two are not necessarily synonymous. If they aren't then, again as I said above, you should know what your theme is anyway.

Instead of the word theme though, I like to use a term I've stolen from screenwriters and that is **INTENT**. It took me almost ten years of writing and 15 manuscripts to realize the absolute critical importance of having an intent to my stories, beyond the one I used to hold onto of simply being entertaining. And having that intent in my conscious mind.

I've heard someone in the screenwriting business say you should be able to state your intent in three words. For example:

Love conquers all.

Honesty defeats greed.

There are others who say you need to be able to state it in one word:

Relationships.

Honesty.

Faith.

Fathers.

Think about what you want the reader to *feel* when they've finished you book. Filmmakers have to think about what they want the viewer to feel when they walk out of the theater. This is one reason there are so few negative endings in films. That's not to say you can't have a dark ending. It's more to point out that you need to be aware of the effect of a dark ending.

I've seen some excellent films where the ending was dark and bleak—and often most realistic—but most of those films were not box office blockbusters. The original screenplay for <u>Pretty Woman</u> was called <u>Five Thousand Dollars</u>. And the Richard Gere character drives away at the end. Realistic, yes. Would it have succeeded as much as the rewrite?

I'm not saying you have to have happy endings and make your reader happy. I'm saying you have to know what feeling you want the reader to experience and make sure you deliver. Larry McMurty is a master writer and most of his stories have rather bleak endings.

I think that the more negative the intent, the better you have to be as a writer to keep the reader involved. To take readers on a dark and relatively unhappy journey, you have to be very good to keep them in the boat.

Another interesting thing to do is to compare the book with the movie. Yes, I know, the book was always better. Maybe. I've seen one or two films that were better than the book.

Pat Conroy novels are always interesting to watch on film. Many times entire subplots are left out without the other subplots changing at all. Sometimes what seems to be the main story is left out; for example, in <u>The Lords Of Discipline</u> the love angle between the main character and his roommate's pregnant girlfriend was very much downplayed. In <u>The Prince of Tides</u>, the Prince, Luke, was practically non-existent in the movie and never on-screen.

40

An example where the loss of original intent can hurt: <u>Courage Under Fire</u> was a good movie but it missed out being as good as it could have been. I saw the movie first. I was perplexed about the reaction of the Denzel Washington character. He seemed to me to be overreacting to a mistake. Granted it was a tragic mistake, but he seemed to be taking it a bit too far. When I read the book, I saw what had gone wrong. In the book it had not been a mistake. He had been a coward. The subsequent actions then made sense. But I could see a production meeting and Denzel Washington saying: "Hey, I'm not going to play a coward." So the story was changed. But in changing that, not only did it take away from the motivation of his character, it took away from the core of the book, which juxtaposed the cowardice of the lead male and the bravery of the lead female, and, how through the male's investigation of her heroism, he came to understand his own cowardice.

The longer I've been in this business, the more I've realized that it is one based not on logic, but on emotion. That is why predicting if a book will sell or if a movie will be a blockbuster is so difficult. The more a reader *feels* about a book, the more he or she will get into it. I believe feeling comes out of the three aspects of a novel:
1. Idea.
2. Intent.
3. Characters.
Most particularly the third factor. If you know and, more importantly, have a good "feel" for each of these three before you begin writing, you increase the quality of your work.

Idea is not story.
To me, there is a very big difference between the idea and the story. I've had great ideas that I couldn't transform into a story. On the other hand, I've taken some not so great ideas and pumped them up with a very good story.

The original idea is the foundation. It's that one sentence beginning. Then you have to figure out how you are going to tell that idea. That's the story. It's the building that goes on top of the foundation.

The difference between idea and story is one reason I don't get very hyper about sharing my ideas with others. I believe two people can have the exact same idea but they will come up with two very different stories.

An idea is usually an abstract. I have found that many fledgling novelists start with the abstract, then got bogged down trying to take that into something concrete (black and white on paper). This is why I beat to death being able to state your idea in one sentence and then writing it down. It makes it real. It makes the distance from idea to story less of a chasm. Even just thinking your original idea is not good enough. You have to state it out loud and write it down on paper. I always find putting thoughts down on paper forces me to focus and I find that this great idea I had in my head suddenly becomes much more difficult to state clearly.

It is a big jump from idea to story. Story includes characters, timing, point of view, pace, locale, etc. etc. Story has to answer all the questions that come to mind the second you tell someone your idea. Story answers: Who? What? Where? When? How? It also answers the Why of your intent.

Ambiguity is *not* good in most novels. You have to be a damn good novelist to take your reader along on a vague ride. There are courses dedicated to taking apart and analyzing what exactly did James Joyce mean in his books, but it is not likely they're going to start a course next week on *you* and your book to analyze it. Several authors who teach at universities have really impressed upon me this big problem they have with literature students who think being vague and ambiguous is a good thing when they write. Many times being ambiguous is more of a sign of the writer not knowing exactly what they want to say in the first place.

Watch the movie, The Player. Watch the writers try to pitch their concept to the character Tim Robbins plays. His line to them all is: "Tell it in 25 words or less." As a novelist pitching to an agent or editor you get at most one paragraph to "hook" them, usually only one sentence. If you can't do it, you've got a problem.

I was watching Biography on TV last night and they were covering Clint Eastwood. He would talk about one movie or another and say, "The thing I liked about this screenplay was . . ." And he would sum it up in a sentence or two. He didn't go on and on saying, "boy I really liked the great scene on page 28, and the twist on page 43, and . . ." I find many writers get too caught up in the minutiae of their story and lose sight of the big picture.

What do you like about your proposed book?

Another of my favorite lines to go from idea to story is: "Take it one step further." After you "what if", play the one step further game. You will be surprised where it can take you. What if things aren't as they appear? When you are first starting out, don't use this very much, but as you get more proficient at writing, it helps you develop more complex and interesting plots. It allows you to add layers to your story.

I can not overemphasize the need to be able to have that original idea in your mind at all times and to be able to state it in one sentence. It will prevent you from making many of the common errors in manuscripts.

If you cannot tell someone quickly and concisely what your story is, you are going to lose your way when you try to write it. Try talking your story out with someone who knows nothing about it. If you can't succinctly explain it to another person, you are going to have difficulty writing it.

Another thing to remember is that almost everything has been done before. The secret is to do it somewhat differently. Many best-selling authors are writers who have "launched" a genre. There was horror before Stephen King but he took it to another level. He even admits, for example, that The Stand, was inspired by the idea of an earlier book, Earth Abides, but King took the idea to a higher level.

Do not write for the "market." Because you really don't know what the market is going to be in the two and a half to three years it will take you to get published. The bottom line is to write whatever you feel you want to. But remember if you want to sell it that you need to write it so other people will want to read it.

The original idea is also critical when it comes to marketing your manuscript, as you will see when we get to the business section. Guess what the opening line of your query letter is going to be? Guess what is probably the only thing an agent or editor is going to read?

I know you may think this is terribly unfair. You may feel that taking four hundred pages of brilliant manuscript and trying to sell it on the basis of just a sentence or two is a travesty, but here is something to consider—how do you buy a book?

Most people buy because they know the author and like reading him or her. But if you are a new writer, then you don't have this option. So how do you buy a book from an author you never heard of? Do you stand in the bookstore, read the entire book, then go and pay for it?

Go to your local bookstore or even better, local supermarket. Stand near the paperback racks. Watch how long each person peruses the books on the shelves. How many seconds do they give to each book? Then, when they pick a book up, how long do they spend looking at it?

Why should it be any different for agents and editors?

5. RESEARCH

Once you have figured out your original idea, before you race off and start your story, the next step is to do research. I try to keep my mind open when I'm doing research for all sorts of possibilities for my story. In fact, before you start writing the first word of your novel, I think you should go through the creative process outlined in the rest of the chapters in this section and make sure you know what you want to do before you trap yourself.

There are two types of research: primary and secondary. Both are important. Primary research is related to specifics of the story you are going to tell. Secondary goes on all the time and should be second nature to a writer (pun intended). You should be observing things about you all the time. You should also be well read. Many times your ideas come out of research in the first place.

I had a demolition's man on my Special Forces team and whenever we went anywhere he was always looking at things around him and figuring out how he would blow them up. Every dam we passed, power line, bridge, etc. he was estimating how many charges and where he would place them. As a writer you should be always thinking like that—how you would write things you see, describe people you observe.

Several times in this book I say that the number one thing a writer must do is write. I would say the number two thing is read. Read for information and read for style. Read for format. Every book you read, you should be taking it apart as I describe in the next chapter.

You should also watch as many films as possible. Although the medium is different, the dramatic concept is basically the same.

In many cases, research helps you construct the story after you have your initial idea. Research is not just looking outward for information, it is also looking inward. You have to develop your storyline, your locales, and your characters. Also question why people are acting the way they are. What do they think their motivation is and what is really their motivation?

You can never have enough information. Even while writing I look for more information about the topic I am writing about. All my books have started from the original idea and then the story developed out of the research I did on that idea and related areas.

One question people ask is how factual their stories should be? Where is the line between realistically portraying something and making things up? That's a difficult question to answer. My science fiction books are only science fiction in that I give a different explanation for things that actually exist. It is a fact that there are large statues on Easter Island. The fiction in my book Area 51 comes in when I give my own explanation for why those statues were made.

If you are writing a mystery you can't be too far off base with your police procedural information. I think many people are lulled by the inaccuracies portrayed in movies. Books have to be more accurate for several reasons; one is that the average reader is more on the ball than the average movie goer; second, you can slide something by in a couple of seconds of film but remember the reader can linger over and reread a paragraph again and again. A reader can also turn back from page 320 to check page 45 where you mentioned the same thing and compare the two.

In chapter 2 I mentioned many of the things you use for research. Another place that is growing in popularity is the Internet. I don't have too much experience on the "net" but I have found it to be useful in gathering information.

Another strength of the Internet is networking. There is every possible organization out there with a web site. There are numerous writers' organizations and writers' resources groups. I even taught a writing class on the Internet. While the pay was excellent, I haven't done it again because it's the only time I've taught that I felt the students didn't get their money's worth. I found it very difficult to coordinate with students, to look at material sent as part of e-mails or attachments, have meaningful dialogue, etc. I'm sure there are some good Internet writing courses, but it just didn't work for me.

The Internet is a useful way to get in contact with other writers and even agents and editors. I maintain a web site of my own through which people can e-mail me.

Be warned though: you should spend the majority of the time on your computer writing, not surfing.

If you look in the front of many books, you will find a list of acknowledgments where the author thanks those who helped with the book. For a mystery this might include a police department, the forensics department, the coroner, etc. etc. This is primary research and can be very useful.

One problem I have found though in talking to experts about their particular field is they are usually more concerned with "getting it right" than telling a story. As a novelist, telling a story is your priority. You have to listen carefully to the expert and shift through the mounds of information they are shoveling your way and pick the nuggets of gold that you can use to make your story sparkle.

My recommendation if you have to write about something you are unfamiliar with, is to "cheat". Find another fiction book that writes about the same subject and see how that author did it.

In fact, that's one of the reasons you need to read a lot and watch a lot of film—to add to your toolkit of techniques and information. Every now and then I read or see something that really strikes me as being different and I file it away in my mind. You have to do the same thing when researching material for your book.

6. BOOK DISSECTION

You've got your original idea and you've done your research. Now, before you begin to write your book, you should find a novel similar to what you plan to write that is already published. Then you should sit down with your razor sharp brain and cut it apart to see all the pieces. Then put them together again to see how they all fit.

45

You have to ask yourself a number of questions:

1. What was the original idea the author started with? How close is it to mine?
2. How did the author translate that idea into a story? What twist did the author put on the original idea? What's my twist?
3. What is the theme/intent to this story?
4. Why did the author begin where he or she did?
5. Why did the author chose the perspective he or she did?
6. What scope did he or she place on the story?
7. What is the pacing of the story?
8. How did the author bring the story to a conclusion?
9. What did the author do that you liked?
10. What did the author do that you didn't like?
11. What didn't the author put in the book that you might have? Why didn't the author put that in?
12. What was in the book that you feel could have been left out? How would the story change if it were left out?
13. What were the subplots? How did they connect with the main plot? Did all the subplots get resolved?
14. Why did the author pick the settings he or she did?

If you will notice, all the above questions relate to chapters further in this book. These are questions you are going to face in your own manuscript. If you can understand how someone who successfully wrote the same type of book answered them, you greatly improve your ability to answer them.

Here's another interesting exercise to do. Take a book that was made into a film and compare the two. For example, <u>The Great Santini</u> by Pat Conroy. If you read the book, then watch the movie, you will notice several subplots are missing from the movie version that are in the book. How did the screenwriter do this yet maintain the original idea and story of the book? Did these subplots add or take away from the book?

I was talking to producer Dan Curtis (<u>Winds of War</u>) and he told me how he works on taking a novel and turning it into a screenplay. First he breaks the novel down into a list of one or two sentences summaries of every major scene or action. Then he writes the screenplay off that list. Then he breaks the screenplay down into a list of one or two sentence summaries and sees how that compares to the one he did for the novel.

Use the narrative structure in Chapter 14 to lay out the structure of the novels you read. What is the hook? What are the progressive complications? What is the choice the protagonist has to make? How is it made? How is the main plot resolved? How do the subplots support the main plot?

It is essential that you be well read in the area in which you wish to write. The more you read, the more you will get imprinted in your conscious and subconscious brain the style and manner in which those types of stories are written, which will aid you greatly in writing your own.

You should also read more first novels, rather than the latest by a best-selling author. Since you are trying to get published, see what kind of novel it takes to get published at various publishing houses. Some best-selling authors can crank out anything—which would not get published if a no-name author did it—and have it become a best seller.

Another thing that book dissection can help you with is determining how "realistic" your book needs to be and in researching your topic. For example, in most mystery novels, police procedure lies somewhere between detective shows on TV and the way it is really done. You'll find if you interview a homicide detective about how they cover a murder scene, that you will be overwhelmed with detail and the scene you write in your book would have to be many hours long and slow your action down. So see how such scenes are generally written in most novels that are published in your genre and proceed accordingly.

A question you should ask yourself after dissecting a book like what you want to write is this: How is my book going to be different? What is my unique twist? Every idea has been done—it is in the development of your story off that idea that you have to bring your originality.

7. 1 of N does not equal N. And: Never Complain, Never Explain.

Yes, a rather long title for a chapter but those two phrases have grown in importance to me the longer I am in this business and the more students I teach.

1 of N does not equal N.

Arrghhh. Math in a writing book. Sorry, but it's the best way I can explain this concept. What this formula means is that just because you can go to the bookstore and buy a best-selling book written by so-and-so, the famous writer, that does not mean you can write a similar book and get it published.

Ahh, now you're really mad at me. I'm contradicting what I wrote in the last chapter. No, I'm not. What I'm talking about is those people who sit there and complain that their book is just as good as such and such and, damn it, they should not only be published but have a bestseller. Also, those people who look at book number 5 from a best-selling author and complain about how bad it is. Yes, there are many book number 5's from best-selling authors that if they were book number 1 from a new author, would not get published. But the primary thing that sells a book is author's name. I've always said

Stephen King could write a book about doing his laundry and it would be on the bestseller list. Stephen King earned being Stephen King and to misquote a vice-presidential debate, I've read Stephen King and you ain't no Stephen King. Neither am I.

Another thing people do is they see a technique used in a novel and use the same technique, and then get upset when told it doesn't work. They angrily point to the published book that has the same technique and say, "SEE." Unfortunately, what they don't see is that that technique is part of the overall structure of the novel. It all ties together. I said in a previous chapter to do a book dissection to study various aspects and techniques and I still stand by that; however, I also remind you of the story of Frankenstein. Just because you can put all the pieces together, that doesn't mean you can necessarily bring it to life. There are some techniques that only work when put in context of other parts of the novel; thus using it in isolation can be a glaring problem. You can't take the type of beginning of one bestseller, tie it in with flashback style from another, and have a similar flashy ending as another and expect the novel to automatically work.

Every part of a novel is a thread connected to all the other parts. Pull on one piece and you pull on them all. Tear apart a novel or a movie and see the pieces, but then be like a watchmaker and see if you can put them all together again as the writer did and if you understand *why* they go back that way.

It is also more important to figure out what is working and why rather that what you feel didn't work in a book you read. An attitude that will serve you little good is the "There's so much crap on the shelves in the bookstore." I admit that there are times when I am looking for something to read, and I stand in the local supermarket looking a the paperbacks, that I really can't find anything I want to read or that sparks an interest. But that doesn't automatically mean it's all crap.

I had to do this many times. I'd read something I might not like, but it seems to be selling quite well. Instead of dismissing the rest of the world as stupid, I try to find what it is about the book that people like. That doesn't mean I'm going to do the same thing, but it does broaden my horizon.

I don't think there is anything wrong with a little fire burning deep inside believing you are better than those people getting published, but I think that's the sort of thing that should be used to fuel your writing, not expressed loudly so everyone can hear it.

John Gardner once said that every book has its own rules. Remember that when you examine a book to see what you can learn from it. Look at the parts from the perspective of that book's specific rules.

I think Henry Ford uttered the famous line: **Never complain, never explain**. This applies in the writing world in several ways.

One thing I do when I critique material is ask a lot of questions. I tell my students, 'Hey you don't have to answer those questions to me' (in fact I would prefer they don't), but rather they are to get the students to think. What I don't tell them is that the more questions I have to ask, the worse job they've done.

The reason I don't want answers is because you don't get any opportunities to explain your book once it's on the shelf in a store. You also don't get any opportunities to explain your submission when it's sitting on an agent's or editor's desk. So if they don't "get it" the first time around, they won't *get it*. Get it? All your explanations and defenses mean nothing because you not only won't get the chance to say them, you *shouldn't* get the chance to say them.

I've gotten five page long, single-spaced letters back from students answering my questions or challenging points I made and my reaction is that such letters are a waste of paper. If I couldn't figure it out from the material, it needs to be rewritten. This ties in with my theory about the original idea. If you can't tell me what your story is about in one, maybe two sentences, *and* I understand it from that, then you are going to have a hell of a hard time selling it. You don't get to put those letters in the front of your published book.

The never complain comes from the fact that there are people running this business. You won't agree with some things, particularly rejections, but do not complain or write nasty letters, make obnoxious phone calls, send dirty faxes, etc. etc. Because you never know when you are going to run into those people again. My first book was published by a publisher that had rejected my own query reference that same book. I had disagreed strongly with some of the things they put on that first rejection letter, still do as a matter of fact, but I ate it and drove on. If I had sent them a nasty letter, methinks they would have remembered me and not even considered the manuscript when my agent submitted it.

I even find this with students I've worked with. They get angry and upset with my comments or questions. And they let me know it. What they don't understand is the fact that their anger expressed that way will get them nowhere. Take the energy and put it into your book, which is the only place it will do you any good.

Agent Richard Curtis' first piece of advice in his book <u>Beyond the Bestseller</u> to writers consists of a few simple words: "Keep your big mouth shut."

The longer I have been doing this for a living, the more I realize the profundity of those words. Go ahead, laugh. But here is the golden rule that I take out of those words: If an action you plan to take, words you plan to utter, a letter you want to write, could have anything other than a positive reflection back on you, DON'T DO IT. Negativity begets negativity. Acting out of anger, frustration, righteous indignation, etc. will bite you in the butt, to put it mildly.

It is hard sometimes not to react. I believe publishing is a very poorly run business in many aspects. And those bad business decisions in New York can adversely affect you. They can destroy you in some cases. But you have to drive on and you have to accept that you, by yourself, are not going to change the entire publishing industry. Also, you can take comfort, if you want, in the fact that the business is in the throes of change as I explain in Chapter 37.

At one publishing house, I have been through five editors over the course of three years. I've had half-a-dozen people assigned to me as my "publicist." None of my publicists returned my phone calls for the first two years. For my most recent book from that publisher my assigned publicist never even bothered to give me a courtesy phone call to tell me all the things they weren't going to do to promote the book.

For the same publisher I submitted an outline for my next book. I asked for feedback on the outline and received none. So I wrote the book and turned it in. Then got a phone call a couple of weeks later saying the book didn't go in the direction they envisioned for my series. Was I angry? Yes. My gut reaction was to tell them it would have been good to have heard that when they sat on the outline for half a year, *before* I wrote a book that faithfully followed the outline.

What did I do? I kept my mouth shut and listened. And I realized that, ultimately, they were right. The book was going in the wrong direction. I spent three weeks, seven days a week, totally rewriting the manuscript and produced basically a new book. It sucked doing that. I didn't get paid any more money for doing it. But what were my options? Scream and yell and rant and rave? And then what? And, getting back to admitting you're wrong, their way was better than the way I had been going.

Most of the time, I have found that comments made by editors and agents, even when I very much disagreed with them initially, turned out to be very worthwhile. I never respond to anything right away. I always take some time to digest it.

At the same time, with the same publisher, they screwed up my royalty check (and it was *their* mistake) and issued it two weeks late, which almost cost me the closing date on the house I was trying to buy; plus the check was short money they owed me. Did I call up my editor and scream? No. I sent a polite letter detailing the situation and sucked it up.

I'm not saying be a patsy. Or go along with every single thing you are told. But I am saying don't shoot yourself in the foot and understand reality. They didn't sit there at the publishing house and decide to screw up the royalty check on purpose, even though paranoid people like us writers like to believe such things.

For example, I am often asked how long a writer should wait to hear back on a query/submission to an agent or publishing house. My answer: Forever.

I'm not being a smart-ass with that answer. Rather I am defining the reality of the situation. What are you going to do if you don't hear back in two months? Send *another* letter to be ignored? Move on.

I said above that publishing is poorly run, but that doesn't mean the people who run the business are incompetent. Like many other businesses, publishing goes through changes and it takes time for bureaucracies to catch up to change.

One of the bitter realities of being a writer is that you have very little leverage. If something isn't happening the way you would like, there is little you can do. In the past year, several major writers, flagship writers who carry publishing houses—who have leverage—have switched publishers. They didn't do it over money, they did it over the way they perceived the publisher was treating them. How much publicity effort they were getting. When I discuss the publishing business I will get into more detail about this area.

I stated earlier that this is an emotional business. If you want to succeed you have to have positive emotions working for you. This is very difficult for many writers. I switched agents because the original agent I had, while good, was a little too negative. I realized I had enough negative traits on my own (as you can see by reading between the lines on some of these pages). I didn't need my agent to amplify my negativity. I switched to an agent who is more confident and positive. Who also, coincidentally, is the most professional individual I've worked with in this business as far as correspondence and doing what he says he's going to do. However, he also doesn't 'hold my hand'. He expects me to be a professional and deal with the emotional issues of this business on my own. But he is also like a psychologist in that he leaves me alone a lot to figure things out on my own after giving me a few comments to chew on. Many people want the 'answer' right up front, but they don't realize they're not ready to accept the answer yet. In the same manner there are things in this book that you intellectually understand, but emotionally disagree with. I have often found that the things I most strongly react to with negative emotions are the things I need to pay most attention to.

Be positive.

Another aspect of this comes whenever you read a book or see a movie. Stop trying to find what's wrong with it and try to figure out what is working. It's easy to be a negative critic—much harder to find the elements that were successful. I believe that learning to do this was a significant achievement for me. I used to look at some best-selling novelists and think their work was totally worthless. Because of that, I failed to look hard enough to see the things in that work that *was* worthwhile and well done.

I recently got a letter from a student where the student first told me all the things he *didn't* like. He didn't like thrillers. He didn't like horror. He didn't like serial killer books, etc. etc. etc. My first reaction was why is this guy telling me this? Second, what good is it doing him to know what he doesn't like? Third, some of what he doesn't like could teach him a lot about writing. Fourth, he was telling me, in so many words, he didn't like what I wrote. Not a good way to start a working relationship.

The bottom line is I've learned to shut my mouth even if I have to bite my tongue in half to do it.

2
How to Write a Novel

E ven the Beatles did a song about being a writer with the basic phi-
losophy that it is an easy road to fame and fortune. It is a profession where anyone with access to paper and ink thinks they can
join the ranks. The longer I do this, though, the more I believe
that it is very important to learn the basic craft of writing a novel before
exercising one's genius. If you talk to coaches of teams, they always stress
learning the fundamentals first, and I feel the same way about writing.
Too often, inexperienced writers jump deeply into too complicated a
story before having the tools in order to set up the basic structure to
make that leap.

I just spent several days looking through manuscript submissions and
saw so many basic mistakes it made me wonder if the writers even read
books, never mind had studied writing. It's like the architect I mentioned
earlier. Before one can build a spectacular bridge, it helps if one has built a
couple of simple bridges to gain the experience.

Here's a checklist of things that I constantly find in manuscripts. I address each of them in the various chapters that follow, but I want to list these up front to gain some focus:

1) <u>Hooking the reader</u>. Many writers spend too much time giving background information, introducing various characters, etc. before they introduce
    a. the plot, and
    b. the main character.

2) <u>Dialogue tags</u>. The words inside the quotation marks have to get across to the reader the necessary information and emotion. Trying to make up for the lack in written dialogue by overusing dialogue tags is very common and very jarring.

3) <u>Repetition</u>. Using the same words over and over again, or same phrases, is very jarring to the reader.

4) <u>Time sense and pacing of the story</u>. I call this the remote control effect. A story should flow in some sort of logical time sequence. Too often stories fast-forward, then rewind to a flashback or memory, jump forward, slow down, speed up, etc. etc. until the reader's head is spinning.

5) <u>Setting the scene</u>. Often I begin reading a scene/chapter and am totally lost for several pages as to where this action is occurring, who is in the scene, when this scene is in relation to the last scene.

6) <u>Italicizing thoughts</u>; the same with putting a character's thoughts inside of quotation marks. I'm not a big fan of either, although I'm sure I could go to a bookstore and find this technique successfully done. Putting a character's thoughts inside of quotation marks can easily confuse the reader who expects this to be dialogue. My problem with italicizing thoughts, while a common technique, is pondering the difference between those character thoughts the author italicizes and those he or she doesn't.

7) <u>Characters talking to themselves</u>. This is a weak technique to give expository information or thoughts to the reader. What do you think of someone who wanders around talking to himself or herself all the time? Also, this technique used in conjunction with an actual conversation can be very confusing because the reader will not be sure which dialogue is directed at the other participant in the conversation and which is directed back at the speaker.

8) <u>Misuse of pronouns</u>. If you have two men in the room and use the phrase *"Blab, blab, blab," he said*. It had better be very clear which he you are referring to. The technical definition of a pronoun is: <u>one</u>

of a class of words that function as substitutes for noun or noun phrases and denote persons or things asked for, previously specified or understood from the context. It needs to be very clear whom your pronoun refers to. Don't confuse the reader.

9) The difference between a memory and a flashback. This is also covered elsewhere.

10) Slipping into second person point of view. Any time you address the reader as I am now addressing you, then you are into second person POV.

Now let's get into the actual tools so we can learn about them in order to avoid these common problems.

8. IDEA INTO STORY

Given that you have now worked your way through deciding **what** to write, you face the second critical hurdle: Deciding *how* to write the what. It may be difficult to believe, but sometimes this hurdle can loom much higher than the 'what' question. In fact, you may find that it causes you to reconsider your what. This is the transition from idea to story and it is not an easy one.

As I said earlier this is when you must decide the who, what, where, when, how and why of your story. There are an almost infinite number of ways to approach a story. This is also where the same idea can turn into two very different stories. I said that every idea has been done before, but every story hasn't been done before. Every story will be different.

When I was living in Korea the power would get shut off on the average of once a day. No matter how often I remembered to save what I was working on, I would still lose some material. If I rewrote ten minutes later what I just wrote, it would be different than the original. I know there are days when I write something that if I had waited another day and written, the entire book would have turned out very differently.

I cover each of the questions about story you must ask in various chapters in this book. There is the who (characters), the what (narrative structure and plot), where (setting), when (beginning, pacing, ending), how (point of view) and why (intent, motivation).

In getting your original idea across to your audience, you have to decide the best mode and method to do that. What perspective or point of view should I take? First? Third? Omniscient? A combination? Where should the story start? How do I work in necessary background information? What subplots are needed to make the main story work? Can I tell my story that way and keep the reader interested? Can I pull off my surprise ending without cheating the reader? What sort of timeline should I use? How should the chapters be ordered? Should there be a prologue? An epilogue? All those and many more questions have to eventually be answered when deciding how to translate your idea into a story that will span a novel. And you have to remember that all the answers interrelate and affect each other.

For example, you have this magnificent idea for a novel spanning three centuries and multiple generations of a family on a farm in upstate New York and their trials and tribulations growing as America grows. You feel so good about your idea that you are ready to sit down at the keyboard and start typing right away. But first there are a few questions you have to ask:

-Where will I start? With the first settlers in the family or back in the "old country" to show how and why the family ended up in America? Or in the present and go backwards in time? How will I do the latter if I choose to go that way? Will I have someone find an old trunk in an attic full of papers, a diary, and photos? Why were they in the attic? Is the family moving and giving up the land and that adds a special touch and urgency to the story? Will I do parallel timelines? Jump back and forth? Will my reader be able to follow my moving in time?

-What will my perspective be? Will I focus on every member of the family? The women? The children? Maybe I'll take the perspective of the land itself, which is one of the constants through the story—but here I might not be able to talk about the son who goes off to the Civil War, you say. But if he is brought back and buried in the family plot and becomes part of the land itself he can tell his story, can't he? (see how every opportunity limits you only by the limit of you imagination?) Or perhaps I will tell the story of the family I want to highlight through the eyes of *another* family on the next farm.

-How will I deal with the family secrets, given that not everyone in the family knows everything?

-What is my intent? What do I want readers to feel when they finish reading this story?

-What is the climax of the story?

-Where will the story end? Can I close out all my subplots with that ending? Is my ending enough pay-off to the reader?

-And on and on—

Do you see how you must think through many things before you start locking yourself in? The minute you write your first page you have reduced many of the possibilities of your technique and style, so it is best to answer many of your style questions before you start writing in order to pick the one you feel best suits the story you want to tell.

One way to view a novel is as a cross-country race. You line your characters up at the starting line and fire the gun. You have a pretty good idea of where you want the finish line to be and a rough idea of the course, but things happen along the way that will change the route. However, by the time all your characters get to the finish line, they will have to traverse the entire length of your story page by page.

There are six good questions to ask yourself before you begin writing:

1. What do I want to write about?
2. What do I want to say about it?
3. Why do I want to say it?
4. Why should anybody else care?
5. What can I do to make them care?
6. What do I want readers to do, think or see?

What I have found is that most writers can answer the first three, but not the last three. The last three focus on the reader, while the first three on the writer.

The key to all the techniques and tools listed on the following pages is that they must be used to insure *smoothness*. By smoothness, I mean that your writing must not jar the reader either in term of style or story. The reader is interested in the story. Reading is the means by which they learn the story, but it is only a medium. The medium must not get in the way of the story. When the reader is pulled out of the story into the writing because you didn't use the proper technique, or didn't use it correctly, you stray away from the story.

A good maxim to keep in mind is: "Don't let them know you're writing."

Sometimes I have mentioned the differences and similarities between writing and filmmaking. I do it to emphasize technique and also because we have a very visually oriented society. Many more people rent videos each night than check books out of the library. The "camera" concept can help you, as the author, to understand what you are portraying to the reader, especially in our first area of perspective or point of view in Chapter 11.

There are two concepts I think it is important to understand when trying to think like a novelist. A successful novelist has to be able to do two contradictory things well. She has to be able to see a story with 360 degree vision (envisioning all possibilities), yet at the same time, be able to focus in one direction well enough to be able to see over the horizon where that particular possibility will lead to. What I mean is that an author, when writing a novel, has to be able to see a multitude of possibilities in the story from the very first idea through the editing and rewriting stage. That wide range of vision allows one the ability to take the story in different directions that will make it more interesting and viable. Having blinders on severely handicaps an author. There are so many story possibilities inherent in every idea and the writer must see as many of those as possible and pick out the best one at each juncture (note we are touching on writer's block here.).

At the same time, a writer must be able to see where each possibility leads as regards the original idea, subplots, characters, timeline etc., much like a chess player has to be able to look twelve moves ahead for each move he can make and see how the possible scenarios will unfold based on each move. And see not only the possible scenarios for the piece he moved, but for all the pieces on the board (including the opponent's which greatly increases the possible variations.).

I have found that people usually have the mental capacity to work either way, but rarely have I found someone who can do both well. Some people see all the possibilities in every situation, but they cannot see the ultimate outcome of each possibility. Others can envision the ultimate outcome for the few possibilities they see, but they miss many of the possibilities.

As I said above, a successful writer must be able to do both. Since most of us might not be capable of doing both very well, that is where you might want to consider discussing your work with a good friend who has a different perspective or reading your work in a writers' group and receiving feedback. The problem with a novel is that it is very large and a one-hour discussion is not going to do you much good. To get adequate help, you need someone who is not only good in the area you are lacking in (if you are), but also someone who is willing to put the time and effort in to do a realistic and good job.

I think very few novels in the bookstores were written in a vacuum. Certainly there are geniuses who have both talents and can do that, but for us mere mortals, we need help. And the help should be an ongoing thing. To write four hundred pages, then give it to someone to read and have them say, "Hey, in chapter one, why didn't you do this?" can be quite frustrating. Remember all this when you read about writer's block later on. Quite often the "block" is the author trying to expand her mind to see other possibilities in the story, or trying to project out possible paths.

Warning. We are now moving into dangerous territory. We're going to be talking about theories, styles and techniques. Most novice writers want formulas and rules. They want the **answer** that will make writing easy and get them published. Unfortunately writing is never easy and it takes much hard work to get published. Read the following words very carefully: *There is no right or wrong way to write. There are only the right or wrong ways to use techniques and the right and wrong times and places to use techniques.*

Does that make sense? In simpler terms, the word <u>never</u> and <u>always</u> should never be used when speaking of style (no pun intended). I emphasize the advantages and disadvantages of every technique and concept in the following pages. You need to do two things: learn how and when to use the technique, then know the advantages and disadvantages. Knowing those two things will allow you to properly utilize them. It's like having a toolkit full of various implements. If you know how to use each one, and where and when to use them, you will be proficient in your craft. But none of the tools are *wrong*. You can only use them improperly, or at the wrong time or place or for the wrong job.

Carrying that concept a little further: the more you understand the tools you have in your "kit" the better you can use them. The more I have written, the more I have come to understand the importance of knowing what I'm doing. That might sound a bit simplistic and naive, but in retrospect, I can quite honestly say I didn't really know what I was doing when I wrote my first several manuscripts. I think the majority of my writing was based on the fact that I had read a lot. So when I chose my perspective, or my timeline, or "developed" my characters, I didn't do so consciously.

Now, when I work on a manuscript, I may be doing the same thing I did on my first manuscript, but I am *aware* of what I am doing and this awareness allows me to improve my writing and opens up more story possibilities and allows me to deepen my characters.

I liken this to self-help books. It is my theory that self-help books only help people *after* they have already gone through the experience of change. Then the books serve two functions: first, they confirm what the person has just learned; second, they explain what the person has learned. In this manner, it is difficult sometimes to understand some of the tools or the way I have explained them in this book if you have never written a manuscript. Study them anyway. Then, after you have written some, go back and reread these chapters. They will make much more sense in light of your writing experience.

I know for myself that I didn't quite understand some of the things in writing books when I first started out. I also smugly thought some of what was written in them was too "simplistic". Well, after many manuscripts, I am going back and saying, "Oh, yeah, *now* I get it."

Further, and I shudder to say this because I know someone will take this and run with it in the wrong direction, understanding the tools of writing may even allow a few of you truly innovative people out there to invent a new way to use an old tool. Your imagination is your only limit. I mentioned above that there are ways around practically every limitation or disadvantage.

Another thing that I have learned over the years is that there is an exception to every rule. Before you start worrying about what tools or techniques to use, it is important for you to know where you are going, what your objective is.

For example, I am not a big fan of self-publishing. But if your goal is simply to see your name on the cover of a book, then self-publishing might be the best move you can make. I'm not a big fan of book doctors, but I've had people get really irate at me for saying that. I know people who have spent over $1,600 on a book doctor and been very happy with the work done. I also recently read where the state of New York indicted a book doctor company and a bunch of agents who were running a kickback scam. If the goal is to clean up a manuscript and to learn about editing, maybe a good book doctor would be a smart idea, then again, maybe not. More on this later.

In the same manner, I'm not hot on the idea of fee charging agents (more on this in the chapter on agents). Yet, I am sure there are people out there who have gotten published using a fee-charging agent.

The bottom line is: know your goal and then evaluate everything in terms of that goal.

Again, please do not feel limited by the discussion that follows. They are tools to be used or not used, as you desire. Whatever works.

At this point, you have done the following flow in your creative process:

1. Stated your original idea in one sentence.
2. Researched everything that you can about your original idea.
3. Done a book/movie dissection on someone else who used a similar original idea.
4. Are prepared to translate idea into story.

I estimate I spend 25% of my time on a novel before I even write word one. I feel that every day spent outlining and preparing, saves me at least five days of actually writing.

9. THE FIVE BIGGEST PROBLEMS

After looking at manuscripts and concepts for years, I made a list of what I considered the top five problems. Initially, the first several years, I focused on perspective as the major problem. As time went on though, and I learned more about writing, I changed that opinion. If a manuscript's major problem is perspective, then at least the writer got out of the starting gate. To my dismay I have found that many writers never make it out of the starting gate. I then decided that not having a good idea was the major problem with most manuscripts. Years after making that decision, I revised my list once more and what you have below has been updated several times.

So my ranking of problems is more of a creative flow ranking rather than perhaps a percentage as determined by Mayer, Doherty, Donegan, Dalton and McGuire, Certified Public Accountants and Statisticians of Writing.

1. Characters. You engage the reader on the emotional and intellectual levels. Good characters can overcome everything else because they touch the reader emotionally which is the most important aspect of a novel. When Anne Tyler wrote <u>Breathing Lessons</u> the basic story was two people driving from Baltimore to Pennsylvania for a funeral and then back home. Not the world's most startling idea or story. But the characters were done so well the book is a great read. For me, this was one of the greatest lessons I've had to learn over the years: people are more interested in people than anything else.

I just read a book about the battle of Thermopylae that is selling quite well now. What I realized reading it was that the aspect of the book that intrigued readers was not so much the battle, but the Spartans—readers were fascinated to learn how men could become soldiers that would stand and die to the last man in that mountain pass in Greece.

Why is Stephen King the #1 horror writer? There are other writers out there who do horror as well as he does. But he does great characters that draw the reader into the story, and then when the horror strikes, it has more of an impact because of that emotional involvement.

If you want to see a great example of introducing characters and engaging readers with them, read the first ten pages of LONESOME DOVE. Larry McMurty introduces Call, Gus, Newt, Jake Spoon, Deets and several other characters in such a way that you immediately have a feel for them. McMurty is a master of multiple points of view.

2. The Idea. You've got to have a good idea to start with. Too many manuscripts are written about something that really won't interest anyone enough to plunk down hard cash to read it.

I beat to death earlier, and will later, the ability to state your idea succinctly. After you master that, find out if it works as a hook. When you look at a complete stranger on the bus going to work and say: "I read a book the other day about—(insert your idea)." How do they react? Are they interested? Do they call the police and have you carted off? Or, most likely, do they stare at you blankly without interest?

The idea is the thing that will intrigue readers more on the intellectual side of the house. You put good characters together with a great idea and the sky is the limit.

3. Story. If a manuscript has an intriguing original idea and good characters, then the next issue is: is the story interesting? How many times have you picked up a book or heard about a movie that sounded interesting and then got turned off by the manner in which the story was told?

My first novel published, Eyes Of The Hammer, was about US military forces going to South America and attacking drug labs. Tom Clancy came out with Clear and Present Danger at the same time my book was coming out. The original ideas in the two were similar. But the way in which we told the story was quite different. He told it from the top looking down, while mine

61

was from the bottom looking up. I focused on the Special Forces team, which I knew well, while he took a more global view.

The story is a major stumbling block. I can pitch you ten very good ideas at any moment. But each of those ten would take me quite a while to come up with a good supporting story. In fact, in eight of the ten, I probably would not be able to come up with a good story.

I spend a lot of time working on story after I have an idea. I war game various stories with my partner and we discuss them. Ultimately, and you are going to cringe to hear this, I don't proceed with a storyline until it *feels* right. This is part of the artistic craft in writing, but a pretty realistic one. You have to feel comfortable that you can write your story and that it is interesting not only to the reader, but also to you the writer.

4. Perspective/Point of View. I have a whole chapter dedicated to this style problem so I won't beat it to death here. But I have found that when a person has trouble writing action scenes the first thing I look for is to see if the author is handling perspective well. When dialogue drags, I check. As a matter of fact, when there is any style problem, the first thing I look at is the perspective the story is being told in, rather like you would check to see if there was any gas in the tank if a car's battery (the idea) was putting out juice, but the engine wouldn't fire.

Perspective is your voice as a writer.

5. Timeline or pacing of the story. I have several chapters dedicated to this area. This comes up very quickly at times because too many writers don't knock the reader's socks off with their opening two chapters. Most of us aren't a good enough writer to spend a hundred pages slowly drawing the reader in. You have to hook them and hook them fast. I have chapter on how to start your novel and a chapter on pacing that addresses these problems.

10. CHARACTERS

I've heard it said that there are two ways to write a book. The first is to come up with a plot and then find characters to live the story. The second is to come up with characters and write their story. I squirm out of that by saying do both. Remember one thing though—it will be people who read your book and people identify primarily with people, not plots or facts. Another thing to consider is this: many times, your characters *are* your plot.

Regardless, you need people in your story. Or maybe aliens. Or maybe an interesting rabbit such as in <u>Watership Down</u>. Or maybe a wisteria vine as in Clyde Edgerton's <u>Floatplane Notebooks</u>. You need characters, even if they are inanimate. The antagonists in Krakeur's book <u>Into Thin Air</u> are the weather and Mount Everest.

I remember in the army we used to get asked which came first: the mission or the men? The approved solution was the mission (read plot). My answer was always the men (read characters), because without the men you couldn't accomplish the mission. In the same manner, you need good characters regardless of the story, and if you keep them "in character" they will dictate what is going to happen in your story because they will react appropriately and not according to your whims as the author.

I was slow to appreciate the importance—indeed the pre-eminence—of characters in a novel. It was a three-stage process. First, I had to accept that characters were the most important aspect of the story. For many that's a given, but coming from a background where plot ruled, this meant I had to make a 180 degree turn in perspective. I've found the opposite is true also. I've read manuscripts that were so character oriented there was little to no plot. There are writers who need to understand the importance of having a story in which the characters exist.

The second step was to spend as much time developing my characters *before* starting the novel as I spent outlining my plot. Some people might be able to invent plot or characters on the fly as they write, but I find the time spent before starting, is time well invested.

The third, and most difficult step, is to figure out how to *show* who the characters are, instead of simply telling. What actions, dialogue, decisions, etc. will show the reader the nature of the character while the character is usually unaware themselves of these aspects of their personality.

The first question is: who are my characters? Do I have a good feel for whom each person is? If you don't, you will find that your characters are two dimensional and not consistent.

What do your characters *look like?* You may know, but you will be surprised how many times characters are never really described to the reader. I felt very stupid when I finished a 450 page manuscript and handed it to someone to read and when they finished, they gave it back and said: "Very interesting, but what did your main character look like?"

It is important to describe characters as soon as possible. If you don't, the reader will formulate their own vision of the character and then you can jar them three chapters down the line when you finally get around to describing the character and it doesn't fit the reader's mental vision.

Try to describe characters in such a way that something about each one should stick in the reader's mind. This gets more important, the greater the number of characters you have.

Sometimes, authors choose not to describe their characters because they *want* the reader to think of 'everyman' or 'everywoman' when they think of each character. That's fine as long as there is a purpose to it.

In the same manner, *names* are very important. You have to decide if you are going to use a character's first name, last name, title (i.e. the doctor, the captain, etc.), or nickname. Try not to use different ones for the same character very much as it will confuse the reader.

How does a person get a "handle?" You have the name you were born with. Michael Jay Porter. Then you have what you call yourself. Mike. Then you have what others call you (with or without your liking it.): Mikey, Jay, Port, Bud, Skinny, etc. Then you have your title: Captain, Vice President for Operations, the butcher.

I saw a great carton from the Far Side once. It had on the top: "What we call dogs: Fido." On the bottom it had what dogs call themselves: "I am Fido, terrorizer of the neighborhood, sniffer of trees, master of all that I see." Or something to that effect. Get the idea?

Given the above two paragraphs, how do you pick names for your characters? The phone book is helpful. Go to the library and wander the stacks and look at author's names. High school and college yearbooks.

You do need to consider that the name fits the character. Many names denote ethnicity. Think about detectives—don't they all have hard sounding names like Magnum PI? That is done deliberately to affect you subconsciously. Also make sure two characters don't have similar names. I try to avoid even have names that start with the same letter.

I recently bought <u>The Writers Digest Character Naming Sourcebook</u> by Sherrilyn Kenyon. I find it helpful in finding names. More importantly, I find it useful in uncovering what names mean.

You should try to stick with one name for each character. Above I mentioned the number of names/titles each of us has. But if you start using all those various names interchangeably throughout a manuscript you can confuse the reader. If you alternate using first name/last name for your characters you are doubling the number of names the reader has to remember. Try to pick one name and stick with it as much as possible. Of course there will be times then other name/title comes in, such as in dialogue, but in your prose make it as easy on the reader as you can.

So what else do you need to know about a character (I will stay with the female here, no discrimination intended)? The absolute most important thing you have to know about your character is: what is her motivation? Then you also need:

1. What does she look like? How does she talk? How does she act physically? Any mannerisms?

2. What is her background? Where was she born? What were her parents like? How was she raised? Where did she go to school? What level education?

3. What is her job? What special skills does her job require and how will they affect her role in the story? What about hobbies and talents learned from them?

4. What is her family? Husband? Her relation to him? Children? Relation? Why not kids? Divorced? Why? Why not?

5. Where is she from? Did she grow up in a city or on a farm?

Some other aspects of a character to keep in mind:

-movement	-dress
-attitudes	-gestures
-manner	-culture
-context—class	-values and beliefs
-needs	-motives
-dreams	-fears

-stressors
-1st family, which is the family of origin
-2d family, which is the present family

The list could go on and on. I highly recommend putting some brainwork into your characters before writing your first page and not make it up as you go along. I say this from my own experience. The review on my second novel from the NY Times said, "The characters are right out of Action Comics." Not very nice, but true. But I think I have finally begun to learn my lesson after many manuscripts, not that I am necessarily any better at it, but I am aware of it and awareness is the first step in changing.

Now, here's something to consider: You can make your characters up out of the blue using the questions (and more) listed above. But reality says that you will be more realistic using parts of people that you have met like your mother and father and the loan officer at the bank. This runs you the danger of getting sued, of course. No, no, listen. Look at people you know as character types and use some of their traits but not them as a person. Confusing enough? Try psychology. There are several books on the market that have tests you can take that will define people by type. Get some of these books and use them to help round out your characters. They list out traits of certain personality types. Traits you can use to round out your characters.

If you deal with non-English speaking characters, it helps to let the reader know what language they are speaking in, especially if they conveniently (as so often happens, luckily for us writers) speak English besides their native tongue. Otherwise how could they shout all those dire threats and have our hero understand them just before he makes his great escape.

You make believable characters by showing how they react/act in a crisis. "Actions speak louder than words." True. Also remember, though, that the same action done for two different reasons, makes the action seem very different to the reader. Your main character kills someone. Is that bad? It depends, you say. Depends on who they killed. Why they killed them. Under what circumstances.

Remember all those answers. Because eventually you will have to answer all those to the reader and they also give you the opportunity to put some twists in your story. For example, character C kills Character J in chapter 3, making C look like a bad egg. But in chapter 7 you reveal that the deceased, J, was in reality a mad scientist about to let loose a plague upon the world and C stopped that by killing him. That certainly changes the reader's perspective on C. A rather dramatic example, I know, but I believe it gets the point across.

You say a lot about your characters by showing what choices they make under pressure which you make by conflict (go to the narrative structure.) I have found that sometimes a person's character totally changes when they are under stress and the "real" person comes out. This can be useful in your plot and storyline.

Also use the back story (doesn't necessarily have to be in the book, but you have to know in order to be able to write believable characters). All of your characters have a background prior to the beginning of the novel. Make sure you know it and where applicable, let the reader know parts of it in order understand the characters better.

Now, the astute reader is saying: "Hey, you're contradicting yourself. Earlier you said to let a character's actions speak for themselves and to try not to get into a character's head to reveal thoughts. How am I going to reveal motive without getting into thoughts?"

Although that is an apparent contradiction, in reality the two are congruous. My question to you is: How do you know anyone's thoughts in day-to-day life other than your own? Through conversation, through watching their actions over a period of time and interpreting, through various means, all short of saying "Jim thought . . ..". Taking it a step further, if you are always in your characters' heads, how can you keep a motive secret, something that might be essential to the suspense of your story?

I also recommend against using quotation marks to delineate a character's thoughts. I see this on occasion in manuscripts and think it is a poor technique for several reasons: First, you confuse the reader who naturally assumes quotation marks mean dialogue. You're making the reader work, and the reader bought your book for enjoyment, not to work. Second, if you are writing third person, how do you draw the line between those thoughts that go inside the quotation marks and everything else in narrative, which to a certain extent is also from a character's point of view? Third, it's telling not showing.

Conflict keeps a story going and reveals much about your characters. Conflict is the gap between expectation and the actual result. There are 3 levels of conflict for your characters:

-inner (inside the character) In many cases inner conflict occurs when a person has a disagreement between values he or she holds to be important. By adjusting a character's circumstances, you can develop internal conflict.

-personal (between characters)

-universal/societal- (characters versus fate/God/the system)

You have to consider what your main character faces on each of these levels.

There are five major sources of conflict for people (although you can probably come up with more):

1. Money
2. Sex
3. Family
4. Religion
5. Politics

Keep these sources of conflict in mind when developing your characters.

Remember all characters have to have an agenda/goals they want to achieve. That gives them a driving force, even if it is a passive or negative one. Characters can pursue their goals aggressively or subtly. Or they could not pursue their goals, which also says something about them.

Motivation is the most important factor to consider when having your character make choices or do actions. Once you have a feel for your characters' motivation and they come alive for you, then to a certain extent you lose control over your story. For your characters to be realistic, they have to react like the people you have developed them to be, not like you want them to react in order to move your story ahead. Every time a character acts or reacts, I ask myself if that is consistent with who I projected the character to be.

For example, I wrote a scene where some people were trying to talk my main character into traveling back to Cambodia where he had last been over thirty years ago. Where his Special Forces team had been wiped out horribly and my character had had nightmares about for years. And I needed my character to agree to go (or else the book would have been rather short). But I had to sit and come up with a legitimate reason for my character to go. I had to figure out what would motivate him to agree to do something that he normally would not do. And it had to be believable to the reader, which means it had to be believable to my character.

Remember also to consider extremes when writing about characters in order to involve your reader more intensely. You can have a good character and a bad character. But would the reader prefer to see an evil character and a noble character? Think of personalities as a pendulum and understand that the further you swing that pendulum, the more involved the reader usually will be. Therefore, take any very positive trait you can think of and try to find its opposite. Do the reverse. Then use those traits to develop your characters.

You need to study people and also remember that you were not the original mold for mankind. Some people are very different than you and have different value systems. I think authors who have very good characters understand this very well. Much better than the average person.

I read an interesting thing that other day in a psychology book: the author said that everyone has a religion. What he meant was that everyone has something they believe in, even if it's not to believe in God. To write good characters, you need to know what their value and belief system is, then keep them acting according to that system. Even a crazy serial killer character has a belief system, skewed as it may be. In fact, dissecting that belief system is often the task of the novel's main good character in order to catch the serial killer.

In fact, a book I recommend reading is John Douglas's <u>Mindhunter</u>. Douglas was one of the founders of the Investigative Support Unit that specialized in profiling. What an author does is actually the opposite of what his unit does. A profiler looks at the evidence then tries to figure who the person is. An author invents the person then needs to come up with the evidence that would be representative of that person. Another interesting aspect of profiling is that it shows that people have character traits that are locked in and that those traits dictate their actions.

For me, the hardest thing to do as a writer is develop an agenda for a character that is something I don't personally have, and then keep in mind that the character is not totally aware of his own agenda and as a writer *show* the reader this agenda.

Continuing on in the field of psychology, you can learn about personality types with a little bit of study and apply those personalities to your characters. The Briggs-Meyers Test divides people up into 16 different personality types. It is given in a book called: <u>Please Understand Me: Character and Temperament Types</u>. The title tells you this might be a good way to get insight into character.

Not only are the 16 types listed, but also the good and bad tendencies of each type are listed which helps making well-rounded characters. Also, the typical interactions between the various personality types are also listed. I found that when I took the test, the personality type I fell into, described me very accurately, both good and bad. The author also lists the percentage of the population that falls into the various types and the types are labeled.

A mistake can be to make a character a composite of several people that the author knows (even though above I said this is a good technique.). The problem is that various parts of different personalities often don't fit together in a smooth mesh in one person. Be careful if you are making a composite character. Make sure that all the parts fit together or else your character will appear to have multiple personalities. Unless, that is what you want.

Another thing to keep in mind is that every character trait is double-edged. Sometimes I read a student's character sketch and I ask: what's wrong with this person? What's bad about them? Too often the characters are pro-jected as two-dimensional, perfect people. All female characters are beautiful. All male characters are over six feet, know several martial arts and are deadly with a gun, yet still a loving father to their children. Right.

Remember, if someone is very loyal, is that a good thing? Can't loyalty carried to an extreme be very bad? Isn't that true of every so-called good emo-tion? Can't love slide into obsession? By working with these emotions, you add depth and interest to your characters.

I've noticed that British TV seems to do more with characters than American TV. I've recently watched two series, <u>Cracker</u> and <u>Kavanagh</u>, where the main characters had flaws, in some case severe. In <u>Cracker</u>, the main char-acter is a psychologist who consults with the police. He also is addicted to gambling. Smokes like a chimney. His wife is leaving him every other episode. He is truly the flawed 'good' guy. Hollywood has gotten away from that, but writing hasn't so much. Give your main characters some rough edges. Readers relate to that.

Unless of course you're writing a Star Wars book. Or a 007 book. There are some types of books where the 'pure' main character is necessary.

Even in an action oriented book, it is useful to look at your characters and try to have each major one have an ongoing personal crisis as a sort of subplot that moves along with the major action crisis. This helps keep the readers as interested in the character as in the plot. This is not as easy to do as it sounds. The character subplot—to be successful—usually has to do several things:

1. Not jar the reader and take away from the action of the main plot, but rather supplement it.

2. Have a conclusion before or at the same time the main plot concludes.

3. It should support the main plot in some manner, beyond the simple fact that the character is involved in the main plot. For example, if your detective

69

is going through a divorce while she is working the big case, is there a way the divorce itself can be connected to the big case beyond the effect it has on the detective? Maybe the prime suspect's lawyer also represents the detective's husband? I talk quite a bit about this in the section on subplots.

I think one of the hardest things to do as a writer is show something about a character rather than tell it. Since most people/characters are not walking around self-actualized on Maslow's fifth level, they are often unaware of the reasons for their own actions. In fact, psychology indicates that people build up their strongest defenses (read 'denial') around the weakest parts of their character.

To give you an example of how a writer shows something about a character rather than simply telling the reader, in Lisa Alther's book Kinflicks the author wanted to show how one of the female characters was always greatly influenced by whatever man was in her life. A brilliant writer like me would have said: "And she was greatly influenced by whatever man happened to be living with her that year." Someone like Lisa Alther shows this by having the woman be dressed totally different each year when she flew home to visit her mother.

Some writing instructors say a main character has to change by the end of the story. My question to you is how many people do you know who have really changed? This gets down to the definition of what change is.

Here is what I think happens to a character when they change. A character has a moment of enlightenment, makes a decision based on that moment, than has to live with the consequences of that decision which ultimately does change both them and the story. But the 'burning bush' type of change is hard to pull off realistically. Most of the time if you do that type of complete change it will ring false to the reader—like an author manipulation.

99% of what people do day-in and day-out is habit. And habits are extremely difficult to change. A great example of character 'change' is in the movie The Verdict. Paul Newman plays a drunken, down and out lawyer. He has one case left—a wrongful injury suit. He's in the hospital taking pictures of this woman in a coma. Suddenly, he stops taking pictures and just looks at the woman. Not a word of dialogue—but he has a moment of enlightenment. The thing in the bed is suddenly not a case, but a real person. He decides there that he will try this case and win it.

What's so good, though, is that he's still a bum and a drunk. He still screws things up. He suddenly doesn't become a brilliant, sober lawyer. But with his decision he does do some things differently. Because he has to live with the results of that decision, he is forced to change.

Another factor to consider is reader empathy for your protagonist. Too often I get character sketches or stories from writers where the main character is someone who the reader won't like. Now, once in a while, a really good writer can pull that off, but it's hard to do. I bring this up right after talking about 'change' in a character because sometimes writers want to start with a negative main character and have the character change into a likable one by the end of the book. The difficulty with that is getting the reader into the story with a character they might not like. If you try to do this, you should have some sort of redeeming quality scene very early so the reader knows there is a seed of hope.

In screenwriting, it is generally accepted that within the first ten minutes of the film (i.e., the first ten pages of the screenplay) the nature of the main character has to be shown to the audience in some manner. As a novel writer you should 'set' your main character pretty early in the novel.

The problem I've run into and others writers I've talked to have is how to make characters who aren't 'cardboard' cut outs. Who have depth, but yet at the same time we aren't blatantly telling the reader about.

Something to consider is this: can you look at someone who is different from you, who has different values, and not only understand him, but empathize with him to a certain extent? I think many smart people have a hard time understanding characters who do things that are obviously not smart. Yet those same smart people have blind spots in their personality where they do corresponding not-smart things. The difficulty as an author is to have characters that you know their faults, yet write them as real people who don't see those same faults. *And*, you can't spell those faults out to the reader—you have to show those character traits.

You will always have a protagonist and an antagonist. In <u>Butch Cassidy and the Sundance Kid</u> who is the protagonist?

Butch.

Why? Because he always comes up with the plans.

Remember that your protagonist is only as good as the antagonist is bad. There would be no Clarice Sterling without a Hannibal Lecter.

Try to give you antagonist as strong a motivation as your protagonist. That way the conflict between the two rings true.

However, there are different ways to look at those. Something I've just recently realized is that the antagonist can be a situation. If you're writing a book about the Alamo, while Santa Anna and the Mexican Army might seem like the antagonist, in reality the situation is what everyone, including the bad guys, are up against.

Good characters should be:

1. Heroic: They struggle to meet every day challenges or extreme challenges. Either way they show courage and dignity in their battle. They don't have to be nice, but they do have to be good. If you start with a negative

71

character there must be a glimmer of hope the reader can discern that they could change for the better.

2. Believable: Give them strengths *and* weaknesses. Often it is the latter that readers identify with more. And you must give consistent evidence of these traits, not just show it once.

3. Sympathetic: Readers like characters who make things happen; who actively respond to the world around them instead of constantly reacting. Readers don't particularly care for victims. Remember I said above that you get to truly know someone by how they react in a crisis—in the same manner, characters grab our attention when they face a crisis. Also remember that opposing external traits cause inner conflict.

4. Memorable. Think back about your favorite book and what do you remember? The characters.

Sometimes *less is better.* What I mean is that occasionally I'll get a manuscript to read and as soon as the main character is introduced, we get their entire life history. How do you feel about meeting someone like that in real life, where you know everything about them at the first meeting? What's the point in seeing them again?

You, as the author, have to know everything about your character, but you don't have to tell the reader everything. A little mystery is intriguing. You know how your character developed a quirky trait, but by not telling the reader up front, you make the reader curious. For example, in the movie LA Confidential, we meet each of the three main characters in three opening scenes and each of them shows us something about who they are by actions they take, but we don't know *why* they're taking those action until much further in the movie.

The best way to think about your characters is as if they were real people your readers are meeting for the first time on a blind date. Make the meeting a memorable and make the character someone the reader wants to go out with again.

11. POINT OF VIEW

After years of writing and teaching novel writing, I firmly believe that perspective or point of view is the number one style problem for most writers. It is also one of the easiest problems to correct with a bit of awareness of both the problem and possible solutions. For the sake of simplicity, in this chapter I will stick with the term point of view, although it is interchangeable with perspective.

When considering how to tell your story, the first thing you have to do is select a point of view. This may be the most critical decision you have to make. Often the type of story you are writing will clearly dictate the point of

72

view, but a good understanding of the various modes of presentation is essential because this is one area where beginning novelists often have problems. They may select the right point of view, but it is often used poorly because of a lack of understanding of the tool itself.

Regardless of which point of view (or points of view) you choose to use, there is one thing you must have: <u>you</u> as the author must have a good feeling about the point of view with which you are telling the story. If you don't have a warm and fuzzy about that, this confusion will most definitely be translated to the reader. Remember, ultimately, point of view is your voice as a writer.

Some people write like an MTV music video: point of view flying all over the place, giving glimpses into each character but never really keeping the reader oriented. I say this because the best analogy I can give for point of view is to look at it as your camera. You as author are the director: you see and know everything in your story. But the reader only sees and knows what the camera records: the point of view you choose. You must always keep that in mind. You see the entire scene, but your lens only records the words you put on the page and you have to keep your lens tightly focused and firmly in hand.

The key term to know, like a director, is the word 'cut'. A cut in film terminology is when the camera is either a) stopped, then restarted later, or b) stopped and another camera is then used. To a writer, a cut is a change in point of view. In an MTV music video, you can go about three seconds before having to 'cut'. Robert Altman, in the beginning of <u>The Player</u>, uses an extremely long single camera sequence before the first cut—another reason to watch the film.

The most critical thing to remember about point of view is that you have to keep the reader oriented. The reader has got to know from what point of view they are viewing the scene. Lose that and you lose the reader. Thus, as with everything else, there is no wrong point of view to write in, or even mixture of point of views to write in, but it is wrong to confuse the reader as to the point of view through which they are 'seeing' the story.

Take the camera point of view a bit further. When directors do a scene, they immediately look into a viewfinder and watch the recording of the take. They do this because, although they saw what happened, they have to know what the camera recorded. As an author, you have to get out of your own point of view as the writer and be able to see what you write as the reader sees it.

There are three common modes of point of view in novels: first person, third person and omniscient.

First person means you use the word "I" quite a bit. It is giving the camera to one character and letting that character film a documentary while doing a voiceover.

This point of view has its advantage in that the narrator is telling his/her own story. The major disadvantage is that the reader can only see and know what the narrator knows. The narrator can be a witness or a participant in the story. You, as the author, are absent in this mode, thus you surrender part of your control in writing. Remember, the first person narrator is not you the author, but rather the character in the story.

Note that there are certain types of genre that fit first person very well, most particularly mysteries/detective stories. That's logical if you understand the advantages of first person: by using that mode, the writer can bring the reader along for the ride, disclosing clues as the narrator discovers them.

The major disadvantage of first person is that your narrator has to be present in every scene. Because of this, many writers make their narrator the protagonist. A problem can crop up in that the narrator will then be a critical part of the plot and have many things happen to them and around them. Will the narrator be able to react realistically while still telling the story in a coherent form?

Another problem can be the logistics of getting your narrator to all the key events in order to narrate them. I have seen writers end up with very convoluted, and unrealistic, plots in order to do that. If the narrator isn't present at these important scenes, then they find out about them by other means, which can lessen suspense and definitely lessens the immediacy of the action in the story as you have major action occurring off-stage.

Some authors use a narrator who isn't one of the main characters—what is known as a detached narrator. The narrator is more of an observer. This has some advantages. Think of the Sherlock Holmes stories—who is narrating? Watson. Why? Because this allows the author to withhold what Holmes is thinking from the audience.

Something else to think about—should the reader believe your narrator? If everything your narrator says is fact, then there might not be much suspense. But think about the movie <u>The Usual Suspects</u>. The story is narrated by a character, who it turns out, is the man everyone is searching for. In a book, you can raise suspense if your first person narrator is caught in a small lie early on in the story—the reader will then have to be more judgmental about everything else the narrator says.

Another big issue of first person narration is the issue of tense and time. There are two ways to view time in a first person story:

1. *I remember when.* In this case, the narrator is telling the story in past tense, looking backward. This immediately reduces the suspense of whether the narrator survives the story. There is also the issue that the narrator is thus withholding information from the reader—the narrator obviously knows the ending, yet chooses not to reveal it to the reader.

2. In real time. The narrator is telling the story as it unfolds around him or her. A problem with this is what happens when the narrator is involved in an emotionally overwhelming event? Will he still be able to narrate the story?

The big problem with time sense is that even the best writers tend to mix 1 and 2 above. At times they will be in real time, then every so often slip into past time.

A further problem with first person is many writers tend to slide from first into second person point of view. Any time you put *you* in your narrative, addressing the reader, you have moved from first to second person. You should avoid doing that.

There are ways to get around the disadvantages of first person. Examine some first person novels and you will discover them. Interview With A Vampire by Anne Rice is an interesting use of first person and the title tells you why. She has the first person of the reporter start the story but shifts into a first person narrative by the vampire Louis through the medium of the interview. She can go back in time with Louis and then return to the present with the reporter, both in first person. She has two levels of interest and suspense: the present fate of the narrator, and the fate of the vampire in his own tale.

There are other novelists who have come up with novel ideas (pun intended) to tell first person stories while getting around some of the disadvantages.

I place great emphasis in my own writing career and when teaching upon reading and also upon watching movies/videos, but I watch videos and read books in a different mode as a "writer." I study them for structure. To see what the author/ screenwriter/ director did with the subject matter. How it was presented. When you pick up a novel, the first thing you should note is what person it is written in. Then ask yourself why the author chooses that point of view. What did the novel gain from that point of view?

When I give examples in a little bit, you will see more clearly the advantages and disadvantages of first person.

One thing about first person to keep in mind. It is the voice most novice writers naturally gravitate to, but it is one of the most difficult voices to do well. Because of that, there is an initial negative impression among agents and editors when confronted with a first person story.

Third person allows the author to be like a movie camera moving to any set and recording any event, as long as one of the characters is lugging the camera. It also allows the camera to slide in behind the eyeballs of any character, but beware; do it too often or awkwardly and you will lose your reader very quickly. Perhaps one of the hardest things to master is to not get in your characters' heads to learn their thoughts, but rather letting their actions and words let the reader figure those thoughts out. This is the infamous "show don't tell" rule of writing and for me, the most difficult aspect of writing.

When you are in third person, everything that happens is filtered through the five senses whatever character whose point of view you are in at the moment. The character, in effect, *is* the camera.

There is a strong tendency, especially when first starting out, to write everything from the point of view of your characters. If you approach every scene with the question: Which character am I primarily viewing this scene through? then you are doing this. While this is the most common and accepted mode of point of view in writing novels, it also presents several problems if handled poorly:

It can be confusing to the reader as to whose head they are in or which character's point of view the scene is viewed from unless you make the breaks clear—a common technique for this is to change POV with each chapter. The reader then grows to expect a different character POV each time they start a new chapter.

Larry McMurty is a master of POV. In <u>Commanche Moon</u> the last book in the Lonesome Dove series, he would change third person POV every paragraph. Larry McMurty also won the Pulitzer Prize. Most of us aren't that good. He is able to completely change his writing style for each character so that you truly can feel that you are seeing the scene from that specific character's unique point of view.

You are cheating the reader if you are constantly in your characters' heads, yet you hold back something the character knows (which is sometimes necessary for your suspense). Try to keep a consistent depth of insight into each character's thoughts.

You give the reader the characters' thoughts, rather than letting the reader figure out the character from actions and dialogue. Unless you are very skilled, you will tend to have all your characters seem alike in the way that they think.

You will also tend to give each of your character's point of views on various topics, most especially other characters, and this can be confusing to the reader who has his/her own point of view from the story you have presented so far. You also might confuse the reader if the characters themselves have disagreeing point of views which is normal if the characters are realistic. This can be an advantage if handled well—differing point of views on the same scene can make for intriguing reading.

All the above is not to say don't get inside your characters' heads—indeed, as I mentioned it is the most common form in published books—but it is to say that when you do it, do it carefully. Keep the number of characters you do it with to a minimum. Make sure switches between characters' point of views are clear. The easiest way to do that is to stick with one character for each section/chapter of the novel so that when the reader flips the page to a new chapter they grow to expect to be moving to another character's head.

Another interesting problem with third person omniscient is that there's a tendency to say, "he (or she) thought" some other character acted in a certain way. Well, did the other character act that way? It's not fair to the reader to not let them know. Remember that if you stay with your characters' point of views, you are controlling the lenses through which the reader sees the story unfold. You must be very careful with that control because that also means you are controlling the reality the reader sees.

If you stay with one character (everything seen from that one point of view throughout the novel) then you might write first person because what you end up doing is writing a third person/first person story. I have, however, read quite a few books that were third person where the POV stayed with one character throughout. Some mysteries are written that way. An author might do this if they want a little distance from the main character—- i.e. they don't want to do the first-person voice-over.

While there is an issue in first person in terms of time—looking back—the issue in third person is more one of distance. How close does the author get to each character? How much of inner thoughts are revealed? This is the distance between being in third person point of view and omniscient. An omniscient narrator can get into any character's head but from an outside-in view, not an inside out. Thus, the author can bypass the character's own flaws and deluded perceptions. This is an advantage if you want it, but that deluded perception is what some entire books are built in. It is all a question of what you are trying to achieve.

The way I think about is this: are you simply assuming the character's five senses to tell the story? Or, are you going to assume their emotional and intellectual reactions also? The depth you do the latter is the depth of the insight into the character you are giving.

Something I have found to be generally true is that you have to very seriously look at the number of characters you are going to use to frame your point of view in the story. The reason for that is, the second you go into a character's mind, the reader assumes that that character is as essential to the plot as every other character whose point of view you have taken. A general rule of thumb that I try to keep in mind is that I should spend as much time on every character whose point of view I use. That general rule cuts out using too many characters' point of views.

Also consider what you are going to do when two or three characters whose point of view you use are going to be in the same scene. Are you going to shift from one to the other? Or stay with one? But then the reader wonders what the other characters whose point of view you've used elsewhere think and feel. A trend I have been following the more I write, is to limit the number of point of views I take in order to strengthen those characters in my story. I had a tendency early on to use too many characters' point of views and this weakened my characters.

Omniscient point of view. This is also known as authorial narrative. When I first began writing I felt I had to lock in third person on a character for every scene. And that worked. But the more I wrote, the more I wanted to use an omniscient point of view at times. I tend to use it for giving the reader expository information.

I liken authorial point of view to the camera getting pulled back in order to show the viewer more. There are times you might want to pull back so you can tell the reader more information or show the reader more than the characters who are in the scene might be able to see or know.

For example, a battle scene can be written much better from omniscient point of view if you want the reader to understand the battle. But if you want the reader to see how one specific character is responding to the danger of combat, you might stick with third person from that character's point of view.

One of the most difficult obstacles for me as a writer was accepting that I could write from the authorial point of view. That I can describe things as they are or were using my own voice as the author of the work. The more I write, the more I find it important to be able to do this. There may be some information that is not going to fit using third person. Also, you may get very tired of writing "he thought" over and over again and the reader may grow weary of seeing it.

<u>EXAMPLES:</u> You have to consider point of view before you begin your book and before you write every scene, much as a movie director has to.

Say you are going to write a thriller about a female FBI agent tracking down a vicious serial killer. You want to open your book with a scene that will grab the reader and set the stage for the suspense of the novel so you decide to open with a killing. What point of view will you use? Now, remember, no point of view is *wrong*—you just have to understand the advantages and disadvantages of your possible choices and make a knowledgeable decision.

You can decide to use third person from the point of view of the victim. This can build tension well, but also means the chapter will end abruptly.

You can use third person from the point of view of the killer, but remember that the killer knows who he or she is and therefore you have to be careful how much insight into the killer's head you allow. A technique some use to overcome that limitation is to have the killer think of himself in different terms than his reality. The killer is Joe Schmo, but when he's in killer mode he thinks of himself as Captain Hook, thus hiding his identity from the reader in third person insight.

You can do third person limited, which means seeing the scene from *behind* the killer. You're seeing the same thing the killer does, but you're not in his head.

Or, you could use omniscient, placing your 'camera' above the scene. Here, though, you have to be careful not to show too much and give away the killer's identity. Much like a director might choose a dark basement where the viewer can't see the killer's face, you will do the same.

Another example of considering how to write a scene is if you have two characters meeting in a pub for an important exchange of dialogue. They sit across from each other. How are you going to 'shoot' this scene? From third person of one of the characters? That means you get that character's thoughts and you describe the other character's reactions—i.e. the camera is on your POV character's shoulder. Is it important that the reader know one character's thought more than the other's? Or is it more important to show one character's reactions than the others?

Or, do you keep switching the camera back and forth across the booth, going from one to the other? If you're Larry McMurty and won a Pulitzer Prize you might be able to do that, but for most of us, such a constant switching of POV is very disconcerting to the reader. Or do you shoot it omniscient with the camera off to the side and simply show actions and record dialogue?

I've written in all the above points of view. I tend now to mix third person with omniscient. I use omniscient for expository information that would be awkward to continually push through a third person POV, but I move to third person to give more depth to my characters and give their reactions and thoughts to situations.

Here is the difference between an expository scene in third person limited and omniscient:

Third person limited:

Joe walked up the dirt road leading to the Giza Plateau. As he cleared the rise he saw the Sphinx off to his right and the three massive pyramids ahead. He knew that historians believed the largest of the three had been built by the Pharaoh Khufu, more popularly known as Cheops. He'd read that it was 138 meters high. He was impressed with magnitude of the construction, noting the massive blocks of aged stone and wondering how they had been moved so long ago.

Omniscient:

Joe walked up the dirt road leading to the Giza Plateau. The Sphinx was to his right and the three massive pyramids in front. Historians believe the largest pyramid was built by the Pharaoh Khufu, more popularly known as Cheops. It was 138 meters high, built of massive blocks of aged stone that must have taken a marvel of engineering to move.

The second presents the information directly, without having to be processed through Joe's head. If you want to break yourself of always using a character's point of view to write, try using the word THE to start sentences. This will help you in writing narrative. Remember that you are the AUTHOR. You can actually write down what you want to say without having to have it come from the point of view of one of your characters.

For more examples of the various points of views try to visualize the following: Your point of view character, Joe, is sitting in a room looking out a window into a courtyard. Two men walk into the courtyard, speaking to each other. They proceed to get into a fight. Notice the various ways I can write this scene:

1. First person:

I saw the two people walk into the courtyard. They began to argue with each other, and then suddenly, they began to fight.

Note: Because I wasn't out there, I couldn't hear what they said, which is a limitation of first person. However, I could find out what was said later on by talking to one of the two people. (There are always ways to get around disadvantages.) Or, I could change the story and have my first person character in the courtyard in order to be able to relate what happens—but the presence of that character in the courtyard could also change what occurs.

Another issue is identifying the two men. My narrator would have to know them in order to do that.

If I changed the story and made my narrator either of the characters, then the issue would whether I am telling this as it occurs, or looking back. If I am telling as it occurs, then can my narrator still narrator while fighting?

2. Third person, deep insight, (which is what I call getting into one of your character's heads) It is as if you are telling the reader what is happening out there from Joe's point of view and he knows something about what is happening

Joe saw John walk into the courtyard with Ted. Joe could see that they were arguing and he knew they were still probably upset about their earlier confrontation over Madeline's boyfriend.

He saw John hold up his hands in a placating manner and say something. Then he noticed that Ted was yelling something back and John dropped his hands.

Joe jumped to his feet as he saw John grab the collar of Ted's windbreaker.

80

Note that everything that happens is being filtered through Joe's senses. And we have to 'trust' Joe's assumptions about the scene; for example, that the two are upset over the earlier confrontation. For all Joe knows, it might be something very different.

What many writers do to overcome this is use one of the advantages of third person, which is switch POVs from one character to another who has a better camera angle.

3. Third person, deep insight, shifting point of view
The same scene. We start in Joe's point of view, and then shift when it is necessary.

Joe looked up from his cup of coffee and saw John and Ted walk into the courtyard. Joe could see that they were arguing and he knew they were still probably upset about their earlier confrontation over Madeline's boyfriend.

In the courtyard, John could see Joe watching them but he could care less. John was still uneasy about their earlier confrontation over Madeline's boyfriend.

"I still don't accept it," Ted muttered. "It's wrong."

John held up his hands. "I don't want to talk about it any more. We've discussed Philip enough. It's up to Madeline."

"No, it's not up to Madeline. We have a responsibility. He's not good for her and I don't approve of their going out together."

John dropped his hands and glared at Ted; he could never just let anything go. "I said, I don't want to talk about it again. Period."

Ted wasn't to be dissuaded. "We have to. I think—"

John felt something snap inside of him and he grabbed the collar of Ted's windbreaker. "Goddamn it. I told you I didn't want to talk about it again."

Note: here I describe what is happening in the courtyard by getting into one of the two men's heads. Note that I make sure the reader knows I've shifted character POV by reversing the camera angle. I let the reader know a little background simply by having one of the character's thinking about it. We can hear what is said and we know what the argument is about. The camera is on John's shoulder with a feed into his brain. We know who the characters are because John, the POV character, knows. We also know that what Joe suspected was true, by having John confirm what they were fighting about.

4. Omniscient (author as narrator) here the author simply records observations, showing, not telling:
John and Ted walked into the courtyard. Ted's face was tight, his forehead wrinkled in thought, his eyes smoldering. "I still don't accept it. It's wrong."

John held up his hands. "I don't want to talk about it any more. We've discussed Philip enough. It's up to Madeline."

"No, it's not up to Madeline. We have a responsibility. He's not good for her and I don't approve of their going out together."

John dropped his hands and glared at Ted. "I said, I don't want to talk about it again. Period."

Ted wasn't to be dissuaded. "We have to. I think—"

John's hands shop up and his fingers wrapped around the collar of Ted's windbreaker. "Goddamn it. I told you I didn't want to talk about it again."

I manage to impart all the information needed and describe the scene. The best way to describe this point of view is to pretend you, as author, are a movie camera that can move around freely throughout your scenes, you show. Also, and this is difficult for new writers, you can make authorial comments such as Ted not being dissuaded because, as God, you know what everyone is thinking.

You could also write this scene with an omniscient point of view and give *both* characters' thoughts and inner reactions.

Note that in first person, because I had the glass between the character, and me I couldn't hear what they said. If I was in the courtyard with them, so I could hear what was being said, I also might affect the action, because of my presence. In third person I am free to either lock onto one of the characters. In omniscient I am floating overhead, and not affecting the scene at all.

The bottom line is: Every time you use a point of view, make sure you look at the advantages and disadvantages. Recognize what information you are imparting and ultimately try to see things from the reader's point of view. In the final analysis, you must make sure your reader is smoothly imparted the information you wish for him or her to have.

More on point of view:

Staying in a character's head also makes your character inconsistent if the thoughts are not in line with what he/she says or does. And if it is in line, then why have to tell thoughts when the words/actions will speak for them? That isn't to say don't get into thoughts at all, but don't do it exclusively.

When you do have your characters' thoughts, make sure they think differently from each other. Don't write the same way for every one and have them react the same or they appear to be cardboard cutouts.

A word on **2d person**. It has been used but is difficult to work with. 2d person is using "you" or "we" in telling the story. This has an advantage in that it can bring the reader into the story more intimately, in fact, making the reader part of the story in the role of participant or close observer. There are occasions where the author might address the reader using 2d person.

TEST. What point of view is this book in?

ANSWER: 2d person. Why did I choose that point of view? Because I wanted you to be involved when you read it. I wanted you the reader to feel that I was talking directly to you.

Overall, though, 2d person rarely works in a novel.

How about *mixing* the various points of views in the same novel? Can it be done?

Remember my premise: there is no wrong way. Yes, it can be done. A certain fellow named William Faulkner did an OK job of it in a novel called The Sound And The Fury. The first three sections of that book were first person (indeed, three different first persons). The last third person. You can do anything that works. It certainly worked for Faulkner, but remember: SMOOTHNESS.

I just finished rereading The Last Picture Show by Larry McMurty and in the forward he presented an interesting angle on point of view. He said that on occasion he has written a story in first person and then rewritten it in third. I've tried it and it's not as hard as you would think.

When you watch TV or film, start paying very close attention how the director filmed the scene. Think about something as simple as two people sitting in a booth at a restaurant. Does the director film it from the side, showing both people? Or does the camera shift back and forth from one side of the table to the other? And if it does, when do the shifts take place? Does the director want to show the person speaking or the person listening and reacting to the other's words?

Do you see how many different ways a scene can be filmed? You, as the author, can write the same scene many different ways.

Please don't think from all that I have written above that it is wrong to get in your characters' heads. If you go into the bookstore today and pull the top ten fiction novels off the shelf, I think more than half would have varying degrees of insight into the characters' thoughts and feelings. The key is to do it right. I have beaten this point to death because I have found this area to be the number one style problem for new writers. I think as long as you are aware of it and use the tool properly, you will be all right.

Remember: consistency and smoothness.

The most important thing about any point of view you use is that the reader knows where the 'camera' is.

12. DIALOGUE

It is important to remember that psychologists say that a very large percentage of communication is non-verbal, yet on the printed page all you have are the words. There is no tone, no facial expressions, no hand gestures, nothing that in normal face-to-face communication can drastically affect the message being communicated. Because all you have are the words, you must choose them very carefully. A conversation in a novel is *not* exactly as it would be in "real life". Because you are lacking the things you would have in real life, you make up for it with your word choice. You also must be aware that you can't bore the reader, thus your written dialogue is usually more concise than spoken.

Purposes of dialogue: You use dialogue for many reasons beyond the simple fact that your plot calls for a conversation at a certain point. Dialogue is a good way to overcome limitations of some of the tools you are using. For example, if you are writing a first person detective story, dialogue is useful in giving your main character (and in turn the reader) important information. It is also useful in imparting backdrop information or exposition (more on this in the chapter on where to start your novel).

Dialogue reveals a great amount of information about your characters. It is their chance to express themselves directly to the reader. Make sure, though, that the voice they use is consistent. If you want to check this, go back through whatever you've written and highlight everything each character says, using different colors for the different characters, then trace each character's dialogue by itself, making sure it is the same voice. Also, make sure that all your characters don't sound the same. Dialogue can reveal motivation, which is critical to character. Remember, though, just like in real life you have to consider whether what a person says is the truth.

Dialogue advances the plot. It can also sharpen conflict between characters. Another thing it can be used for is to control the pace of the story. Sometimes if you are going full speed ahead with action, dialogue can be a good way to slow things down a little and give the reader a breather. But it more often creates suspense and intensifies the conflict in the story.

Movies tend to beat dialogue to death, always searching for that greater line. Who can forget Clint Eastwood's "Go ahead, make my day."? While your dialogue should keep the readers' attention, don't beat them to death with stilted dialogue.

Dialogue must fit the characters but try to avoid excessive slang as it usually interrupts the smoothness even though it is natural for that character and locale. Think about it: the reader is going along, your smooth prose has them absorbed in the story, and all of sudden the writing changes to slang. It can be disconcerting. Again there are places where it works, but understand what the disadvantage is and weigh it before using.

I liken this to going to see a play by Shakespeare and not being able to see the stage, but only being able to hear. So you have a friend sitting next to you who describes all the action. I don't know about you, but it takes me several minutes to get used to listening to 'olde English'. But what if my friend is describing the scene in 'new' English to me? Would I be able to keep track of everything?

Dialogue tags: A dialogue tag is any words you use to indicate who is speaking. A tendency is to feel that you have to use terms such as "he exclaimed"; "she gasped"; "he shrieked"; etc. etc., to make up for your lack of tone, gestures, etc. It can, and often is, be easily overdone. I noticed an interesting thing while reading Larry McMurty's Lonesome Dove: in almost every instance of dialogue, he just simply wrote the word "said". Seemed to work for him. Use strong "dialogue tags" when absolutely necessary, but don't overdo it or it will take away from the words themselves. This is very common mistake among new writers.

Make sure the reader knows who is talking. I've seen exchanges where there was no indication who was speaking for seven or eight lines and while (with just two characters) one assumes that you are switching character each time you hit a new quotation mark, it can become irritating to the reader to have to keep track.

If you have more than one male in a scene you can't use "he" even if in the context of the writing it's pretty evident who is speaking. Same with more than one female. Also, don't have bystanders who you forget about. I've read scenes with three people in them, where one says nothing and sort of fades into nothingness by the end, then startlingly reappears at the end of the dialogue.

Dialogue is usually much shorter in a novel than it would be in real life. There are several reasons for that but mostly it is because people expend numerous words in real life to make a point. Words that in print would quickly cause the reader to lose interest.

An example of how difficult it is to write dialogue is an on-line chat room. When people are forced to use only the words, communication often breaks down and misunderstandings abound.

Other points to consider on dialogue:

1. I said above that you can use dialogue to give expository information but if you do it so obviously, then guess what—the reader will notice and be distracted. This is also true of films. For example, Jim turns to his wife Marge and says: "Gee, Marge, your uncle Bill, the famous artist, is coming from his home in France, to visit us next week." Now, you did give the reader important information about Bill here: that he's an artist, Marge's uncle, and he lives in France. But. Don't you think that Marge would know her own uncle is an artist and lives in France? Do it another way.

2. Although dialogue in a novel is usually much more concise and to the point than dialogue in real life, be sure it doesn't appeared stilted or formal. Your characters can use contractions.

3. While you should be wary of dialogue tags, there are times you have to get across more emotion or attitude than the words themselves can convey. Make up for the lack with the actual scene, with action and setting rather than dialogue tags. Also, there are times in extended conversations where the reader can get so caught up in the dialogue they lose track of where the characters are at and the environment around the people. Occasionally, you should throw in a little bit of action in the midst of your dialogue. For example, when you are talking to someone on the phone, do you sit totally still? Or do you move about? Play racquetball while on your portable? When you talk to your boss, does he sit totally still on the other side of his desk and respond to your questions like Data on Star Trek: The Next Generation? Keep the reader oriented to the place the characters are speaking are in, and what they are doing. You can give more emphasis to your dialogue by having them make movements or gestures but don't overdo it.

4. You can use dialogue to give expository information that is necessary for the story but beware of slowing your action down too much with this. This is a place where you must consider using your author's voice to give narrative information instead of contriving scenes where your characters have to sit around and discuss something in order to give that information to the reader (I should know this as I just got an editorial letter back on one of my books with just this point.).

5. If you have only two characters in a scene, the reader knows when they hit an end quotation mark that they are going to the other character; however, you should only do about three or four exchanges like that before reorienting the reader as to who is speaking. We've all read scenes where we had to go back up and count the end quote marks to figure out who is talking. Don't make the reader work that hard.

Keep the story flowing. Don't stop the story to let your characters have a discussion and then jump-start it at the end of the discussion.

13. SETTING

Setting establishes mood. Go to the bookstore and open up a bunch of books and read the first line. You will find the majority of opening sentences have something to do with setting and evoking an emotion in the reader. That's why "It was a dark and stormy night" is such a cliché—there is always a large degree of truth in clichés.

Setting can be a character in your story—think who the antagonist is in Krakeur's Into Thin Air. Mount Everest and the weather. Some writers have totally wrapped their story around their setting and it's what makes their book unique. Caleb Carr's stories are mysteries set in New York City in the 19th century and it is the setting, which sets them apart.

Next time you're sitting watching your favorite sitcom or TV drama pay a little attention when the scene shifts. In NYPD Blue, every time the scene shifts back to the station house, don't they show the outside of the building for a second or so before moving inside? In Ally McBeal, don't they show either the law firm or courthouse for a second, before jumping into the scene? Ever wonder why the director does that? They do it to orient you as the viewer. As a writer you have to keep your reader oriented.

Setting consists of two parts, even though most people only think of one. It is the where and the *when* of your story. And there is so much more to the where that most people see at first glance. Think about the different places you've lived (if you've lived different places). There was more than just the place being different. Weren't the people somewhat different? The weather? The socio-economic structure? The yearly seasons? The physical terrain? The architecture? The list could go on and on, but the key is not to get caught up in simply describing what a place looks like. It takes much more than that to come alive.

I have found this to be particularly true in writing science fiction. Maybe it's simply because I've become more aware of the entirety of the setting when I can't take anything for granted. When my main character steps through a portal and gets sucked into the fourth dimension, I suddenly become much more aware that I have to describe *everything* down to the very texture of the air they breath.

However—you knew there was a however coming didn't you? However, like everything else, you just can't slam the breaks on your plot and wax eloquently about the fierce north wind roaring through your chapter. It has to come when the reader needs to know about it.

How much is too much detail? If you can take it out and the reader who knows nothing about your story other than what he's read so far doesn't miss it and doesn't need it.

One thing I do highly recommend though, is a thing I call "set", short for "set the scene." When you start a new chapter or change perspective I think you have to relatively quickly (in first two paragraphs perhaps?) orient the reader as to:
-Where is the locale?
-When in the timeline is this?
-What is the point of view, and if it is a character's, which character?
-Who is here?
Answering those questions "sets" the scene.
And by the end of the scene, you have answered the most critical question: WHY?

14. NARRATIVE STRUCTURE & PLOT

If you'd like a blueprint for a novel then I give you the narrative structure. There are 5 elements to narrative structure:

1. An inciting incident (hook)
This is a dynamic event and should be seen by the reader. It upsets the balance of forces and the rest of the novel is usually an attempt by your protagonist to restore the balance.
A good way to twist the inciting incident is to have what appears to be a good thing turn out to be the worst thing that could possibly happen. We've all heard stories of someone winning the lottery and it ruining his life.
I have the next chapter devoted to how to begin your novel.

2. Series of progressive complications (ever rising risks)
I heard an interesting story one time that goes as follows:

There once was a very poor man who lived in a kingdom. All he had was his son and six beautiful horses. One day the king came riding by and saw the horses. The king offered to buy the horses for a very large sum of money. The man refused. His neighbors told him he was crazy not to take the money because the king's offer was a very good thing. He replied: "I don't know if it's a good thing or a bad thing. It just is."
Two days after the king had made his offer and the poor man had turned him down, the horses disappeared. His neighbors looked at the poor man and said now he should feel very bad because he not only didn't get the king's money, but he also no longer had his horses. He replied: "I don't know if it's a good thing or a bad thing. It just is."
A few days later, the six horses came back with six more wild horses, just as beautiful. The poor man's neighbors said: "What a good thing you didn't

sell them to the king. Now you have twelve horses." He replied: "I don't know if it's a good thing or a bad thing. It just is."

While trying to break in the six new horses, the man's son was thrown and shattered his leg, crippling him for life. The man's neighbors said. "What a bad thing those six new horses are. Now your son is crippled for life." He replied: "I don't know if it's a good thing or a bad thing. It just is."

A year later, the kingdom went to war with a neighboring kingdom, a war everyone knew they were destined to lose. When the levy came for young men to go fight, the poor man's son wasn't taken to go because of his crippled leg. The man's neighbors said: "What a good thing that your son is crippled so he doesn't have to go and die in this foolish war like our own sons." He replied: "I don't know if it's a good thing or a bad thing. It just is."

And such goes life and such go stories. Keep the reader along for the ride. They want to turn the pages and find out what happens next.

Suspense is a very integral part of practically any story. This can range from the hero saving the world to wondering what is going to happen to a main character. There are many types of suspense. I just watched an interesting movie call <u>Dancer, Texas, Pop. 87</u>. It chronicles a weekend in a small Texas town. It starts on Friday, with a high school graduation of a class of five, four boys and one girl. It follows the four boys over the weekend and ends on Monday morning. The four boys, when they were sophomores, all bought bus tickets for the Monday morning after graduation to get the heck out this small town and go to LA. The suspense comes from wondering which of the four will be on that bus Monday morning and which will stay. Since you come to care about these characters, you care about the decisions they will make.

Suspense in a thriller can come from a clock ticking. Or in a mystery from the classic 'who-done-it.' One thing that many mysteries I see are lacking is suspense—if it is a one-time murder, how are you going to generate suspense? Sometimes it's from *how* the good guy catches the bad guy. But if you have just a body, and there's not threat that the killer will kill again; or that the hero is in danger; or some pay-off, then there's little suspense.

3. Crisis (a choice)
The protagonist is forced to make a choice whether or not she wants to attempt to restore the balance that was disrupted by the inciting incident. It should not be obvious to the reader how this is going to be resolved. You raise suspense by keeping the reader guessing.

4. Climax (make choice)

The choice is made and balance is either restored, or a new balance is worked out.

Make sure your protagonist is involved in the climax.

5. Resolution (wrap up plot and subplots)

Don't leave any loose ends dangling. The reader cares about all the characters and all the events. Tie it all up.

The above are very simple and self-explanatory. I won't go into depth on them because I don't want you to feel that you <u>have</u> to do anything. Just keep the five elements in mind as you outline your novel and as it progresses.

There are certainly novels that do not follow the narrative structure. I present it here as a guideline for those who wish to use it. Certain types of genre fit into this structure much more clearly than others.

Near the end of this book, I list the way a screenplay breaks down into three acts with plot points. I think this is also an effective way to break down a novel.

Use the narrative structure to break down the novel you dissected in chapter six.

You can also use it when approaching the question of story. Your idea might be the hook, or it might be the crisis, or it might be the decision that is made. The question is, can you lay out a complete story that has a resolution?

I talk about outlining later, but I think the more you know before you start writing, the better off you will be.

PLOT:

I looked up the definition for plot in the dictionary and it said: *A secret plan to achieve a hostile or illegal purpose.*

Just joking. The applicable definition is: *The series of events consisting of an outline of the action of a narrative or drama.*

In the next three chapters I'm going to cover major parts in detail: the beginning, pacing and the end. In this chapter I want to talk about some structural issues regarding the development of a story.

First, notice the definition says a *series of events.* That means something has to happen. Most of us can't get away with writing a story where your characters stand around doing nothing. Action, in whatever form it takes, moves the story forward and carries the characters with it. Sometimes your characters act, sometimes they react. Regardless, they're doing something.

One thing I do that helps me considerably while I am still working on developing my story (before I've written my first sentence) is try to have an idea what the climax of my story will be. After all, that's where all the action is driving toward. I think it helps to know the climax because it gives the story direction. It also focuses me on the main plot, and helps from getting side-tracked and making a subplot develop into the climax of the book. Without an idea of what the climax is, you might end up with the book that will never end.

Real life is full of coincidences, but there is great debate over how much coincidence can be in a novel. Some people say you can have no coincidences at all in a book; that everything must happen for a reason. The thinking behind that is to prevent the author from manipulating the plot too much. But, the author is, after all, the supreme ruler of the novel, so in essence the entire novel is a manipulation.

When does a coincidence work? When it is an integral part of the novel.

Example: In Michael Connoly's novel BLOODWORK, a retired FBI agent is asked to investigate a murder by a relative of the victim. He is recovering from a heart transplant operation and doesn't want to take the job on—until he finds out that the heart he received came from the victim. A staggering coincidence, right? Not when you find out that someone murdered several people in an attempt to get a different type of transplant. Thus the 'coincidence' turns out to be a plan by someone that drives the entire story and provides the climax.

When doesn't it work? When it comes outside of the plot to change it.

Example: Your hero is trying to find out who the bad guys are. The phone rings and the secretary for one of the bad guys gives your hero much needed information. We never hear from or see the secretary again; she was an obvious plot device to jump-start the novel and give needed information. However, the phone call works if it's an attempt by the bad guy to lure the good guy into an ambush.

The term you should think of is *internal logic*. A plot needs to make sense inside of itself.

15. WHERE SHOULD MY NOVEL BEGIN?

There are actually two beginnings to a novel: the first words the writer puts down to start the manuscript, and the first words the reader sees when they open the completed book. Only rarely are those two sets of words the same. When I teach novel writing, I find most students spend an inordinate amount of time trying to have the perfect beginning, but if the first sentence of this section is true, then much of that time is wasted. My advice always is: just start somewhere and sometime. You can always go back and redo the beginning. In many of my books the published beginning is not where I began writing on that first day starting the manuscript. The number one rule in novel writing is simply: WRITE.

Now that we've cleared that hurdle, let's discuss the beginning of a novel in conceptual terms. Understanding the diagram below will help us in doing that:

Let me explain what each part represents:

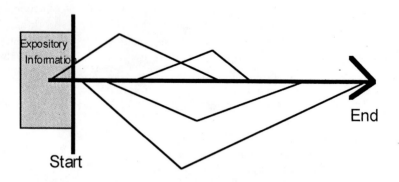

The thick vertical line on the left, labeled Start, is where the novel begins. Page 1.

The tip of the arrow on the right, labeled End, is where the novel ends. Last page.

The thick horizontal arrow, going straight across, is your original idea or the main story line.

The thin arrows are your subplots and ancillary action. Note that all subplots eventually end up supporting the original idea.

When trying to decide where to place the start line, keep in mind the purposes of the beginning of a book. Your opening chapter has to bring people in the door. The beginning must hook the readers and also serve a second purpose: either introducing the story theme/problem or introducing the main characters. It could do both, but don't overwhelm your reader by putting too much in the first chapter. By knowing all the information in your background box, you give yourself the ability to dip into that box and write a new beginning. Sliding the start line to the left. If you slide the start line to the right, you simply have to expand your background box by removing the information you originally had in your beginning and working it in as expository information. Understanding this concept gives you an almost unlimited freedom to be able to eventually have a dynamic opening chapter.

I believe by the end of your second chapter you should have accomplished two things: introduced your core problem that will be resolved in the climax; and introduced your protagonist.

Think about the message you send with your opening. If you lead with your problem, you are telegraphing to your reader that the problem is key. If you lead with your main character, then you are telling the reader the character is more important. That's not a hard and fast rule, but it's a tendency.

Start noticing how books and movies start. Figure out why the writer started them the way he or she did. There is a reason.

<u>The most important thing to remember about your beginning is you have to hook the reader very quickly.</u> Within a few pages. Hopefully within the first sentence. James Hall, a best-selling writer, said that he spends an inordinate amount of time going over his opening once the manuscript is done, refining it, making it the best it can be.

Some writers spend too much of the beginning giving background information setting up a hook. You don't have that luxury. I recommend going to the bookstore and simply taking books off the shelf and reading the opening paragraph, the opening line. You'll start seeing a common thread, where the authors try to evoke a mood, an emotion very quickly to get you interested in the story.

If you have to use a flashback or memory in your opening chapter, seriously consider moving the Start line back so that the flashback or memory happens in real time.

Remember I mentioned that a book's impact is emotional and intellectual. I think you have to do your best to engage a reader's intellect and his emotions as quickly as you can.

The shaded box before the start point is what I want to discuss right now. This is known as your expository information, or more simply, the background or the back-story. There is always a history prior to the start point of the novel—a history of the characters, the locale, the environment, the crisis to be faced—the list goes on and on. Depending on the type novel you are writing, this box can be very small, or very large. For example, a science fiction writer, setting a story in the 24th century, has a very big box that he/she has to understand and develop before he can even begin to write the START.

Beyond that, though, is the fact that you can see that the start of the arrow of the original idea—and many of the subplots—begins prior to the start point of the novel. This means to you, the writer, two things. First, **you** must know all the information in this box prior to beginning your writing. You must know about your characters; your locales; all the background information necessary to make a believable story. Failing to do this essential background work sabotages the story before you type your first word and becomes very apparent to readers as they progress in your work.

If you have invented a fantasy world of magic, you must have a basic working idea of the rules of magic in your fantasy world. That isn't to say that you can't adjust and change it once you get into the writing, but you have to start somewhere.

Secondly, it means there is usually vital information the **reader** must eventually have about events and things that existed/ occurred prior to the book start point in order to comprehend what he or she is reading. How you relay this information to the reader is extremely important. Naturally, it must be worked in smoothly. Work in the background information the reader needs in glimpses, when it's required to understand the present story. In most cases, try not to use whole chapters to do this as it usually sabotages your story by slowing it down too much. A common mistake is to write an excellent opening chapter presenting the crisis or hook, and then have three chapters of 'necessary' background material presented to fill in all that the reader needs to know. Once you initiate action, you have to keep it going.

Move your action and slip in background when needed and when it answers questions the reader will have. Give the reader background information when the normal reader would get to a certain part of your narrative and start picking up his hand to scratch his head because he needs to know something he doesn't. Give him the information before the hand reaches the head.

Try to use dialogue or authorial narrative to present that information; this is preferred over simply having characters thinking and remembering. You can also use flashbacks but use them correctly. You must have a good lead into the flashback and a smooth lead out, back into the action of the narrative. Flashbacks work when you do that, and when you put them at that point where the reader is interested in finding out the background information you are going to present.

Also, remember there is a difference between a flashback and a memory. A memory has the additional factor of a character's viewpoint on a past event. This gives the event more relevance to the current story.

You must not only slide into and out of flashbacks smoothly in the storyline, but you must also do it smoothly style-wise. The first and last paragraphs of the flashback should move out of and back into the last and first paragraphs on either side of the flashback. For example, you can be writing about a man sitting at his desk at work, getting ready to make a life-changing phone call. You move into a flashback giving necessary information as to why the phone call has to be made by starting the flashback with *another* phone-call in the past. Then you can move back to the present with the phone in the present ringing, bringing both character and reader back to the present. A simple and obvious ploy, but better than just plunking down the flashback in the middle of your chapter.

I once saw a very interesting movie where the story began at the end and progressed back in time. The writer presented the resolution of a crisis and then proceeded to show how that resolution came about and what started the crisis in the first place. My point, though, is: did the writer originally write it that way, or did the writer script it in normal time sequence and then reverse the whole story? This has a direct application to my point that you can always go back and adjust the start point. In my diagram, it is a sliding line, that can move along the arrow of the original idea, but most of the time you can't decide the correct place to put it until you have drawn out that original idea to its conclusion. In this particular instance the writer reversed the flow of the story line.

There is another aspect to consider when deciding where to start your novel and that is the timeline of your story. This greatly affects your writing and style.

There are many ways to arrange the timeline of the story but the most important thing to remember is to keep the reader clued in. It is extremely confusing to the reader if their time-sense of the story gets screwed up.

I used "headers" before each new scene in some of my manuscripts. These give the time and location of the upcoming scene. While that is an easy way to keep the reader oriented, I have to remember that not all readers (including myself.) read such headers. More on this in the next chapter.

Almost invariably, you are going to have to move back in time to give expository information in a story. I've already discussed this, but make sure your reader knows what you are doing.

Let me give you an example of timeline problems: I just recently looked at a manuscript telling the story of two brothers caught up in the Civil War. He had to pick a start point and then move his story from there. At first he picked Appomattox. The problem was that he was constantly going back to battles during the war, such as 1st and 2d Bull Run, Antietam, etc. etc. The shift in style required to do this was very jarring to the reader.

He then rewrote the story starting at 2d Bull Run. The only problem he now had though, was in style. Once you "freeze" your time frame for the story with a start point, you must make sure your tenses indicate to the reader whether they are in the normal time frame of the story or moving back, prior to the start point, or even moving around in the normal sequence. The reader assumes that you are going to progress in a sequential fashion. You don't necessarily have to, but you must remember to take the reader along with you when you do make your shifts. There are numerous ways to do this (a good reason to read a lot and study others' styles)—just do it correctly.

Another problem this writer had was by starting at Appomattox, he lost all his suspense during his chapters that went back into the war because we knew who was alive at the end of the war, Appomattox, also the beginning of the book.

Some writers start their books with a prologue, others with Chapter 1. What is the difference? A prologue is used when whatever is in the opening chapter is out of time sequence with the rest of the story.

In the next two chapters I am going to discuss pacing and the ending of a book. I think it is important to consider 'bookends' to your story—a time framework in which to put your storyline.

16. THE PACE OF THE STORY

The beginning can be fun to write and the end is, most certainly exciting, but the bulk of the novel lies between. Wherever you decide you want to start, you must get to the end in a manner that doesn't lose or confuse the reader. What you want to avoid is what I call the 'remote control effect'. This effect is when you write as if you have pause, slow motion, fast-forward, stop, etc. etc. buttons. A novel should play out with a smooth pace but many writers jerk the pace around and in the process jerk the reader around.

There are two ways to look at the pacing of your story: overall, and by chapter.

Overall, the reader will quickly grow to expect a certain time sequence and pacing in the book. This includes not only in the time that goes by in the story (even if you are going *backwards* in time) but also in locale. Remember the number one rule of writing is to not jar the reader.

You can find pretty much every possible time sequence published. You can find books that go forward in time every fifty years, those that bounce back and forth between the present and the past, those that go past, present, future. Those that use parallel time sequences. You name it, it's been done and you can do it. But remember the poor reader. Make sure they can follow what you're doing.

There is no law about chapter length. I usually envision a chapter to be a set length of time in the story. I have chapter breaks when there is a change, usually in time, point of view or setting. If I'm reading a chapter and it comes to an end, then turn the page to the new chapter and it the same point of view, the same time, the same setting, the same characters, I wonder why the writer just didn't continue and not have a chapter break.

Pace within the chapter, within the writing itself, is also very important. I just looked at a sample chapter from a writer who in the opening paragraph had the main character packing up to leave her home; in the second paragraph the character was in the new town; in the third she was in a job interview for a new job, a part which went into much more detail and extended for several paragraphs; then another paragraph jumped weeks ahead; etc., etc. There were two major problems. One was that is was disconcerting to not know where I was both time and location-wise every time I started a new paragraph, never mind a chapter, but also, in one paragraph the writer would cover a major event such as a move, then several paragraphs later spend a whole paragraph describing an office. In my mind, it made the two equal in significance because of the amount of writing given to both, even though they obviously aren't. This is a classic example of remote control effect.

The reader will tend to think if you spend two paragraphs on A and two paragraphs on B, then A equals B. It might not be to you, but as I will get into later, you always have to consider what the reader thinks.

The best analogy I can use is it is like watching a video and you can either watch it in normal time or you can use the fast-forward. But every time you use the fast-forward—or the slow forward—you lose something. Keep it steady.

Of course, you say, might not use of a time sequence change catch the reader's attention and be used in a positive manner? Of course. Just make sure you understand that there *is* a pace to a story and do it consciously. The major problem I have seen is writers unaware of how they are jerking the pace around.

Of course, you often have to move the reader forward or backward in time. We've already discussed some such as flashbacks. There are many techniques to do that and if you think of a new one, more power to you as long as—you guessed it—it works and does not jar the reader (unless of course, you *want* to jar the reader.).

One method used to get the reader oriented quickly is to use headers. I have used headers extensively. I open every chapter, and even inside the chapter when I switch locales, with a header like:

<u>West Point, New York</u>
<u>14 November 1997</u>
<u>10:23 AM local/ 1523 Zulu</u>
Quite honestly, while a valid technique, it is also a bit of a lazy one. I used it because my stories shifted so quickly to so many locations, across numerous time zones. The Zulu time is Greenwich Mean Time, which is used internationally to keep people in different time zones on the same sheet of music time-wise.

One thing I have learned about using headers is that often readers don't read them. Quite frankly, they are a not a particularly good way to start a new scene. I try to back up the header in the first paragraph by letting the reader know where they are at and when they are at and which characters they are with. For my last half-dozen manuscripts I've stopped using headers.

If you don't use headers—and odds are you won't—you really must make sure you orient your reader quickly, usually in the first paragraph. If the reader spends too much time wondering where and when they are at, then they will start losing interest in the story.

If you are writing suspense, there is usually a 'clock ticking' in the story. A deadline approaching adds suspense to a story and gives your story a definite timeline.

17. WHERE SHOULD MY NOVEL END?

The end is the conclusion of your beginning, the climax of your original idea. But remember all that expository information that you worked into your story? You must also close out all your subplots by the end, which sometimes can be quite difficult to do.

Study endings as much as you study beginnings. Why did the author use an epilogue? How did he explain all the hidden details that bring the conclusion together? How many chapters did the author write after the climactic scene?

The "end" line on the diagram in the chapter on the beginning is not as flexible as the "beginning" line. When the end comes in your story it comes. Because you have all those pages prior, you have lost some degree of control over your ending. It should be a *natural* conclusion of the story itself. Sometimes I'm asked how long a manuscript should be and I always say long enough to reach the end.

The end should answer the question posed in your original idea to the satisfaction of the reader.

I believe it is important that you have an idea what the climax of your book is going to be before you start writing it, as that is where the story is driving toward. Some writers don't want to do that—you have to find what works for you.

I think we have all read books where the ending rang flat or disappointed us. The question you should have asked yourself, as a writer is *why* did that ending disappoint?

Some writers work from their ending backwards. By this, I mean they know in their mind how they want the story to end and they write the entire book with that in mind.

I think you should have a good idea of your ending when you start writing because if you don't, your writing may tend to wander. It all goes back to outlining and whatever you feel comfortable with. Another problem with not having an idea of your ending is that if your plot is complex you might not end with an ending at all as everything simply unravels—or, more likely, you can't tie together all the loose threads to end the book succinctly and in a satisfactory manner.

Stephen King says he doesn't have a clue what his ending is when he starts a book, but I think he is the exception rather than the rule. And he's Stephen King. And recently he's changed that opinion.

The most important thing about the ending is to close out your main storyline and all your subplots. Don't leave the reader guessing.

Also note that in the narrative structure the climax is not the same as the resolution. The climax ends the crisis. The resolution explains how the crisis is over and also lays out the effect on the characters who must now go on.

Series and Sequels: I often see unpublished writers trying to pitch trilogies or a five book series. While later in this book I talk about how you will almost always get at least a two book deal if you sell one, that does not mean you can sell two books in a series or a book and its sequel.

I think the first book you try to sell should stand alone, but it should also potentially be the beginning of a series.

There is a difference between writing series and sequels. A series consists of books that have a link such as the same main character, but each book stands alone as far as story goes. Sequels are books that flows out of the ending of the previous book and really don't stand alone.

THE LORD OF THE RINGS are sequels.

Sue Grafton's novels are series.

The reason you should keep in the back of your mind a series, is that a publisher might want some continuity beyond simply your name on the cover.

"If I knew then what I know now—" My first book contract was for three books. I had two manuscripts in hand, but they were not part of a series. The publisher said they wanted the books to have the same character. So I rewrote one of them to have the same main character as the first one. But the mistake I made was to not title them so that the reader would know they were connected.

Think how brilliant Sue Grafton has been with her alphabet series. Don't count on your publisher to think of something like that for you. I'll discuss this more in depth later in the business section. The thing to remember at this point, as my agent just told me last week after he read my latest manuscript: "Don't kill off your hero."

18. OUTLINING

I have grown fonder of outlining the more I have written. A novel is very complex when viewed in its entirety, most particularly mainstream fiction. Working without an outline is sort of "winging" it. I say this after have done that for eight straight manuscripts. I think I have finally learned my lesson and have actually gotten to the point of outlining in some degree of detail (about a page per chapter) the entire proposed novel.

I'm updating the above paragraph after 22 manuscripts written and I believe even more strongly now in outlining. I think every hour spent outlining prior to starting a novel, saves you many hours in the actual writing process. It also helps to make a better novel as you will 'tighten' down the story in your outline before you write, rather than having to do it in rewrite.

To be honest, I only outlined my first complete novel when I had a contract that called for a complete outline to be submitted to the publisher prior to final approval for the project (and more importantly a portion of the advance was to be paid on acceptance of the outline.). You are going to have to "outline" sooner or later when writing. You can do it as you go along or you can do it before you write. Doing it as you go along often causes you to have to waste a lot of time writing material that either has to be thrown out or be extensively rewritten. It is prudent to do a lot of the thinking work ahead of time.

The major problem in working without a good outline is that you tend to get "stuck" about halfway through. When I first began writing this wasn't a major problem. My stories were basic and relatively straightforward action/adventure and, while I didn't have a detailed outline, I did have a good idea of where I wanted the story to go (as they were based somewhat on personal experiences) so I managed to blunder my way through. As I tried writing more complex stories, I found myself getting stuck more and more often and having to take days away from the keyboard to work out where the story was going and keep the subplots in line.

When you start your manuscript with your one sentence original idea, you have a relatively blank slate to work with. The further along you get, the less options you have. If you work without an outline, you may find yourself with *no* options at some point. Or at least no good options. This is, to slightly understate the predicament, not good.

If you combine many of the other chapters in this book such as narrative structure, the beginning, characters, etc. you get a good overview of the pieces you need to put together a novel. Outlining is putting those pieces into a framework. The basis of your framework is that one-sentence original idea that I beat into you early in this book. Then you decide your basic storyline and the characters who are going to live the story.

I cannot overemphasize (OK, I probably could) how important it is to have a feel for your characters before you begin writing. I consider getting that feel part of outlining.

Outlining is also very critical in keeping your subplots tight to the main plot. You will restrict yourself from going off in tangents if you know at which point in your main story a subplot develops and where and how it will eventually come back and tie into the main story line.

Another advantage of outlining is that since the outline is tight to start with, as you write and add flesh to your outline, you can make the story even tighter.

One of my biggest obstacles to outlining was that I just wanted to get started writing and didn't want to take a couple of weeks doing the outlining. Now I realize how much time in the long run it saves me to stay away from the manuscript and do the outline first.

The degree of detail in your outline is personal. In fact, you may chose not to have one at all. But don't treat it like the gospel once you do devise one. As you go along the characters will develop a life of their own as will the story. As you fill in details, occasionally these details will cause you to change parts of your story as opposed to what was outlined. None of my recent, more complex novels, turned out the way I thought they would way back in the beginning when all I had was the original idea and some research.

Also remember that outlining is an ongoing process just as the writing is. If you view a novel in the beginning as a large blank slate, then the original idea is a sentence you write at the top of the page. From there you start your outline, tracing characters and events along the timeline of your story. When you feel you have an adequate outline, you start writing. As the story progresses, you must go back every once in a while and redo the outline, tightening your story down.

I view this for me as writing in surges. I project out my story as much as I know at the time (nowadays to the very end.). Then I proceed to write. When I sense that I am losing track, I go back over my outline and fill in what I've already written, adding in all the details. With these new details, I redo the outline, tightening down what has yet to be written and making sure it is in congruence with what has already been written. Sometimes, I also have to go back and add a layer to the story, or take a layer away.

There are some critical questions that you must answer before you begin your manuscript. Answer these questions in writing, not in your head. To me, the bottom line on outlining is writing down everything I can possibly think of with regard to the story. You will find that the process of actually writing down those great thoughts you have might knock you up against the harsh rocks of reality. Sometimes it looks very different in black in white on paper, than in color in your brain.

Here are the questions:

1. What is my one sentence original idea?

2. Who are my main characters? What are their primary motivations? Do their primary motivations naturally lead them to assume the role they must, in this novel? How did they get these primary motivations? How do I *show* the reader the characters primary motivations?

3. Where and when is my setting?

4. What is the climax of my story?

5. How do I maintain suspense/reader interest throughout the novel?

Caveat. Be careful that your writing doesn't appear to be just a blown up outline. When that happens, the writing appears to be stilted and a little forced. Also, just expanding an outline leaves little room for creativity and allowing the characters to react and "live". You may have outlined certain events occurring, but when you actually sit down and write your characters experiencing those events, usually you will find that it turns out not exactly as outlined. Sort of like real life. Go with it. Allow your characters to be living beings involved in the story.

Find the degree of outlining that you are comfortable with, but at least consider doing some sort of outline, even if only in your own head. There are some very successful authors who can break a novel down by sections and structure and crank out certain genre novels according to a "script" they have for that type of book. And, although many don't like hearing it, there is a formula to some type of novels. Although we all want to be original (or maybe we don't?), realize that if you are writing a romance and you produce something totally unlike any other romance on the bookshelves you've done two things: you haven't written a romance in the first place, and secondly, when you try to market it, it won't be viewed as a romance. You may be the trailblazer like those I mentioned in an earlier chapter and start a new field, but the odds aren't good. If you feel strongly about your writing, don't let that dissuade you, just be aware of the reality of the situation.

I definitely feel that updating your outline is important every day when you sit down and try to write chapters. Pick a start point and an end point for every chapter. Then ask yourself how do I get from one to the other? What is the purpose of this chapter? Also look at the chapter in terms of the overall story. Where does it fit? Is this the right time for this to happen? If you don't have a definite end point, your chapter will meander.

Appendix 1 is an example of a chapter outline. While some of the notes might not make sense to you, they certainly do to me because I did the research and know what the original idea is. The keys things to note are:

1. I list the date at the top, putting it in time sequence for the story.

2. I have the characters who will be in the chapter (which makes me cross-reference to my one page character summaries.)

3. I list the events in sequence, giving the major action and where it occurs.

4. I make notes on key material that must be dealt with later, in other chapters, or already has been dealt with. This is very important to insure continuity of story.

5. I have a definite start point at the beginning of the event sequence and a definite end-point. I have listed all important events that I need to occur in between.

6. Perhaps most importantly I give the *purpose* of the chapter. Where does it fit in the overall story? How does it relate to the original idea? This will prevent having extraneous material.

This is not to say that once I start writing the chapter things won't change. But it is a heck of a lot easier to write with all the information thought out beforehand rather than making it up as I go. Basically, what I'm saying here is that the outline allows you to concentrate on the writing since you know what you are going to put down. I find my writing is better when I have a good outline.

An outline can grow out of your original idea when you start doing your research. For me, research is one of the "fun" parts of my job. Going to the library and looking through the stacks, checking magazines, videos, the computer, etc. all are interesting. Keep your eyes open. Just because you are looking for a book filed under U410.L1 E38, doesn't mean you ignore the books to the left and right of it. I usually scan all the books that are shelved together and have often come up with goldmines of information sitting three books over from what I thought I needed.

A last word on the Catch-22 of outlining. Not to contradict what I've written above, but there is a problem with trying to sit down and outline your very first manuscript. The problem is that since *you've never written a manuscript, you are trying to outline something you've never done.*

I opened this chapter by saying that I have grown more fond of outlining the more I have written, but that is also a natural outgrowth of gaining more experience in novel structure and style. I have learned enough in knocking out manuscripts that I am able to outline now. I don't think I would have done anywhere as good a job on outlining my first manuscript. This is also why I emphasize starting out writing about something you know quite a bit about and keeping the story as simple as possible.

My recommendation on outlining is simple: write down everything you think you know about your book. I say 'think you know' because the transition from what you think are startlingly clear thoughts to black and white on paper can be very difficult. I've had great ideas that I thought would make great stories, but when I start actually sketching it out in the real world—on paper or on computer—rather that in my head, I find things change considerably.

One phrase I always say is "Details drive the story." This is why, even with an outline, a story takes on a life of its own. No matter how detailed you outline, you can't think of everything. As you actually write the story, details will start popping up that will cause you to make changes. Most of the time these are details of reality.

For example, in your thriller you have a scene where your protagonist is searching out a series of tunnels, looking for the bad guys. The way you wrote your outline, the bad guy isn't in the tunnel and your secondary main character is sitting in her car on the surface and she sees the bad guy escape. So she calls the protagonist on the radio and he rushes to the surface for your climactic scene hanging off the skid of the helicopter, right? Wrong. You can't use radio to get hold of someone underground. Or cell phones. This is a detail you might not have thought of when doing your outline but as you write it you realize it. So you change, you adjust.

Just as details can limit you, they can also give you more opportunities. This goes back to research being an ongoing process, which I mentioned earlier.

If you have been following the flow of these chapters, they represent the way you might want to consider approaching your manuscript. You've done a lot of legwork that you can put together to begin your outline at this point.

19. SUBPLOTS

Subplots are everything in your story other than your main storyline. Basically a story is similar to a bunch of threads woven together to make a rope. You've got to make sure everything in your story ends inside of that rope to make it a strong one. If strings extend beyond the main area of the rope, those strings will unravel the entire rope.

The rope, from the diagram I used earlier, is that storyline that springs from your original idea and drives to the climax/resolution of the story. Note that all the subplots (the smaller arrows) all eventually end up at least once coming back into the main storyline (and staying there. Don't let them wander off again and not come back).

Don't have loose ends. If you put something in your story make sure it serves a purpose and that you close the loop by the end of the book. Don't put things in your novel just because they are neat or you like writing about them. And use everything you do put in as much as possible. The best stories are very tightly woven with almost every single occurrence/fact/character serving multiple purposes in keeping the story going.

Don't write something just to make a point or move the story along. Sometimes you get to a place where you need to present a scene or action to keep the story going; spend some time and make the scene or action have more than one connection to the original idea. Have it serve multiple purposes.

Chekov once said: Don't have a gun in Act One unless you fire it by Act Three. This is true of writing. Don't throw superfluous things into your story. The reader doesn't know the significance of whatever you write so the reader assumes that *everything is* significant. You disappoint your reader if you have a scene that appears to be important, but you never refer back to it, and wrote it only to keep your action moving.

I have often been misled when reading manuscripts for critique because I misjudge the importance of something in early chapters that is never mentioned again. In one case a writer had a large explosion occurring that destroyed quite a bit of property and killed many people. I assumed that this explosion was tied into the main plot; in fact, I figured that the "bad guys" had caused the explosion. Yet the explosion was never mentioned again nor really explained. The author had simply used it to set up the circumstances causing the hero to have to use a different escape route. It totally threw me off the original story for over fifty pages as I kept anticipating a reference back to that explosion.

To keep suspense and different levels of intrigue you present something and allow the reader to make the "casual" inference/supposition. Yet you know there is a more complex level with a different reason/purpose that eventually will be unveiled and the reader can look back and say "Oh Yeah."

In the process of writing a book look at everything that is said and something minor can later turn out to be rather important.

An example is in Pat Conroy's The Lords Of Discipline when the main character is in his roommate's father's study talking to the father and he sees the man's journals on the bookcase. A minor observation there, as the conversation is the critical thing in that scene, but later the journals turn out to be extremely significant when the main character breaks in to read them and discovers the truth that brings about the conclusion.

Another example of what I mean when I talk about having your subplots serve multiple purposes is as follows:

The primary purpose of Chapter 2 in my manuscript, Cut Out, is to introduce my main character, Riley. Since he is not yet involved in the crisis (introduced in Chapter 1), I have to introduce him outside of the main story line. I do this by having him in as exciting a situation as possible (to keep the reader hooked). In that chapter I also start the following supplementary loops:

-I introduce another character who will have a role to play later on.

-I introduce a tactical situation and have Riley react to it—although in and of itself, this situation only appears to introduce Riley, I bring some of the factors in this situation in to play later on in the novel when Riley faces other situations and reacts in a similar manner.

-I introduce Riley's relationship with the main female character by having him get a letter from her. We learn about him and his relationship with her when he reads the letter. Furthermore, we also learn about her (she gets introduced here, even though he's in Ft. Bragg and she's in Chicago).

What could have been a pretty straightforward chapter, simply introducing my main character, now serves multiple purposes, some of which will only become visible to the reader, as he gets further into the story.

Be careful of having a subplot that is bigger than your original idea/ main plot. I once looked at a manuscript where one of the subplots had the President of the United States being assassinated. While this certainly moved the main plot along, it also kept the reader wondering how this major event was going to be resolved, to the point of distracting from the author's main storyline.

You must close all your loops. It is very frustrating to the reader to have loose ends when they finish a book. This presents you with a hard task. It forces you to limit your subplots as much as possible. In my second manuscript, the initial storyline was very complex and, quite frankly, it got away from me. I could no longer write because I had too much going on in too many different directions and, most importantly, I could not close all the story-lines at the same time to conclude my story. I had to dump all but the main storyline.

Remember the narrative structure and my beating home the concept of being able to state your story idea in one sentence? There is only *one* main story. There is only one main crisis. There is one main resolution. Everything else must support that. Sometimes beginning writers get too carried away and overwhelm themselves with subplots to the point that the main idea gets lost. In most cases the writer gets lost writing it, and the reader will certainly be lost reading it.

When in doubt use the KISS technique—Keep It Simple.

Every character, incident, location,—everything—you put into your novel has to be examined very carefully. What additional use can you make of it? The more uses you can make of each subplot, the tighter the story. The tighter the story, the better the manuscript. I cannot over-emphasize the point to you, because I cannot overemphasize it to myself.

For a good example of an extremely tightly written book, try reading <u>A Thousand Acres</u> by Jane Smiley (a modern King Lear), which won the National Book Award. Or try <u>The General's Daughter</u> by Nelson DeMille.

A method I use to keep a handle on my subplots is in Appendix 6. I list major characters across the top, and then go down the page in chronological order, playing out each one's actions. Then I draw arrows, lining up the order between these "subplots" in the manner in which they occur and I will write them. I usually find that by the end of the "outline" that I am left with all my characters at the same place (or having died along the way) for the resolution.

This sort of visual outline allows me to keep my subplots from unraveling from the main plot. It also allows me to properly sequence my story, having events happen in the correct order.

I mentioned earlier in this book the power of the subconscious, but let me give you an example of where it can play a role. I have found that in many of my manuscripts I do what I call "planting seeds". I put things into the story that might not necessarily seem important at the time. Minor things—like the journals in the Pat Conroy scene I described earlier. Later on, when I get to a part of the book where I'm 'stuck', I go back through my book and look for these seeds and grow them into solutions. Many times you have already put the solution to a problem late in your book, somewhere earlier in the manuscript yet you're not aware of it until you open your mind to alternate possibilities and go back through the manuscript searching for these seeds.

Here's something to consider: There are three ways Pat Conroy could have written that scene in <u>The Lords of Discipline</u>. Examine these three because you will see it gives you *three* ways to use subplots and to rewrite:

1. He knew from the very beginning that those journals would be the key that unlocks the answers to the mystery his main character was trying to uncover. In that case, Conroy wrote the journals in when he got to the scene in the study and then when his main character needed to find a key, he already knew what he was going to use.

2. Pat Conroy wrote the journals into the study as part of giving the reader the setting and telling the reader something about the character of the roommate's father. (What do you think of a man who would keep such journals?). When the main character got to the point in the book where he needed a key to unlock the mystery, Pat Conroy, as author, was in the same predicament as his main character (a situation every good writer finds themselves in.). Conroy found himself then working with the same information his main character had. He went back through the book, searching, as the main

character would, for a key. When he re-read what he had written—voila.—he realized the journals were the key. He had his main character break in, read the journals, etc. etc. This is a case where Conroy's subconscious gave him the answer before he knew what the question was.

3. There were no journals in the study the first time Conroy wrote this scene. Conroy got to the point where his main character needed a key. Conroy sat and thought about it and realized—voila—he would put the key into the study in the form of the journals. So he went back and wrote them in, thus planting the seed for the flower he would need later on. This part of the ongoing rewriting process that every author must do as a book progressed.

I don't know which of these is what happened. The point is, that every writer uses *all three* techniques when writing.

20. SHOW, DON'T TELL & SYMBOLISM

If you've ever attended a writing class or conference, the first phrase has fallen upon your ears again and again. What exactly does it mean?

First, let me say that it isn't completely true all the time. There are indeed times in a novel when you should tell. In fact, telling is one of the advantages a novelist has over a screenwriter who must stay completely in the showing mode.

Also, the line between showing and telling is non-existent at times. It's a sliding scale. At one end (telling) is pure exposition; at the other end (showing) is dramatization. Telling tends to summarize information, giving it second-hand. Showing allows you to see, hear, feel, smell and taste, first-hand.

Some things to keep in mind when considering whether to show or tell:

1. Don't do information dumps. Too often people lead with information rather than plot. Information should only be given to the reader when it is absolutely necessary *at that moment* for the reader to understand the plot. Too many writers give information too soon and the reader doesn't know why they are being given this material.

Also, many people open a book with a nice opening line or paragraph and then suddenly go into memory or flashback. My recommendation is that if you have a memory or flashback in your opening chapter, you are starting the book in the wrong place. Move the start line I discussed in Chapter 15 earlier so that the flashback/memory becomes a real time event.

2. Match the two to the inherent pace of your story. If you have a fast-moving thriller, a lot of telling can really slow down the story. On the other hand, if you are writing a multi-generational family saga, there will probably be a lot of telling. Also, mix the two. If the reader gets too much telling, they

might get bored; too much action might overwhelm. You can balance the story out by using both.

    3. Always show action. Don't have your action occur 'off-stage'. Summarized action is boring.

    4. Always show the climax of the book. And hopefully, have your protagonist and antagonist in the scene.

Symbolism:
Remember those Literature classes where the teacher went on about Faulkner's use of the color yellow in <u>Soldier's Pay</u>? Did they call it symbolism?

    The example I'm going to use is Richard Russo's superb book <u>Nobody's Fool</u>. It was also made into an excellent movie, from which Paul Newman was nominated for an Oscar.

    The opening of the book is several pages spent on the old trees overlooking the main street in the town the story is set in. The trees were once the pride of main street but now they are old and diseased and the people who live there fear them, that an unexpected branch will collapse on their house. This foreshadows a large part of the story. The trees are a symbol for the way the entire town has become.

    Then there is the symbol for conflict. The main character, Sully, has a running feud with a man he worked for, Carl. So Sully steals Carl's new snowblower. And Carl steals it back. And Sully steals it once more. And in the process Sully poisons Carl's dog, which Carl gives to Sully at the end, a symbol of Sully having changed.

    Some symbols are most blunt. Sully hates his departed father. Every time he drives by the cemetery where his father is buried, Sully gives the grave the finger.

    Symbolism, to tie it in with the first part of this chapter, is how we *show* things to the reader, rather than tell them.

21. GENRE

Decide where your book fits (if it does fit). No one likes hearing it, but there are certain guidelines to follow when writing in specific fields. If you are writing an action/suspense novel, then your primary emphasis is on action. That's not to say that you shouldn't have good characterization, but you should not emphasize the characters at the expense of slowing down the action. Remember the perspective of the reader: when they bought your book, or picked it up to read, why did they do that? What are they looking for?

    As I've said before, the second most important thing an aspiring writer should do (with writing being number one) is read. Read everything you can get your hands on in the field you are trying to write in. Read the published authors in your field. Read the good ones. Read the bad ones. Dissect the books and try to find commonalties, then find where some authors were a little different.

Walk into a bookstore and look at how it is laid out. You have a fiction section; a mystery section; a science fiction section; etc. etc. You should be intimately familiar with the section that you propose to write in. You should know who the authors are. You should know who the publishers are. You should be a member of the appropriate writer's group, for example, Sisters In Crime for mystery writers. Optimally, you should go to a writer's conference where a writer in your field will be and try to get information first hand. Go to the library and look up copies of Publishers Weekly and go through the reviews and see what is being published.

I am not saying that you have to fit into a genre. I am simply saying that most writers do. If you look at the recent history of publishing, there are certain names that stick out: King, Clancy, Crichton, Grisham, etc. What each of these have in common is that they basically "launched" a new genre. That's not to say that there weren't horror books before Stephen King, but it is to say that somehow King did something a little different and broke open the field. In the same manner, Tom Clancy is the leader of the pack in military techno-thrillers.

Sometimes when I talk to other writers, I realize that pretty much everything has been done before. The secret is to do it better and/or do it slightly differently with a new twist.

As I will discuss at length in the business section, though, you really cannot try to beat the market place. The time lag between concept and being in the bookstore for most authors averages around three years. So while lawyer books might be hot this year, don't count on it being hot by the time you get that book done and marketed. *Write what you can write and what you want to write.* I remind you of genre only to make it easier for you to study what has been done to help you do what you want to.

There are times when you don't want to fit in a genre. One of my publishers doesn't want to list my AREA 51 series of books as science fiction because they feel they can reach a broader audience if they label it mainstream. Mainstream is what everything that doesn't definitely fit into one of the categories of genre—which are basically: science fiction/fantasy, mystery and romance—goes.

A key thing to remember, also, is that your story does not have to be enjoyed by everyone. If you are writing a romance and you hand it to someone who has never read—nor likes—romance novels, to read and critique, don't expect very good feedback. If one person in ten out of your writer's group says: "Hey, I really liked that." then think about it—ten percent of the selected population liked your story. If ten percent, or even one percent, of the people who enter a bookstore wants to buy it, then you have a bestseller.

Earlier I mentioned that it seems like most aspiring writers (and writing programs) disdain genre and try to write books about "life". But go back to my analogy to being a student of architecture. The reason I always suggest to a new novelist to write a genre novel or two first before moving on to the Great American Novel is because it is like the architecture professor giving his student a set of blueprints and saying: "Here's a rough set of guidelines of buildings like the one you want to build—and all these guidelines worked. Now, use these as a reference and design your own."

Putting a novel together is so difficult that any way you can help yourself in the beginning is useful and, not to beat this to death, but making not only the subject of your novel, but the format, a familiar one will help you. If you read five romance novels a week, then you have "studied" romance writing quite a bit. You know the format. The flow of the book. You even know quite a bit about the business end (you know authors, publishers, and the market.).

I'm not saying write "formula" books. I will talk about this again in the business section. The point, though, is that genre is not only the way publishers look at books and categorize them, it is also the way readers categorize books.

Another helpful aspect of understanding what genre you are writing in, is that there are writers groups for most genres. Sisters In Crime comes to mind (address in Appendix 4). There are science fiction groups, mystery groups, and fantasy groups. There are also conventions and workshops designed specifically for those areas, such as Boucheron.

Regardless of genre, your goal should be to write the best possible book you can both in terms of plot and characterization.

The Literary Genre
I have added this after attending a writers' retreat where I read one of the participant's manuscript. It was about a woman and the way her life changed in response to events in it and her own growing maturity as a person. It made me reevaluate some of the things I've taught and written in this book. My focus used to be on action driven stories because that is what I did. It is what I did because it is what I was capable of doing. If I were capable of writing War and Peace, The Sequel I suppose I would do that, but I'm not. Yet.

Many writers want to write about people, not specifically action. There is nothing wrong with that. I have perceived though, that there are some things to keep in mind in a character oriented book and I will touch on what little I have learned and experienced.

In a character oriented book you should treat your characters like you would subplots in an action book. For example, don't have a character in chapter 3 if you don't develop and use that character by the end of the novel. To abuse the Chekov quote I used earlier, don't have a character in your story unless that character impacts the main plot by the end. Just as all subplots must be kept tight to the main plot, all your characters must be tight to the main story, which is your main character's development.

Each character must be real and have his or her own agenda, just like each person in real life has his own agenda, even if it isn't a conscious one. The characters must also be consistent.

Also realize that perhaps the greatest flaw most people have is their lack of awareness of *themselves*, never mind others. True characters are not walking around self-actualized on Maslow's hierarchy. Many times they are walking around ignorant of their own agenda. Sometimes authors are also ignorant of their own agenda, specifically why they are trying to write a novel.

I have also found that character oriented books often need to be cut down much more than action oriented books. There is a tendency to wander a bit, because people's lives tend to wander a bit. Now, there are some authors whose style is so good that you like that wandering—say, a Larry McMurty or Pat Conroy. But for most, less is better.

Some authors come to mind for these types of books: Lisa Alther, Anne Tyler, Richard Russo, Jane Smiley, Clyde Edgerton and many more. If you want to write like these people, you should read everything you can that they write. You should study the craft of writing, of putting words into sentences into paragraphs.

You have to judge yourself accurately as a writer. For example, my goal in the next few years is to apply the skills I have learned in plotting to my characters.

One thing for sure: The quality of writing in a character oriented book must be higher because it must evoke emotion in the reader, not just intellectual interest. Marketing character-oriented books is also somewhat different and I will touch on that in the business section.

22. THE READER

I have to occasionally remind myself that I spend many months full-time writing something that will be read by others in several hours. I also have to remember what mindset the reader approaches my novels with. I have to both tell a story interesting enough to keep the reader's attention (intellect) and tell it in a manner that the reader enjoys (emotion). As a writer, you also need to be aware of these things.

Don't forget what the reader knows. If the reader knows something that a character in your story doesn't, it makes the story harder to write and you must be more skillful. You have to do this sometimes, but be very careful to not confuse or bore your reader. Don't go 10 pages with your character agonizing over who killed Aunt Bess if the reader was shown Uncle John strangling Aunt Bess in chapter two, something your character obviously wasn't privy to.

I find this to be a big problem that many new writers have, and it comes about because of point of view. If the writer has a scene that reveals who the bad guy is in chapter 2, but the protagonist doesn't know who the bad guy is until chapter 14, those twelve chapters in between, wherever the protagonist is trying to discover who the bad guy is, are a real turn-off to the reader.

In the same manner if you have an ensemble cast of characters traveling all over the world, you run into the problem of what we used to call in the army 'dissemination of information.' The reader knows all of what all the characters know, but the characters don't know what each other know. I used to have scenes where my characters literally all sat around a conference table and exchanged information—at least that is until an editor pointed out to me how boring those scenes were to the reader.

Don't underestimate the reader. If they can read, they have at least a base level of education. Don't beat the reader to death to make a point. Most writers err on the side of overkill; although a just as dangerous trait is being so subtle the reader misses it. Usually, though, the difference between a book and a movie is that the reader can go back three pages and reread something to check it. Also remember most people read every word and aren't likely to miss what you write. They may miss the significance of what you've written (which is useful in building suspense and having neat twists) but usually when the reader gets to the end and learns what really happened (if it's well written) they suddenly see the significance of things they didn't pay much attention to. Thus mention Uncle John maybe only once, instead of twenty times. Yeah, he was mentioned and the especially astute reader may pick up your clue, but even the most obtuse will get it if you rant on about Uncle John's massive forearms and great hand strength in chapter 10, and happen to mention several times how he likes to pop the heads off chickens in chapter 12 and how he used to set fires and torture small animals as a kid in chapter 14— get the point? Or do I have to beat you to death with it?

When remembering your reader, do not sell your reader short. Give the reader credit for putting some brain effort into the book. There is a tendency for beginning writers to either beat a reader to death with a point that they feel is important (i.e. repeating it several times on the same page) or being too subtle because the writer knows what's going on but forgets that the reader doesn't.

In the first case, overuse of language can be a problem. If a character is upset and you basically say that once, to use very strong adjectives or adverbs further on, to further emphasize the character's state of mind can actually detract. It is almost like using dialogue poorly. Let the actions, not the adjectives and adverbs speak.

An example of this common mistake:

"Listen you idiot," Buffalo Bill angrily screamed at the quivering boy. "You've really made me mad now," he furiously added as he pounded the stock of his rifle into the dead buffalo's already smashed skull.

Think Buffalo Bill is angry? Uh-huh.

Also don't lecture the reader. Sometimes you will write something you feel very strongly about emotionally, but really adds little to the story. Cutting something out of your manuscript is one of the most painful things to do but one of the most necessary. I had a thirty-page chapter in my second novel that I was very proud of. It was a Special Forces briefback that went into superb detail on the upcoming mission. Unfortunately, it slowed down the action of the book and I made the decision to cut it down extensively and Chapter Six went from thirty pages to five in the final version. Concentrate on the overall story, not parts of the story.

I've even heard someone say that you should cut out the part of the manuscript that you absolutely love the most because your emotion is clouding your judgment. I'm not sure I agree with that, but there is a certain degree of validity to taking a hard look at the parts in your story that you feel most strongly about. It might even be just a sentence that strikes you each time you read it, jarring you out of the story, or even a word. Be prepared to cut.

Another mistake is too much foreshadowing. I found that I tended to 'set up' plot points a bit too much instead of allowing them to occur naturally. I mention elsewhere Chekov's rule of not having a gun in Act One unless you fire it by the end of Act Three, but be careful not to mention the gun too much or the reader loses all suspense.

The most important thing you have to remember about the reader though is that you have to interest him. You have to get him involved with your story. You can never assume you interest the reader. You have to focus on making sure you do that.

Even now, when I publish a book, I step back from it and look at it on the racks in the bookstore. I ask myself why should someone who has never heard of me pick up that book and even look at the back cover, never mind buy it? What makes my book stand out?

That leads me to this brilliant observation I made after publishing 10 books and writing 15 manuscripts: **Title is important.**

I look at the titles for my first eight books now and I cringe. There is little in the title of any of those books to interest the reader. So then why should they pick up and even check to see what it is about? Do that yourself. Go to the bookstore and just scan. Besides the cover art (if the book is fortunate not to be spine out), what do you notice? The title. And which ones catch your interest? It is something very important to think about and consider.

Many authors come up with a title that only makes sense if you read the book; i.e. the title comes out of the book. But that's backwards logic. Because no one is going to read the book unless the title draws them into. I recommend spending a considerable amount of time thinking about your title. I believe it is the only marketing device the writer has control of.

The bottom line is that the reader is the most important factor in the entire publishing arc that goes from writer, through agent, to editor, to publisher, to bookseller, to bookstores, to reader.

23. THE WRITING CYCLE

After the idea comes the actual work. I view writing as a continuous four-stage cycle.

Stage 1: The idea. After the main storyline, you need to know where you are starting each time you sit down to write. Where is the story at that point, and where is it going in the immediate future? I usually do this a chapter or two ahead at a time. Always remember your one sentence original idea. I like to start every day of work by reminding myself of it.

Stage 2: Research. Often I find upon researching an idea that there are many other aspects to the subject that I was not aware of. In many cases research drives the creative train. There is a very thin line between being realistic and telling a story. Real life is sometimes pretty amazing and sometimes you have to bend reality a little for the sake of your story. Bend it too far though, and no one will be interested in sticking with you. Also you must make sure you have internal validity to your story. For example, if you are writing science fiction and have faster than light space travel, you must have certain rules as to how that travel works and you must stay within the boundaries of the rules you set up. Remember the diagram? Research is key to building that background box. I constantly research, pretty much every day, even while I am writing, because it gives more opportunities to develop the plot.

Stage 3: Writing. Sit down and write. Just get it down on paper. It almost always looks awful the first draft. But at least it's written. Give yourself a pat on the back for doing that. Worry about the awful later. Use 'bum glue' as Bryce Courtenay says. There is absolutely no other way to finish a manuscript other than writing it, one word, one sentence, one paragraph, and one chapter at a time.

Stage 4: Editing. Go back and look at what you wrote. Clean it up. Throw it out if it doesn't fit (don't literally throw it out—never, never, never discard something you wrote. You never know when you might need it in another story or after the first draft of the manuscript is done. Label it and save it.) To start my writing day, I usually begin by going back and at least reading what I wrote the previous day, cleaning it up as I go. This not only edits the work, but also gets me in the proper groove to continue.

Now I am going to be very honest with you. Unlike most writers (or at least unlike what most writers say) I have no real set routine. Sometimes I wake up and jump right into writing. Sometimes I spend days editing. Sometimes I spend days doing nothing externally, but spinning wheels in my head, trying to figure out what I'm doing with the story (but there are less and less of those days lately because—you got it—I have good outlines.).

There is no typical workday for me other than the fact that I do work at something. I have listed out all sorts of routines and suggestions in this book so far and I have used all of them at one time or another. But don't feel like there is a golden rule. If one day you want to write standing on your head on the New York City subway—then go for it (just be careful—it's a jungle out there.). Sometimes I sit down and outline chapters just like I suggested in the outlining section. Sometimes I don't outline the chapter, I just begin writing it. Do whatever works. But work.

24. EDITING

There are two types of editing: story editing (rewriting) and copyediting.

Story editing:
Ask yourself the following questions: Is there continuity? Does every sentence and action serve a purpose in the story? Does the story flow logically? These and other questions are the ones you ask when story editing. This is the editing that you need most. By the time you finish a manuscript you have read every word dozens and dozens of times. See how the story *feels*. If you read a lot, then you have a feel for a good story or a bad one.

Give it to a friend or acquaintance to read. But beware. A writer cannot have a soft skin. Take criticism and examine it very carefully. If more than two people say the same thing then maybe there is some truth to it. Pick people who read a lot and read the type of book that you are attempting to write.

Ask the following questions when editing:

-Do these words have a purpose?

-Do they relate to my story?

-Is this the time to tell this or should some of it wait?

-Is my timeline consistent?

-Are my characters consistent?

-Are my transitions subtle but clear?

-Is this section necessary? Can it be cut without affecting the main story?

Again do not write things just because you think it's interesting or you want to lecture or educate the reader. A useful technique for story editing is to let the manuscript sit for a while (several days to a week or two) to clear your head and then take a relook.

Rewriting: This is a foul word to most writers' ears but an essential one. *Every* manuscript I have had accepted for publication has had to be extensively rewritten. By that I mean that although the original idea stayed the same, something that initially seemed rather vital to the story had to change.

Rewriting is not something that just happens after the first draft is done. It too is an ongoing process. Every fifty pages of manuscript, I print it out and go over it. Every time I change the plot somewhat further on in the manuscript, I have to go back and rewrite everything before to fit the change.

It ain't over when you think it's over. When I complete the first draft of a manuscript, my work on that manuscript is somewhere between 1/2 and 2/3 completed. Too many writers are so glad to have finally completed all those pages that the thought of having to go back and rework the whole thing is blasphemous. But it has to be done.

I'm writing this section because less than a minute ago I got off the phone with my agent and we were discussing three of my manuscripts, which have been languishing in his and my care. We talked about one and he just threw out several ideas and in the course of them I got a few ideas that might help me re-write and get rid of the weak points of the story.

The most important thing for me about rewriting is to be honest. To very objectively look at a piece of work (which I, as the author, know quite intimately) and find the flaws. Most of the time I know when I'm writing the flaw that it's a flaw. This is a hard area to explain because a lot of times I work simply on gut feeling about what is wrong and needs to be corrected.

Rewriting can vary from having to completely tear apart the manuscript (thank God for computers.) to simply making a few changes here and there. But almost every manuscript needs a rewrite.

I suggest you put away a manuscript for a week or two after you finish writing it to allow yourself some mental distance before looking at it again. Give it out for reads and listen to the feedback. However, *don't* make changes simply because someone suggests them if you don't feel they are valid. I've spun my wheels on one manuscript making change after change, and what I was changing was the wrong problem. If there is a problem, I believe as the author, if I am honest and take my time, I can usually find it better than probably anyone else (usually, though, after someone else points out that there is a problem to me).

I just received an 11 page, single-spaced letter of comments from my editor on a manuscript that needs to be re-written. I know what it feels like to attend a writing retreat and get back a critique that tears the manuscript apart and recommends changes, some of them rather major.

My first reaction to such a letter is, of course, negative. I've learned to take a couple of days to let that feeling past. Then go through the comments and the manuscript. The next feeling is one close to despair. It appears an almost insurmountable task

There is a process that a writer goes through when getting a manuscript back from an editor/agent very similar to Kubler-Ross's five stages: denial, anger, bargaining, depression and finally acceptance.

First we deny there is a problem; then we get angry for not receiving validation for the work that has been done or things that are working with the manuscript; then we try to explain away the problem; then we start realizing there really is a problem and the thought of rewriting sends us into a funk; then finally we accept that it really is a problem and must be fixed. Then we can begin rewriting.

<u>Killing it—The ultimate edit</u>: After attending many writing conferences, I believe that numerous aspiring novelists become too enamored of their first manuscript. If you talk to published authors you will find out that the vast majority did not get their first manuscript published. It was an investment in learning. They moved on to write a second, a third, however many it took to get published. It's a difficult thing, but often you have to take the manuscript and shove it in a drawer, give up on getting it published and move on to writing your next one. You have to take out that trusty .45 pistol and put that thing down.

<u>Copy Editing</u>: This is an ongoing process. If you are lucky, your computer will have a spellchecker. I assume you have a reasonable mastery of the

written word so this is merely a matter of putting the time in with a red pen-cil/pen and paying attention to detail. If you are fortunate enough to be published, you will have professionals go over your work with a fine tooth comb and even then they will miss a few things.

Remember the following basic rules:

-don't repeat words or phrases.

-use a style manual.

-don't have secret agents. Always know who is doing what to whom or what.

-The fewer words the better.

The bottom line is: Is it clear?

A good technique to help eliminate extra words and to make your writing smoother is to read it aloud and have someone listening with a copy of your manuscript and a red pen. Have them note where your *verbal* reading "edits" the copy. You will be surprised how much you change what you have written when you have to speak it.

The most important thing to remember about words is: Verbs are power words. Adjectives and adverbs are weaker words that can dress up your work but can also interfere with the smoothness of the writing. Hemmingway is an extreme example of writing using verbs as power words and trying to minimize adjectives and adverbs.

Active versus passive tense: When characters act they are more persuasive than when they react (passive). When characters react they are less sympathetic to the reader.

Try not to overuse words ending in -ing. For example:

>Don was sitting there.

>Don sat there.

The second sentence is more direct and smooth.

Do not repeat words if you can help it—especially uncommon words, because the first time it will go by smoothly but the second time will jar the reader and remind him/her of seeing it before.

Adverbs: make sure each one is essential. Ask yourself if you can eliminate the need for the adverb by choosing a different verb.

Avoid overusing verbs that end in *-ing*. The primary purpose of an *-ing* verb is to show simultaneity.

Weak verbs. Always see if you can change the word to a more descriptive one.

Avoid vague pronouns. Don't make the reader work to figure out who you are referring to. Always have an antecedent to your pronoun or else it does-n't make sense.

The last word on editing is: Omit all unnecessary words.

Read a lot.... This my final word on writing. Read to study style and also for story ideas. Whenever I feel myself start grinding down at the keyboard, I pick up a good book and read. It's a form of inspiration and rejuvenation. I also go to the mall and wander around the bookstore, looking at what has just come out and vowing to myself that I can write better stuff than that. So can you.

3

Getting your Novel Published

You've finished your manuscript and now it's burning a hole through your desktop. You desperately want to start making submissions.
STOP.

I recommend you do two things before you start marketing a manuscript.

1. Start writing your next one. You learned so much writing the first, that your second is bound to be better. Most authors do not get published on their first try out the gate. Don't pin all your hopes on the first one and the best way to do that is to start writing the second. This also prevents you from spending an entire year trying to market the first and ending up with just a pile of rejection slips. At least at the end of the year, at the very least, you can have a pile of rejection slips *and* another manuscript ready to market.

2. Let the manuscript sit for at least two weeks before making submissions. As you read the following pages, the one adjective I use over and over again with regards to the publishing world is *SLOW*. No one else is in any rush so you have to fight spinning your wheels. You're only going to get one shot at each agent and publishing house you send your submission to; it is best to make sure it is your best one. Let the manuscript sit for a couple of weeks, then pick it up and read it very critically. Rewrite. Edit. Clean it up.

If you've done those two things, then you are ready to start thinking about marketing your book. I recommend you take the book process and work it backward to get to your starting point in trying to sell it. Think of the ultimate buyer, the person standing in the store. How do they choose a book? Don't you think editors and agents think about that quite a bit?

The critical components that editors and agents are looking for in a novel are good characters revolving around a good idea.

Why? Because that is what readers are looking for. Not only does the idea by itself have to be top-notch, but it also has to fit the publisher's needs at the time.

I don't think you should "write for the market" but you most definitely need to understand the market when attempting to break into it. Your original idea is the first thing that gets looked at, long before your writing does. Your background—and I mean more than just your writing background—also plays a determining role in how a publisher looks at a submission.

A common lament among writers is: *"If I could only get my manuscript read. I know a publisher would buy it."* There is a flaw in the logic of that statement that most people never consider. As I mentioned earlier, how many of you go to a bookstore, completely read a book, and *then* buy it? To expect agents and editors to do what you don't do is not fair. Also, it makes no sense. Most people buy a book from an unknown author based on reading the cover copy (your cover letter and partial synopsis) and maybe looking at the first couple of pages. In other words they buy it the same way an agent is going to take you on, or a publisher will offer you a contract.

To expect someone to invest the time into reading something of questionable value to them is naive in this business. A person in the store is going to put down her hard-earned money to buy a book. To an agent or editor, time is money. For them to invest the time to read your manuscript, they have to expect a reasonable return on that investment. And remember, *every* writer thinks his manuscript gives a great return.

Here's a scary thing about the business. When the sales reps for a publisher go out to the bookbuyers to get orders for upcoming books, they don't carry boxes full of manuscripts or even bound galleys. They carry cover flats. These are the cover, front and back, spread out flat. On the reverse side is some marketing information about the book and the author. That's it. The sales rep spreads all these flats out on a table in front of the bookbuyer, like a dealer in poker. They have one or two of the entire list for a month that they pitch in a minute to the buyer. The rest, the buyer thumbs through (maybe) or tosses down the stairs, or whatever, to determine how many copies to order.

By the time an average mid-list paperback hits the racks, maybe three people in the business have actually read the book. The sales reps certainly don't
have time to read them, nor do the bookbuyers for the stores. Scary, isn't it?
But it's reality.

Note: You should not start marketing a manuscript until it is done. I have
seen new writers—with only a partial manuscript and an outline—try to
approach agents and publishers at conferences. Their feeling seems to be that
they will do the work to finish the rest of the manuscript if they find someone interested in it. I'm sorry to say, but that really doesn't fly in the face of
the realities of the business. As I noted earlier, in the majority of cases, writers have several completed manuscripts before they get published. This is true
for fiction, but necessarily for non-fiction.

There is no secret handshake. I say this because I see very strong emotions at
writers' conferences. A constant asking of the same questions (most of which
are answered in this book), with the feeling seeming to be that suddenly some
author or, most especially, some editor or agent will suddenly leap to their
feet and give the "secret" to getting published.

Another thing I see at conferences are writers getting confused by the different perspectives that are offered. I watch writers listen to authors all week
long, then when the editors and agents show up on the weekend, all the same
questions get asked and the answers from those on the buying end are attended to more carefully than those on the selling end, yet writers are going to be
on the selling end. I can tell you how to sell a manuscript—an editor can tell
you how he or she buys a manuscript. The two are not necessarily equivalent
unless you want that specific editor to buy your manuscript. That editor represents his or her own views and the buying policies of that particular publisher. My perspective is being an author in the world of publishing, which
has a variety of places to sell your work to.

For example, I recently heard a panel of editors unanimously agree that
writers don't need to get agents. True—except for the fact that these editors
represented publishing houses that still accept unagented manuscripts. And,
most importantly, from *some editors'* perspective, I agree—a writer does not
need an agent. (Most editors, though, would prefer a writer to have an agent,
especially when it comes to negotiating a contract as they will be on the same
sheet of music as far as the business goes). From a writer's perspective, if you
can get your stuff looked at without an agent, go for it. If you can negotiate
a contract by yourself and know all about joint accounting, foreign rights,
electronic rights, etc. etc. then go for it. The bottom line as far as I was concerned was that these three editors would prefer to negotiate with writers
directly and so would I if I was in their shoes. The majority of editors would

prefer to negotiate with an agent rather than a novice writer because the agent speaks the same language and the deal can be completed more quickly. There are many sides to every issue and listen to them all, but there is no *secret*. There's just a lot of hard work and effort and persistence.

Also, I've noticed at conferences that some editors and agents spend a lot of the time during their talks telling the attendees how to make their (the editors and agents) job easier. While I don't believe in abusing editors and agents, and am a firm believer in being professional, a writer's goal is not to make their jobs easier. It's to work together.

Another thing I see a lot of, is a we-they attitude between writers and the publishing business. I'm constantly asked how much control over cover I have (none), or how much an editor will change the manuscript (always recommendations and almost always for the better of the book), and how the publisher will screw over the writer (only if your interests and there's are in opposite directions). The bottom line is that writers, agents, editors, and everyone else at the publishing house are supposed to be on the same team with the same goals. It should be a me-we relationship. I recommend approaching people in the business with a positive attitude, while looking out for your own interests.

At this point your manuscript is done and ready to market. As you read the following chapters, try to follow the methodology I used. First you must find the right target. Then you must do a submission, which may well be the most important piece of work you do as an author.

25. THE SUBMISSION

The submission is the first step in entering the world of publishing and, for most writers, the last. (Note for the purposes of this chapter consider the terms submission and query mean the same thing—also, this is the same thing you will send to agents). Understanding the flow of the submission will greatly increase your chances of receiving a good look. The process I describe below will make more sense if you think of it as a replication of the flow a person goes through entering a bookstore and perusing a book for purchase.

Step One: Find the right place to send it.
The initial thing you must determine is who to send your submission to, in the same manner that the bookbuyer walks to the part of the bookstore that has the type of books she enjoys reading.

Whenever I look at a book on the shelf, my eye automatically goes to the little imprint on the spine that says who the publisher is. Sometimes, though, be aware that the name listed may be an imprint of a larger house. For example, Spectra is the science fiction imprint for Bantam. To find the publishing house, turn to the copyright page which will usually have the publisher's address listed. Imprints are the way a large house breaks down inside of itself to have various smaller parts. Also, some famous editors, such as Nan Talese, have their own imprint.

(Another interesting aspect of the copyright page is that you can tell what printing the book is in—there is usually a list of descending numbers. Wherever the numbers stop, that is the printing of that book.)

There are numerous publications such as the <u>Novel And Short Story Writer's Market</u> that list publishers and their needs and requirements. These books give both the address and what each one wants in the way of a submission. The information listed also tells you what type of books they specialize in.

Use not only the <u>Writer's Market</u> but also do what our bookbuyer is doing and go to the bookstore and look for books similar to what you have written. Check who published those books and then look them up in the <u>Market</u>. Every publisher has an affinity for certain types of novels. Also, remember that you do not have to break into the top of the line of the market right from the start. There are numerous smaller presses that are more accessible. Clyde Edgerton has done quite well with Algonquin Books of Chapel Hill. I talk about this in the last chapter, but I believe that contrary to what many people believe in these days of corporate mergers, small presses are making a comeback—actually as a result of these mergers.

I have noticed a trend lately: less and less major publishers are accepting unsolicited material and deal only with agents. The process I describe for a submission in this chapter is the same with submitting to agents who I will cover in Chapter 27.

When preparing to market a manuscript, my agent always says you have to "know the scorecard." Know who is who. You have to do the same.

Understand also that the corporate take-overs and buy-outs have changed the face of publishing. Bantam, Doubleday, Dell was just bought by Random House. Houses are eating each other up ferociously and you should know who is who because different imprints in the same house won't compete against themselves for the same manuscript. Ultimately this is one of many reasons why you need an agent, but let's hold off on that until I talk about agents.

<u>Step two: Prepare your submission.</u>

When you find a publisher listed, follow the instructions for submission and address it by name to the appropriate editor. Although some publishers will look at unsolicited manuscripts, the majority of entries in the MARKET read like this:

"HOW TO CONTACT: Query with outline/synopsis and 2 sample chapters with SASE. Simultaneous submissions OK. Reports in 6 to 8 weeks."

Each one might be slightly different but if you send each the same thing you'll get looked at and it will save you quite a bit of time. Ninety-nine percent of agents and editors will accept the general format I give here. Even if a publishing house says it will look at unsolicited manuscripts, I recommend never sending one out unless it's preceded by a query and the manuscript is requested.

What that means is that you must submit four things: A cover letter; a synopsis; sample chapters; and a SASE. Before I go into the details of each, let me give you some general guidelines—and yes, I know you will tell me you have heard different from Agent So and So and Editor What's Her Name at that big New York publisher, but what I'm giving you here are the general rules; ignore it at your own risk.

1. All correspondence should be typed. Hand-written material does not fly.

2. Make sure the typing is clear. Use a new ribbon, laser cartridge, whatever. Hard as it is to believe, agents and editors do get material so faded or poorly printed it is difficult to read. Difficult to read equals a no-go.

3. Use white, 20 lb. paper. Do not use erasable bond paper. Your cover letter can be on higher quality paper. Do not use colored paper to try and get attention. You don't want the attention it will bring forth.

4. Use a plain type style. Don't try using weird fonts or graphics. In this day of a million fonts available in your computer, keep it simple. A courier 12, Geneva 12, etc. work fine. Use a decent sized font, particularly in your manuscript. I often get manuscript pages on which the font is so small it gets difficult to read. I like a font that averages out to about 250 words per full manuscript page, give or take 5%.

5. There should be no visible corrections on your cover letter.

6. Have one-inch margins all around.

7. The manuscript is double-spaced (you might be able to get away with single or space and a half on your synopsis to get it down to one page).

8. All material, to include sample chapters or the manuscript, should be unbound.

9. Your name or title should be on every piece of paper.

10. Anything longer than one page should be numbered.

Now for the details of each part:

A cover letter (query): The first line of your query letter must grab the reader because it is the first (and maybe the last) thing the person opening your package will read. It is the same as the inside flap of the book in the bookstore that our bookbuyer is looking at.

What is the hook for your manuscript? Why will they want to buy it? No matter how good your manuscript is, if you don't write a good query, it will never get read. My suggestion is that you use your story's original idea as your opening line: "What if . . ." Doing that serves two purposes: it gets the reader's attention, and it plants that original idea in the reader's head as she looks through the rest of the submission.

I suggest <u>not</u> starting out with the following lines:

-"Enclosed you will find . . ." Everyone is sending the same thing. The editor/agent expects to find what is enclosed—a submission. This opening doesn't grab anything when it is seen fifty times a day.

-"I've just written my first novel and I'd like you to take a look at it . . ."

-"I just know you will love this . . . "

Go to the bookstore and look at book jackets. Note how they put "NY Time Best-selling Author" etc. on the cover. Well, since you aren't a NY Times Bestseller, look for the ones that have some sort of catchy phrase on the top back. For example on a book I have here: <u>A nuclear holocaust is just a button away . . . and someone's about to push it</u>. This would be a good opening line for your cover letter; except for the fact this storyline has been beaten to death.

Below, in the section on the synopsis, I talk about overusing adjectives and praising your own work. That applies here too. Let the facts speak for themselves.

After a paragraph or two on the novel itself, grabbing the editor's attention and making her drool with anticipation to look at your synopsis, then move on. Include not only a sales pitch for the manuscript to the publisher but also a sales pitch for yourself. The manuscript is an extension of you. What special background do you have that would make her want to see what you have done? This means not only any writing background you have, but also your background as far as the story goes. My years in the Special Forces certainly made some editors take a longer look at my query letter concerning a book about Special Forces. These paragraphs are your writing resume. If they accept your book they are hiring you. This is the equivalent of the author blurb on the inside back cover of a book. Often people buy books because the author has an interesting background; don't you think editors do the same?

This does not mean you won't get looked at it if your background doesn't have much direct application to your subject matter and you have little writing experience, but editors and agents also remember what Mark Twain said: "Write what you know." If your job or background in any way applies to what you've written, make sure you mention that.

As far as the paradox many lament of putting writing credentials in the cover letter, yet they haven't been published, unless you've been published in something noteworthy that you've been paid for, don't clutter up the letter with such information. Editors and agents understand you're a new author trying to break through.

Above I said make a sales pitch to the publisher, but I recommend not marketing the book. What's the difference? The sales pitch to the publisher consists of telling them what the great idea you have is. Marketing is telling the publisher who you think will want to read your novel. I've talked to agents and editors about this and for fiction they pretty much agree that you shouldn't do that for several reasons. One is that they consider themselves the expert on the market. Another is that you will probably be wrong in your estimates. Let the work speak for itself.

Be very, very careful if you try to be humorous. In a contest of submissions I just judged the one cover letter where the writer tried to be humorous was the absolute worst turn-off. I felt as if the writer were treating me like an idiot. Most of us aren't that funny. I advise staying away from trying to be funny. Unless of course you've written a humorous book in which case your cover letter better have the agent or editor rolling on the floor. As an aside here, think about what I wrote earlier about dialogue in a novel. Now think of the difference between someone like Dave Barry being funny using just the written word and a stand up comic. Written humor is extremely difficult to pull off.

Your cover letter must be one page. No more than that. Sad to say it's a volume business. An agent I knew said he knows within twenty seconds if a submission is worth looking at any further. From my own experience a reader can tell very quickly whether something is worth looking further at.

Address it to the editor or agent listed in personally. Don't worry about who is really going to look at it. It's better than addressing it to "Hey you." In fact, give the publisher a call and ask whoever answers the phone if that editor still works there. Editors tend to move around quite a bit. The initial editors I started with at three different houses are no longer there.

End the cover letter with a polite thanks to the editor/agent for his/her time. Naturally, the cover letter should be an example of your best writing. Misspelling or poor grammar and you're not even out of the starting block.

You can also add a last sentence giving some factual information about the manuscript such as: *This is 85,000 word science fiction manuscript.*

When you think cover letter, think book jacket for a hard cover book.

If they like your cover letter, that means they like your idea. The major purpose of the cover letter is to get the reader to want to read your synopsis. That's it. Simply to get them to turn the page and look at your synopsis.

I just talked to an agent who told me he could pretty much tell whether he could sell a manuscript based completely on reading the cover letter! Just like the person in the bookstore who makes a decision to buy or not buy your book based simply on the cover jacket copy.

   The outline/synopsis: Again, one page. You will hear other opinions, some ranging up to ten or twenty pages. I say one page simply because I take the editors' and agents' perspective. I don't think you are going to hook them with five pages of synopsis if they don't read past page one. And you may turn them off on page three if they do. Contrary to what you instinctively think, I have found that the more someone puts down the more chance they turn they reader *off* rather than hook the reader. Remember they were hooked by your cover letter. A long synopsis might make them wiggle off the hook because there's a good chance you'll put something they won't like the more you write. I really, really, recommend no more than two pages in a synopsis, and truly think it should be one page.

   I just read a four page synopsis someone sent me to review and I asked a ton of questions because the more he put in the cover letter the more questions were raised. If he had been more succinct, I would have had fewer questions.

   "Oh my God," you say. "How am I going to get four hundred pages of manuscript down to one page?"

   It isn't easy. This can take weeks to do, but do it you must. Look at the book jackets for similar books to what you've written. Guess what? They were written in collaboration between published writers and publishers. So be sneaky. Write a book jacket for your book except you are also telling the entire story. A book jacket, when spread out on an eight and half by eleven piece of paper is only two or three paragraphs, so you actually have more room than the poor editor does when she tries to prepare copy for a jacket.

   In your manuscript you will have so many important things (*everything's* important you cry) that it is bewildering to condense. Something you can try is letting someone who has read the book summarize it and see what he comes up with. His distance from the writing might allow him to do it more easily.

   The best synopses of my books that I have read were my reviews in Publishers Weekly. In those, the reviewer gets the story down to one paragraph. I suggest perusing PW and seeing how a book similar to your own was summarized. Another method is to go to your local bookstore and get some old publishers' catalogues and see how they pitched their books. Don't you think it would be very worthwhile to pitch your book to that publishing house in the same manner?

   Although many people feel this one page synopsis to be very unfair, if you look at it from a business perspective, it really isn't. What does a reader do in a bookstore? Look at a book cover, then the jacket or back page to read the

129

less-than-one-page partial synopsis on the jacket. If that doesn't interest them, they don't even bother to flip it open. Neither will an editor or agent.

There are some common mistakes to a synopsis and here are a few:

1. Too long. I beat people to death with the one page rule. Can you go longer? Yes. But every page you go over, realize that you exponentially increase the odds of losing the interest of the reader.

2. Too much detail in certain areas and not enough in others. You always have some great ideas and plot twists that you want to mention. Forget about them. The synopsis is an *overview.*

3. Making the synopsis a list of bullets: First this happens. Then that. Then this. Then that. Did you ever see book jacket that looked like that? The synopsis should be prose.

4. Too many adjectives: This is an intriguing and fascinating story about a fierce, dedicated, Viking warrior who plunders his rapacious way across Europe told in a scintillating manner, great blah, fantastic blah, blah, blah."

I can just see an editor responding: "Yes, normally we publish non-intriguing, boring books, but since yours is intriguing and fascinating—because *you* say so in your synopsis—we most certainly want it."

Just as you have to cut the fat in your book, you have to get rid of the fat in your synopsis. Editors expect good manuscripts to be intriguing, exciting, captivating, etc. etc. You, as the author, using those adjectives to describe your own work, is a waste of space. Use verbs as your power words—not adjectives and adverbs. This also goes for your cover letter. Let the work speak for itself.

5. The "I don't know what the story is about?" syndrome. There are few things worse than finishing someone's synopsis and still not having a clue what the manuscript is about. Give it to a stranger you meet on the street— or better yet in the bookstore—and see if they understand it. Have them tell you what they think your story is about after reading your synopsis. You might be surprised at the feedback.

6. The "You have eight great stories here in your synopsis but what's the book about?" syndrome. Too often synopsis turns out to be a muddle of subplots that leaves the reader wondering what the main story is about. Wondering what—you got it—the original idea is.

7. The "I don't know what kind of story this is? What's the market?" syndrome. I've read synopsis and then scratched my head wondering if this was a science fiction book? A fantasy? A children's book? Just where the heck in the bookstore are we supposed to stack this sucker anyway? You are supposed to cover this in—you got it—the cover letter (pun intended) but if it's not clear in the synopsis, it makes the editor/agent wonder if it will be clear when they read the manuscript. If they read it.

8. The "These characters sound very good but what's the story?" versus "This story sounds great but are there any characters in it?" Both are extremes and both are wrong.

9. The "Gee, it sure would have been nice to know your surprise ending, but I don't have the time to respond to your query because you left me hanging," syndrome. Tell the ending. The editor doesn't want to play guessing games and too often people promise much more than they actually deliver in surprise endings.

There is another angle to take sometimes with synopsis, particularly if your manuscript does not fit into a specific genre, is more character oriented, or perhaps is humorous. I think about some books that if you wrote a synopsis on them, first off, there would not be much of a story and secondly there would be no hint as to the real uniqueness of the writing. For example, Anne Tyler's <u>Breathing Lessons</u> would make a most boring synopsis.

I mention this because I think it is important not to sacrifice the uniqueness of your book to try and fit a "format." The page you use for a synopsis might be better used in some cases to give examples of some highlights of the writing. If your book is a series of anecdotes about a family, pick one of the best and make that your "synopsis" and tell the editor this is your book times one hundred.

The major purpose of the synopsis is to get the reader to want to look at your sample chapters.

<u>Sample chapters</u>: Which ones to send? The first two? The last two? The best two? Remember the purpose of the sample chapters. The synopsis gave the reader the story. The chapters are to show the reader how well you write. Some publishers make it easy and tell you to send the first couple. I advise sending consecutive chapters. It makes it easier on the reader to stay with the flow of the story. I recommend, even if the publisher doesn't specify, sending the first couple. Sending chapters from the middle or end could be too confusing.

The major purpose of the sample chapters is to get the reader to want to look at your entire manuscript. Do you see the flow here? Cover letter to Synopsis to Sample Chapters to Manuscript.

To justify or not to justify? I justify my format, but my computer spaces evenly. Some programs do not space the words evenly on the line and if your's doesn't, then don't justify.

The title or your name should be on every page along with a page number.

Chapter breaks should start on a new page.

SASE: Self-Addressed Stamped Envelope. If you want a reply send one. Isn't it nice that you are paying postage on your own rejections?

If you want the submission itself back, send sufficient postage and a large enough envelope. Otherwise it goes to file 13. They deal with hundreds of submissions each week at major publishers and agents, and it gets quite expensive if they paid to send it all back. I recommend not bothering and letting it get thrown out as the cost of postage to return is usually less than the cost of copying or printing a new submission.

You might want to send a stamped self-addressed postcard in your packet that they send back to you to let you know that the packet was received. However, this is only for your sanity. It's not going to make a bit of difference to the people looking at the slush pile.

How quickly will you hear back? From four weeks to never.

What's a reasonable amount of time? Whatever the publisher or editor or agent determines it to be.

What can you do if you haven't heard back in what you consider a reasonable amount of time? Nothing. What can you do? Nothing. You have no leverage; you can't make people work faster than they are going to.

What will you get back in your SASE? This will range from nothing, to a "No thanks" written on your cover letter, to a form slip thanking you but declining to a personalized letter of rejection. If you get the latter (and they are rare), take some hope. It means someone took the time and effort to actually reply.

Multiple submissions: Usually it is all right with publishers if you submit to other publishers at the same time. It takes so long for publishers to reply that you'd be a very old person if you did it one at a time. Also remember that December and August are very dead times in the publishing business when most people are on vacation.

I would not bother to put on the cover letter to publishers that it is a multiple submission. It's a subconsciously negative thing and unnecessary. Don't put anything in your cover letter that doesn't serve a positive purpose. Be very aware of what could subconsciously negatively affect the reader.

If you do get asked to send in the entire manuscript, it must be in the proper format. I am still amazed that people will spend so much of their time writing, yet the manuscript is not in the correct format. I wonder how people edit a single spaced manuscript?

A SPEED BUMP. A word of caution here. Having just read this you are probably raring to go and write your scintillating cover letter and your sparkling synopsis. But I just finished judging (with some assistance from my agent) a contest on cover letters and synopsis and the first place and second places went to people who did not have cover letters in exactly the format I listed above.

"Treachery," you cry. "You have deceived us, you scum-sucking dog," you lament.

No. I'll tell you exactly why those two entries were chosen. The first place winner had the most intriguing **idea and story**. Keep that in mind. Because you can sculpt a pile of horse manure into a shape that is pleasing to the eye, but it is still horse manure. You have to have substance. The second place person had the most coherently written synopsis along with the second best idea.

The formats I have given throughout this chapter are guidelines and only that. They do not guarantee success. They may enhance your possibility of success, but ultimately in order to sell a manuscript you *have to have* two things before even trying a submission: a good idea and good, smooth writing.

The worst thing about being an author, in my opinion, is the need for patience. This business is extremely, extremely slow. I cannot overemphasize how slow it is.

I once had a manuscript at an editor who asked for it and held it for 13 months and I never heard back on it. Once I talked to a well-known actor who wanted me to co-write a book. His last words on the phone were "Come on out to Hollywood and let's do this thing." I've yet to hear another word on the project. My phone calls to his office went go unanswered. My letters, faxes and phone calls to the editor above went unanswered.

A change to the paragraph above now that the dust has settled. I tried calling the editor who had my manuscript for 13 months. I finally got through (you're not supposed to ever, ever call an editor like this according to the rules editors propagate, but after a year, I'm sorry but everyone has their limit) and he picked up the phone and said: "Editorial."

Now I recognized this editor's voice having met him at a conference but I politely asked to speak to so and so. He told me that so and so (him.) was on another line and the he (I guess his alter ego) would take a message.

Here I violated one of my rules. I got upset. After all it had been over a year since this guy had asked to see this manuscript. He had not answered any of my most polite letters inquiring as to the status of the manuscript. He had not returned any of my recent phone calls. So I called back. When he did the same thing, I told him I recognized his voice and asked him what kind of game he was playing. He got irate and told me that was the way he dealt with people calling.

Now, an editor certainly has the right to do anything they please. As a writer your option is do you want to deal with this person? Unfortunately in the world of writing, there are a couple of dozen writers who get their calls returned and have editors do what they want. For the rest of us, you have to suck it up and drive on.

I also know, though, turning it around, that there are many writers who fail to keep up their end of the professional relationship. Writers who miss deadlines. Who refuse to compromise on editorial work. I exercised my option in this case and sent a polite letter to that editor apologizing for calling and asking him not to review my manuscript.

The bottom line is that in my experience nobody is in a rush to do anything. Except you of course.

26. REJECTIONS

Why a whole chapter devoted to rejections? And right after the chapter on submissions? Because guess what's coming shortly after you start sending out your queries?

Rejection is a fact of life in the writing business and something you *will* face. I have approximately eighty rejections for each of my first two novels. Every publisher my agent sent it to soundly rejected my fourth manuscript. This despite both having an agent representing me and having my first novel out in hardcover. I am currently reworking that manuscript years later using all the comments noted in the rejection letters. My fifth manuscript is gathering dust in my agent's office because we have made a mutual agreement that it is not worth marketing right now and might never be.

A publisher who has done the first six books in a series just rejected me for a seventh book.

If you want to be a writer get used to rejections. It's part of the business.

In fact, the prospect of rejection sometimes keeps writers from sending queries out. If you don't ante up, you can't be in the game.

Ninety percent of the time you will get a form letter thanking you for your query and wishing you luck elsewhere. If you get a personal letter that means someone really took a hard look at what you sent and was interested. Take hope, even though it is a rejection. Read carefully any comments made and take them to heart.

It's essential that you remember that the publishing business is exactly that: A business. Too many writers approach it from an idealistic perspective. The dollar is the bottom line for the publisher. If they don't see how they can make money off your submission—no matter what its literary qualities—then they won't be interested.

I've heard someone once had a Pulitzer Prize winning novel (THE YEAR-LING) from about thirty years ago typed onto 8.5 by 11 paper and submitted it to a dozen publishing houses. Every single one rejected it. Even if you have an excellent idea and manuscript, you might be rejected simply because they already have a similar manuscript programmed into their production schedule. That has happened to me several times.

There's a book called Rotten Rejections edited by Andre Bernard. (Pushcart Press, 1990). If you feel bad getting all those form letters, take a peek at this book and be glad you aren't getting some of the personalized rejections others did:

The Bridge Over The River Kwai (Pierre Boulle). A very bad book.

The Good Earth (Pearl Buck). Regret the American public is not interested in anything on China.

The Diary Of Ann Frank (Anne Frank) The girl doesn't, it seems to me, have a special perception or feeling which would lift that book above the "curiosity" level.

Take heart and hang in there.

Learn to control your emotions with rejection. Sometimes you might get a rejection letter back with comments that you totally disagree with or might be outright incorrect. Don't lash out. The publisher who eventually did publish them initially rejected my first two manuscripts. I was very upset when I got that initial rejection letter back and I disagreed with some of the comments the editor made—but think what might have happened if I had picked up the phone and called him up and chewed him out. Also, after I calmed down, I realized that the comments *were* legitimate.

On a cover letter for a military techno-thriller I sent out, I got back a sentence scrawled in the upper left corner of the letter that "We don't do fantasies."

For every acceptance I have (seventeen now) I have at least twenty to thirty rejections on average. I also get rejected for teaching jobs at seminars, magazine articles I submit, etc. etc. It's part of the business and you have to use it to your advantage. Take strength from any positive comment. And also remember that you don't know how and when your break will come—perseverance counts, but you are also dealing with people and courtesy counts also.

Remember that many times the rejection has nothing at all to do with the work itself. There are many reasons for rejection.

Sometimes a publishing house has no room at the inn. Their list is full for the next couple of years and they simply can't buy any more material for a while. Sometimes they don't see how they can market a particular work.

You have to remember who sits at the conference table at a publishing house when they decide whether to buy a manuscript. It's not just the editor who read the manuscript, you also have other editors, the publisher, the marketing people, the sales department, publicity, etc. etc. Sometimes editors may like a work but one of those others sees a problem with it, whether it be not being able to market it, not getting booksellers excited about the type of novel, etc. You have to remember that a publisher has to feel like they can sell the book.

One frustrating aspect of rejections is the second read. The first editor likes your work, but they need a second opinion. Sometimes it will seem to you that everyone can say no, but no one can say yes.

The best advice I received regarding rejection came from an agent at CAA—Creative Artists Agency—when I asked him what the "coverage" was on a manuscript he had sent to a bunch of studios and had rejected. He told me that a rejection is an emotional decision. Then the person who did the rejection goes back and invents reasons for that decision, sometimes correctly, but many times wrongly.

Ask yourself this—why did I buy this book and not that book from the rack in the supermarket last time I was there?

One aspect of rejections I find fascinating is what I call the: "We want something like X, but not like X" theory. I got a rejection back from a studio considering one of my novels and the summary was: "This book is too much like Independence Day and no one wants to be compared to the 4th highest grossing movie of all time." You have to really sit and think about what that sentence says. My reaction is, "Hell, yeah, I want to be compared to such a success."

There's no way around this mindset. In many ways Hollywood and the New York publishing world have 'group-think.' Either everyone wants something or no one wants it. They constantly say they want something different and daring, but they'll reject something because it's different and daring.

The bottom line on rejections is that it is a subjective process.

I recently cut out a newspaper article on a woman who finally had a manuscript accepted. It's her 33rd manuscript—none of the previous ones having been accepted. That's dedication.

There is such a thing as a good rejection if you learn from it and are able to read between the lines. I received a rejection on a new manuscript from an editor who previously bought manuscripts from me at another publishing house. His only comment was: "I like Bob's work, and have bought it before, but this is the same as what he did then."

What I took from that was that I had to get better. I couldn't keep doing the same and expect to move up.

You have to have a thick skin as a writer. It's guaranteed, even if you get published, that someone, somewhere, will not like your book, and that at least one of those people will make it their life's mission to inform you of that.

27. THE AGENT

The agent is a key player in the publishing business. If there were no agents, publishing houses would have to hire more people to wade through their slush pile. There are some major publishing houses that won't even look at material if it isn't submitted through an agent. It's simply a question of economics. In fact, in just the past couple of years, that number has grown considerably. There are very few large publishing houses left that will look at unagented material.

The agent is the link between the author and the publishing world. This is most critical for new writers with no background in publishing. It *is* a jungle out there and your agent should be your guide. The agent should know who, where, what, how much, and when.

HOW TO FIND AN AGENT:

Most writers hate the quandary that searching for agents put them in. They see the Catch-22 of: I need an agent to get published but I can't get an agent unless I'm published.

That's not really true. Agents are constantly on the lookout for new writers; that's how they stay in business. There are several ways to find an agent:

1. You can do direct submission using those agents listed in books such as the Guide To Literary Agents. Just like publishers, agents list their wants and how to submit to them. There are hundreds listed.

2. Get a recommendation from a published author. Remember, though, that this works two ways—the author also should recommend you to the agent. I've had total strangers call me up and ask for the name of my agent and/or editor. Then a few proceed—without asking me—to use my name in a submission saying that I recommended them. Besides being impolite, it really doesn't help. Some people put so much effort (I know because *I* did.) into simply trying to get their work seen, that they tend to overlook the fact that even if it is seen, it might not be worth the look. As I've mentioned in other places, you only have one shot with each person you submit to on each piece of work. Make damn sure it's your best shot.

A thing to remember—it is just as likely that it is the *author's* fault for a bad relationship with an agent as the reverse. Often I hear authors complain bitterly about agents. I always take that with a grain of salt, because ultimately, the person who produces the product is the author, not the agent. If the product is not good, it does not matter how good the agent is. Very rarely will you find an author willing to admit that maybe his writing didn't measure up. Many authors automatically think that if they sold one novel, everything they write from there on out will sell, but actually the facts show the reverse is true.

3. A book editor that you made a direct submission to might recommend an agent. Remember above where I talked about the role of the agent? An editor who feels your work has some merit, but is not quite up to standard to offer a contract for, might suggest an agent so that you can work with the agent to improve the work. Contrary to popular myth, not all editors enjoy rejecting manuscripts and most of them actually do want to see writers succeed. I should know. I found my agent through an editor who gained nothing at all from the deal (he worked for a non-fiction publisher that in my desperation I had sent my fiction proposal to, which by the way violates the advice an agent just gave out last week at a conference I attended).

Also, many editors prefer negotiating contracts with an agent rather than a new author. They speak the same lingo and have experience. It saves time and aggravation all around. A good agent can negotiate a contract in a matter of minutes because they are familiar with a publisher's boilerplate and know what wiggle room there is.

4. Instructors at writing seminars can be a good source but like I mentioned above, it works both ways. You should have something that makes them think it's worth their agent's time.

5. Teachers in MFA programs usually have contacts. This is an old boy/girl network that does take care of its own. If that's the route you take, make the best of it.

6. I've just gotten on-line and I've noticed some agents advertising through web sites. On-line can be a relatively cheap way to network.

Like most publishers, most agents automatically reject unsolicited manuscripts. However, in a recent copy of *Poets & Writers Magazine* there was a survey that said 227 of 240 agents surveyed would read cold *queries/submissions* received through the mail. I do *not* recommend cold phone calls or faxing queries or e-mailing them. An important point to remember is that if you come off as an irritating person during your contact with the agent, it might not matter how good your manuscript is. The agent simply might not want to work with you. I heard a prominent agent tell of letting go of one of his authors because the author bypassed him and was very rude to some of the people at a publisher.

What about multiple submissions to agents? My key adjective for the publishing business is SLOW. I said earlier that agents respond quicker than publishers but you could still grow very old waiting. Most agents will only read your work if they have it exclusively. Here's my suggestion:

Do a query to the number one agent on the list you made up from the sources above. Wait a week, and then send to the number two agent. Week three, agent three. Don't tell them it's a multiple query. If an agent calls to ask for the manuscript they will ask you if anyone else has seen the manuscript. Answer honestly. Send the manuscript. Then hold on your submissions to other agents.

The question that always comes up is: What if *another* agent I queried calls and wants to see the manuscript? My reply is: You should be so lucky. But, in the one in a thousand chance you are, tell them it is with the other agent and that you will contact them as soon as you hear back from agent #1. This doesn't necessarily hurt your chances with agent #2, because it actually confirms their interest. Don't try to leverage agent #1 with #2. Have patience, take some sedatives and wait.

How do I know if an agent is legitimate? I am often asked this. My first reply is to use common sense. It's like the person who offers to sell you the Brooklyn Bridge. If an agent promises you they will sell your work, I wouldn't believe them. No agent can make that promise unless they have some sort of kickback deal going with a vanity press.

A legitimate agent should be willing to tell you who some of their clients are and even refer you to one if they want to sign with you.

Remember, though, there is a pecking order to agents. As a new writer, you might not be able to get the number one guy or gal in town. You might hook up with someone who is starting out and has few clients and sales to her name. The bottom line there is to use common sense.

New York State just recently brought charges against an organization that was giving kickbacks to agents who referred clients to it for book doctoring. So there are sharks out there. Be careful. The next chapter is dedicated to this subject.

WHAT DOES AN AGENT DO? An agent knows the market both in terms of what's selling and who's buying. They also know which houses do which type stories and can direct your manuscript not only to the correct publishers, but also to the correct editors at those publishing houses. They are on top of the latest changes in the publishing industry and should know what the current needs are.

In most contracts, an agent will be the sole source for all literary properties produced by you except if he/she chooses not to take on a work, then it reverts back to you.

Most agents are ex-editors so they have an idea how to make a manuscript marketable. I was under the mistaken impression that my agent would go through my work with a fine tooth comb, looking over every page carefully. That simply doesn't happen. Again, remember it's a volume business. The same is true of editors to a certain extent. If your manuscript is not basically acceptable in its present form, you won't get a contract. On my first manu-

script, my agent faxed me a one page list of suggestions. I made the suggested changes and we eventually sold the manuscript. Ever since then, with
every agent I've worked with, they generally tell me in a letter or phone call
what their suggestions/problems are with a manuscript and it's up to me to
make the corrections.

The key to remember is that if your manuscript is right on the margin of
being publishable, it is much more likely that an agent will work with you to
make it marketable than an editor will. Editors work with authors under contract and they screen submissions. They very rarely work with something to
bring it up to snuff to be offered a contract.

Agents negotiate sale or lease of rights to works, including translation.
This includes sales to foreign markets. Normally they charge a higher percentage fee for foreign rights. Most agents have contacts with various foreign
representatives and with a Hollywood agent for film rights.

An agent reviews and negotiates contracts. For a new writer who has no
idea what the market is like, this is very important. Contracts vary from publisher to publisher and I've seen some terrible ones writers ended up signing.
I'll often hear a writer say they'll get a lawyer to review a contract if it comes
to that point, but unless they are an entertainment lawyer they won't understand the standards of the business; and entertainment lawyers live in
Hollywood and deal with movie people, not books.

Agents collect monies due and render share. This can be very frustrating
for both the author and agent, but having the agent do it at least allows the
author to maintain a semblance of cordiality with his or her publisher. My rule
of thumb is that my agent takes care of all business contacts with my publisher. Once a contract is negotiated, I generally work directly with my editor on the written work unless there is a large difference of opinion.

Agents examine royalty statements (as if anyone could make sense of them
to start with.) They are also supposed to check on the publisher's performance
and how they handle your manuscript. Just because you are getting published
doesn't necessarily mean you are going to make any money. The agent can
help you track what the publisher plans on doing with your book, particularly in such important areas as selling the subrights.

Don't expect any paychecks in the mail quickly. Richard Curtis has a running bet with publishers that a writer can write a book faster than they can
cut a check. You may laugh, but I have literally done that—written an entire
manuscript while waiting for a contract to be drawn up and a check cut.

Like any other business, you have to stay on top of your agent. You are the
ultimate protector of your interests. A good agent will advise you, but it
should always be your decision as to what actions to take regarding you and
your property.

The agent is the business link between you and the publishers. Also remember, though, that the agent ultimately works for himself, not you. Remember, too that the publishers cut the checks, which go to the agent, who takes his/her share and then renders the author his share. So if things start getting sticky between you and your publisher, your agent might not put his or her neck totally on the line to protect your interests simply because they have *other* authors that work with that same publisher and the agent wants to maintain his relationship with the publisher, perhaps to the detriment of your relationship, but this would be a rare case. Ultimately, agents' loyalty lies with their writers rather than the publishers. Also, of course, remember that the reverse is true—your agent holds some power with the editor because the agent might or might not steer future good work toward that publisher depending on the relationship.

Some agents require contracts that stipulate what the roles are and what he/she will do and what you are required to do. Without getting in to too much detail, my main point is that you should work with an agent on a case-by-case basis. What I mean by that is that your agent should have the first chance to look at what you produce. She then should let you know whether she wants to work with you on the manuscript or not. If she doesn't, you are free to do whatever you like with it. This is important because you don't want someone representing you simply because you have a contract—especially if she isn't enthusiastic about a particular manuscript.

TO PAY OR NOT TO PAY? In many listings, agents are broken down into two categories: those who charge a reading fee and those who don't. You can get varying opinions as to the pros and cons of going to one that charges a reading fee. Take the opinion out and look at the reality of what you want: do you want to get published or do you want feedback on your work? If you want to get published, go to those that don't charge a fee.

I have had no experience with a fee-charging agent so everything I say here is supposition. All I can say about that is that some make their money reviewing manuscripts—not selling them to publishers and getting 15% of what you make. My opinion is don't do it. Try quite a few submissions first. Then if they all come back negative and you get no decent feedback, it's your money. In many cases, it's not necessary to get all 400 pages of your manuscript reviewed. When I look at manuscripts, I can usually tell what problems there are within the first couple of chapters. If you are paying by the page, send a submission (cover letter, one page synopsis, and the first couple of chapters) and see what they say about that, before sending the whole thing. Make sure you get feedback not only on your manuscript, but also on the synopsis and cover letter.

I would suggest going to writers' conferences and asking around. Sooner or later you will run into someone who has submitted to a fee charging agent

141

and you will get some feedback as to not only the whole process, but about specific agents.

Here is a good example of taking the other person's perspective (which as writers you must be able to do.). How would I operate if I ran an agency that charged a fee for reading submissions? The advantage to me would be I could hire extra people to go through a larger volume of submissions in more detail, searching for those that are deemed publishable (that is also an advantage to you, the writer). Another advantage would be that I might be able to work with someone who is marginal (given that they're paying me some bucks, that is), whereas I wouldn't be able to if my time was my money. Now both are those are true if I was totally honest.

The disadvantage would be that I would tend to focus a lot more energy on making money out of volume of submissions received and be spending a lot of time on un-publishable material (a disadvantage to you the writer). I would also appear to put a lot of time and effort into each submission but in reality I would work off a computer boiler-plate of common mistakes (much like the how-to-write section of this book) and simply go through, make a few changes in the boiler-plate, and send you back thirty pages of apparently in-depth review, which is actually the same as buying a writing book off the shelf at your bookstore except be a lot more expensive. Now these last two are not dishonest but simply a fact of business. I'm not saying that all fee charging agents do either the good or bad. Again, the bottom line is: it's your money.

When is it time to switch agents?

This is an issue almost every published writer runs into sooner or later. I think there are several times: 1. You are going nowhere with the agent you have. No sales.

2. The agent tells you to go elsewhere.

3. You feel like your work is improving but your current agent keeps trying to market it at the same level you've been at. It is an up or out business so this doesn't do you much good.

4. You are changing genres and your current agent doesn't like your new genre.

5. You want to move up. There are levels to agents just as there are levels to editors. Certain agents can place a manuscript at a certain level in a publishing house. Others can go right to the top.

6. Your agents main concern is selling your next book rather than establishing your long term career. The two are not necessarily synonymous.

Ultimately, though, I think it is the same as doing a rewrite on your manuscript. You should feel good after talking to your agent, not bad. You should feel like the agent is representing you in the best possible and *realistic* light. You should feel that your agent views your career as an upward ride.

The bottom line for more writers though is, is to be happy if you can get an agent to represent you at all. Remember that agents are business people are not there to hold your hand or keep you together psychologically while you write (unless of course you write bestsellers.). Also remember that you are not the only client an agent has.

28. BOOK DOCTORS, SCAMS, & SCHOOLS

Because writing involves a lot of emotion, naturally there are those that prey on others in the business. The first area of concern involves agents. I've seen several articles discussing how to figure out if an agency is for real. Here are some of the warning signs:

-Agency has a PO Box for an address.

-Solicits by direct mail. Very few agents send out mailings hoping to find a client.

-Advertises in writer's magazines. I know a legitimate agent who allowed his agency to be listed in a prominent writer's magazine—he regretted it greatly. He received thousands of queries from which he found not one client.

-Won't give you a client list or at least a referral to a client.

-The agency owns its own 'publishing' house.

-Charges an up front fee. Some legitimate agencies that *are not* fee charging will charge you for some fees such as copying manuscripts, postage, etc. This can be a tricky area as there are some fee-charging agencies that are getting slicker and are trying to hide their fee in such normally legitimate expenses. This is where common sense should help you.

-Commission rate should not exceed 15% for US rights.

-Guarantees to get you published. No legitimate agent can do that. I've seen this in print from some agencies and the best I can figure is that they have a deal with a self-publishing house and thus if you're willing to pay, well the guarantee wasn't a lie.

-Has no sales he or she can refer to with legitimate publishers.

-If it sounds too good to be true—it is. There are sites on the net where you can find listings of agencies that are suspicious or have done shady practices. You have to do your homework.

-Refers you to a book doctor. The latter is a scam that has been going on for a while. Edit Ink was recently caught in an interesting scam involving this. They even set up bogus agencies, which referred every single query to Edit Ink for book doctoring. Regardless of the quality of the query, these agencies (and other agencies that Edit Ink gave a kickback to) would send you a form letter saying that your manuscript was close to

143

being publishable but needed some work before, etc. etc. They would then recommend you work with Edit Ink and get back to them.

Which leads us to the issue of book doctors. Many new writers find themselves in a Catch-22. Since there is no real apprenticeship system as I noted earlier in this book, they desperately want some help with their book. More importantly to most, they want some feedback, an idea of how good their work really is.

There are some legitimate people out there who edit manuscripts for a fee. My recommendation is this: I can tell what is wrong with your manuscript by looking at a cover letter, synopsis and thirty or so pages—i.e. by looking at a submission. I don't really need to see all 400 pages. Neither does a book doctor. So if you have to pay, only do a part of the manuscript, which might save you money.

Another thing, though, to remember is getting honest feedback can be painful. If you just want a pat on the back, you're looking in the wrong direction. There are some schools out there that do this. First there are MFA programs—Masters of Fine Arts in creative writing. These schools usually focus on the creative side, the artistic side of writing. There are some excellent programs, such as the University of Iowa's, out there. While most view this as a rather large investment of time and money, the issue is the one I raised early on in this book: writing is a serious business and no matter which path you take, you will have to invest considerable time, effort and money. An MFA program is a good focus for a writer. Another advantage of MFA programs is that once you get your degree you have an inside track at teaching at other MFA programs.

There are other schools such as Writers Digest. I've taught for it and it's a worthwhile course if you're willing to learn. Unfortunately most people who sign up for it seem to want a stamp of approval of their work and then move on to immediately getting and agent and being published. The positive thing about Writer's Digest is that the instructors are published authors, so they understand the business side of writing. You get as much out of it as you put in.

Ultimately, I believe that if you are a good reader, you should be a good editor.

4

Making a Living in the Publishing Business

Why do you need to understand the business end of novel writing? Because being an author is being self-employed in the world of publishing. The more you know about the business, the more success you will have.

I can already see legions of literature graduate students holding up their collected works of Faulkner to blind me with and sharpening the binding of their Shakespeare Collections to drive through my paltry and rancid genre writing heart, but hey, Faulkner meandered out to Hollywood in 1932 to make a buck and Shakespeare didn't let them do his plays for free. If Faulkner had never been paid for what he wrote, he might have spent the rest of his days in the post office in Oxford.

I feel it is critical that authors understand the perspective of all the other players in the business: editors, agents, publishers, bookbuyers, bookstore owners, reviewers, anyone who has anything to do with the life of a book (including as mentioned earlier, the reader.). Too often authors get on a high horse and decry all those other players in the business, but in doing so they tend to cut their own throats. Some authors feel that without writers, there would be no book industry. (Watch THE PLAYER and see the scene where they discuss how great the movie business would be if they could only do away with the writers.)

It is true that without writers there would be no publishers, but without any of those other people in the business there wouldn't be any books. None of those people may have your interests as author number one on their priority list but they also don't have screwing you—the author—on their priority list either. For many, making money is a priority, but for most agents, editors, publishers, bookbuyers, etc. they do it because they love books. Like me, they could make a better living doing something else, but they are in the business because they want to work around books.

I've had people in the business make moves and do things that were not advantageous to me, but if I were in their shoes I probably would have done the same things they did because it was advantageous to them. If you understand that, you will have more control of your destiny—or at the very least, not as many stomach problems.

Also, most of the other people in the business actually enjoy getting manuscripts published, even though it might not seem that way to you as the rejection slips pile up. Why else would they be doing what they are doing? As an author there are few things I would enjoy more than being able to recommend a manuscript to my agent or editor. Editors and agents feel the same way. They love to find that rare diamond that they can publish but they have to sift through at least 99 submissions to find one worthy of just taking a look at.

I feel the business end is extremely important but I issue one caveat here: just as I recommend not getting so caught up in the actual writing world that you ignore the business end, don't do the opposite. Knowing everything there is to know about the business end of publishing won't get you published if you don't have a well-written and well thought out manuscript based on an excellent idea. I've run into some people who are so concerned about getting to know this person and that person in the business and getting their manuscript looked at, or going to conferences and getting interviews, that they forget to take an honest look at the manuscript and realize it is poorly written or that the original idea of their story is simply not that innovative or appealing.

There is a very thin line between aggressively marketing yourself and your work and being obnoxious. To me a person falls on the obnoxious side when the manuscript is not worthy of publication. They fall on the aggressive side when it is. Of course, that doesn't help you much. My suggestion is to watch the reactions of those you deal with. If five consecutive people, whether they be agents, editors, other authors, etc. shy away from you after taking a look at what you have, take the hint and take a harder look at what you have rather than trying to hunt down more people to look at it.

I have learned to be more truthful about synopsis and proposals that people give to me to look at. I feel not being honest would be misleading. And that brings me to another point; more often than not I receive a synopsis that isn't a synopsis and single-spaced chapters, etc. etc. etc. If someone doesn't take the time to buy (or at least get out of the library) a basic book about how to do a submission, then that immediately turns me off and makes me not as enthusiastic to look at what they sent. Editors and agents feel that way a hundred-fold.

Never, never, (oops, that's right, I should never say never) act out of emotion when dealing with anyone in the business. When you find out your publisher is going to delay releasing your book for another six months, don't grab the phone and scream at your agent and editor. That method is not likely to change anything other than get people you need to work with upset with you. Act professionally even though you might not be treated in the same manner in return. Always take your time and carefully understand a situation before acting. Look out for your interests in every interaction—no one else truly will.

29. THE PUBLISHING PROCESS

As discussed earlier, it all starts with the submission. So let's discuss how submissions are handled. There are two ways: cold submissions and requested submissions.

The first is your brown envelope in the mail to the publishing house you looked up in The Writers Market. No one at the publishing house specifically asked for you to send your query. That makes it a cold one.

The trend nowadays in the major houses is to not even deal with cold submissions which makes the role of the agent an ever growing one. But since almost all the smaller houses and some of the major ones still do, let's discuss the life of the slush pile. The first by-word is <u>slow</u>. Some of the big publishers get hundreds of queries a day. They have very low-paid people wading through the pile. Sometimes, smaller houses will have "parties" every couple of months where they stay late several nights and attack the slush pile, which helps explain why you haven't heard from them in three months. It also explains the coffee and donut stains on the rejection notes.

Think of the attitude of the person who has to deal with those stacks of envelopes. Think of the state of her brain. Imagine yourself, sifting through page after page of, on the average, very bad ideas presented very poorly. I don't say that to be mean, I actually say that inspire you—- after all, *your* query is exciting, professionally done and well-written, right? Those people actually are yearning to see something exciting and good, so give it to them.

You will spend many months waiting for the replies from the publishers you submitted to. Some will never reply. Then one lucky day you get that most happy of news: send in the entire manuscript to be read. Then the wait-ing game starts. Months drag by. Then, maybe, just maybe, you'll get an offer. Often you will be referred to an agent as discussed in the chapter on agents. We will talk about contracts below, but right now, let's shift over to the other type of submission: the requested one.

This usually happens when an agent submits your work to a publisher. You have already gone through the weeding out process of the query and the manuscript review at the agent level. The agent works with you a bit on the manuscript and gets it to a level where he/she thinks it is marketable. They will come back to you with their proposal about where and how to send your work. For example, an agent will say: "I think you have a mid-list, mass mar-ket, paperback. I'd like to show it to the following five publishers."

You may retort, "Why, no, I think I have an original hardcover bestseller." In which case you have a problem between you and your agent. It has taken me almost a dozen manuscripts on the market to get a feel for both my work and the market and even then I still don't really know what's going on at the publishers' end, so I do have to trust my agent. As a new writer, you aren't in a very good position to judge what is going on. I'm not saying roll over and play dead, but be realistic.

After you and the agent decide how and where to market the book, the agent makes copies of the manuscript and mails them out to the editors he/she has already talked to about the manuscript. Note this interesting part of the process: your agent makes a "query" for your manuscript to the publisher over the phone or over lunch. Your agent has got to be able to say, "Well, Ellen, I've got this very good thriller manuscript about—. I think it will work as—" There are two things your agent has to be able to do:

1. Describe your work in a couple of sentences.
2. Place it in the market, usually by genre.

This is another reason why I am very big on that original idea and also genre. I've had my agent call up and say: "Tell me about the book in a sentence or two." I know that what he is going to do is turn around and call and editor and repeat that same sentence or two and ask if he can send them the manuscript.

What is good for you in this situation is that manuscripts placed by agents get read much more quickly. And you will get back a signed rejection letter if it isn't bought.

The Contract:
A typical publisher's contract will include at least the following: (if you are representing yourself, contact the Authors Guild and they will send you a full length suggested contract.)

-Delivery of an *acceptable* manuscript by a certain date.

-Corrections after acceptance cannot exceed 10% or you are charged for composition.

-Who has rights. If you are going with hardcover publisher, that publisher will also usually control the paperback rights (along with 50% of the royalties.).

-You usually retain dramatic adaptations rights, i.e. film.

-Advance and when it will be paid. Usually the advance is broken down into three payments. The first portion comes at contract signing. The second at acceptance of the manuscript, the third sometimes after (may be at time of publication).

-Royalties and how often they will be paid (usually twice a year). Royalties are interesting because they are accounted twice a year, usually the end of June and December. Then the publisher takes three to four months to issue a statement. Frustrating, but again, not much you can do about it.

-Author's copies- usually 10.

-Protection of work -copyright, infringement

-and numerous other details such as audio rights, electronic media rights, etc. etc. (can we see here why an agent might be beneficial?) Electronic rights is a big issue right now and I discuss them in the last chapter.

I very much recommend getting a copy of the Author's Guild suggested book contract and comparing it to any offer you get. The problem is that authors don't seem to have much power (unless you are on the very top of the pile like Stephen King). There is an interesting phenomenon in publishing— there is very little middle class among authors. There is a handful of elite and then there is everyone else, scrambling at the bottom in the pack. I talk about this a little later on.

The most critical word in your contract is: "acceptable." When does a publisher accept a work? Your guess is as good as mine. Horror stories abound of writers cranking out a manuscript under contract, sending it to a publisher who says "Yeah, it's OK", and then suddenly getting a phone call months later saying: "Your manuscript is not acceptable and we want our advance money back." Joan Collins had a very bad experience with just this clause and she had to sue her publisher. And she won.

It would be nice, and you can try, to get a better definition on the term. Of more practicality, try to at least get a timeline on how long a publisher can sit on a manuscript before giving you their decision on acceptability or not.

I recently send in a manuscript to a publisher that was part of a series. It was very close to the outline I had sent the publisher the previous year and been paid for.

I got a call a couple of weeks later and the basic gist was: "This isn't going in the direction we want. Perhaps you need to take a hard look at it."

To say the least, I was a bit bothered, particularly considering the fact that they had approved the outline. And I wasn't thrilled that they were basically saying they didn't want the book. But I had to get through my negative emotions and accept that what they were saying had a gem of truth to it—I was going in a bad direction for the series.

Every time I've had someone say something wasn't quite working in one of my manuscripts, no matter how screwed up I initially thought they were, there was a core of truth to what they said. It is my responsibility as the author to find what it is and then figure out a way to fix it.

In this case I had to basically write a new book in two weeks, ripping apart the old one. It was hard work, but I did it, because it was the best thing for the book all around.

__The publishing timeline__: The following is a typical timeline from the moment you sign that wonderful contract through actual arrival of the book in the bookstore. Pay close attention to the number of months that pass—there's a quiz at the end.

Month 1: sign contract. (usually about two to three months after they agreed to terms over the phone)

Month 4: The "editorial process" begins. The amount of time this takes depends on how much revision the manuscript requires. It is important for new writers to know that publishers won't buy a manuscript if it requires extensive revisions. It is very frustrating to new writers who think they have a spectacular and novel (no pun intended) idea and think that with some editorial assistance they will have a best-seller, to find that if the manuscript isn't pretty much already in a publishable form, it won't get looked at very long.

This process tends to get longer, the more books an author has published. While that sounds contradictory, think about it for a second. It gets longer for those novels put under contract as concepts as opposed to those novels put under contract as a completed manuscript. With the latter, the publisher has pretty much accepted the manuscript. With the former, the publisher has accepted the concept—when they get the first draft of the manuscript, there is more of a tendency to want to change things.

The first stage of this process is when the editor presents a report to the author. This is usually a month or two (or more depending on the production schedule) after receiving the manuscript. It gets a couple of readings at the publisher and then they put those thoughts down in a letter. Those could consist of changing the ending, adding more twists to the plot, deepening characters, etc. The author makes the suggested changes (or argues them, but usually bows to the inevitable—after all, it is the publisher who makes the final determination of "acceptability"). Then the manuscript is sent back for final approval of story, followed by being sent to a copyeditor who does the final polishing up—checking grammar, punctuation, spelling, etc.

Then the author gets the manuscript back for copyediting. It has already been through the proofreader once. This is for very minor changes. The ten percent change rule applies here.

The edited manuscript is then sent to production, which is a group of several small elves who stand around and cast spells over the pages. No, actually, production is where the manuscript is designed and typeset. Nowadays, they usually use computer disks to do this. The page proofs are printed and the author receives loose galley proofs. These are 8.5 by 11 Xeroxed pages showing what the pages will look like. You proofread these and send them back. At this point, the front matter (title page, table of contents, dedication, copyright page, etc.) is completed.

At the same time the elves in production are working on the book, the dwarves over in marketing are designing the cover and developing copy and promotional material (which for a new author consists of "Hey, here's a new book.").

You receive bound galley proofs. These are the exact same as the loose galleys (with the same mistakes, corrections will be made later). They are what are sent to reviewers for advance review. These are also sent to book buyers who help your publisher determine how many copies of your book will be printed based on their orders.

Around fifteen months after signing the contract you get a look at your Xeroxed jacket/cover. It's too late to change anything so you love it. The actual printing takes about six to eight weeks.

Month 18: Your book is published.

From a publishers point of view here is the timeline. Let's use a delivery date of the manuscript as specified by contract of January 1 and a pub date of September.

January: Minor or major editorial changes.
-scheduling. Note for publishers September to November is most dangerous time to schedule a book because it is the most crowded. You're competing with the big boys and girls.
-jacket input.
February: Copy editing.
-1st sketches on cover.
-flap copy
-fact sheet/book brief, used internally
-design pages (font, etc.)
March: pre-sales (launch) meeting. Selling the book to the rest of the house, which of course has no time to read the vast majority of books they are selling.

-publicity planning
-co-op advertising considered (money spent with booksellers)
-set price
-book is positioned
-editor prepares the catalogue copy
April: 1st pass of the galleys
-bound galleys are sent to reviewers
-marketing budget
-press kit
-catalogue comes out
May: sales reps get kits
-BEA, the old ABA convention, although this is getting less and less important as sales break down right now are roughly: Chains= 40%; Internet= 10%; clubs= 10%; Independents= 25%; wholesalers= 15%. These numbers vary depending on whether it is a hardcover, mass market paperback or trade paperback.
June: orders come in.
-pub date confirmed.
July: the book is actually printed.
August: the book is in warehouse.
-the book is shipped—bound book date.
-last week of the month the book is in the store.
September: pub date.

Quiz: How many months from signing the contract to the bookstore? Right. Eighteen. Add in the time it takes you from original idea to finished manuscript. How long does that come to? Two years? Three years? Go way back to where I wrote about your story idea. Factor in a—say at least a 2.5 year, more likely three-year process. What that means is if you are writing about a subject that may change in the next three years then you'd better be careful. My first manuscript in 1989 was overwhelmed by world events. I had the Russian bogeyman as the enemy. Well in 1988 they were. In 1989 the Wall came down. Oops. A word to the wise: Be careful with time sensitive stories.

The publishing company and your editor.
When you get that first contract offer, you will probably be so excited you'd sign anything. Having an agent will help, but even that's no guarantee the contract is a good one. I bring this up because, sad to say, writers as a rule are not treated very well by publishers. Not because publishers are mean, but because usually they don't have to treat writers well. There is no union and your only rights are the ones in the contract and even then, you need an

152

expert to point them out to you. This is not to say publishers are evil (although many writers I've met think that way). It's simply that publishers are doing exactly what you or I would be doing if we were they—looking out for their own interest. So you do the same—look out for your own.

I pay very close attention now to my contracts, but even then, there is only so much leeway a publisher will give you. The Authors Guild, Inc. (330 West 42nd Street, New York, N.Y. 10036.) will send you a copy of a recommended Trade Book Contract for a small charge. Unfortunately, large publishing houses have a boilerplate contract that they offer and the moon and the stars would have to be in very strange alignment for them to change it for you, new author. You can read the Author's Guild recommended contract, think 'wouldn't it be great?' and then probably sign the boilerplate.

Again, even with a contract, publishers will look out for their own interests first, and yours secondly. Remember also, that your agent may have other authors that he/she represents to that same publisher. Thus your agent may be very leery of standing up for you if it means making an enemy of that publisher. It gets back to what I said above—you have to look out for your own interests. On the other hand, the publisher might not want to alienate your agent or you.

You have to understand what your publisher is doing and how they make money. If you are being published hard cover, you have to understand that unless that house also does paperback, then they are going to make a lot of their money off of selling subrights to your novel to a paperback publisher (hopefully) and also foreign rights.

Your editor is usually your 'voice' at the publishing house. But be aware that editors move between houses. When your voice is gone, your manuscript has also lost its voice. Additionally, your editor is not the only 'voice' at the publisher and certainly not the last voice. Remember that your editor works for the publisher—not you. Every editor I started working with at each publisher was not the editor I finished working with. Fortunately for me my works were still published but it is a common horror story that when an editor leaves, those works that that editor acquired might be canceled.

A large problem in the publishing business is simply geography. It is very rare that an author lives in the same town as his or her publisher. While you may have visions of getting jetted in to discuss your work over lunch in downtown Manhattan, I recommend you be thankful you get your 10 free copies when the work is published.

At the ten-year point in this business, with thirteen books published and five more under contract, I had met my first agent once face to face. That was it.

When I teach, I tell the story of the first glimpse I had of a copy of my second novel. I was at Fort Bragg on active duty (I'd anxiously waited weeks

153

for my copies to arrive via UPS, but by the time I had to leave, they weren't there). So there I was at Bragg and I met another fellow from New Jersey who looked at my nametag quizzically. We started talking and he said my name sounded familiar and he asked me what I did. I told him I was a writer and the cloud on his face cleared up. He reached into the backpack he was carrying and pulled out a copy of my second novel, which his wife had gotten out of the library for him to read on the plane down.

The lesson I learned from all that is that New Jersey has a very efficient public library system. No, actually, it was another of many lessons I've learned about patience.

You will most likely not meet anyone at your publisher for several years unless you live close by and make the effort to visit. You will also rarely meet your agent unless your travel arrangements happen to coincide. Dealing with people exclusively over the phone and in letters is very difficult and requires some care and consideration. It takes time to get a good feel for someone under such circumstances (remember what I wrote earlier about dialogue. How the majority of communication is non-verbal, yet here is a case where the majority has to be verbal). The next chapter will discuss some of the care that needs to be taken.

People in the business.

At one publishing house I have been through five different editors in the course of three years and three books published. I've also been through five different publicists in the same period of time at that house.

Talking to some people on the inside, what I have learned is that editors and others in the trade work their way "up" by playing musical chairs. They don't work up at their house; they work up by stepping up the ladder to another publishing house.

This causes a tremendous problem, given that it takes over a year to actually publish a manuscript once it's been accepted.

There is an advantage to this though. It means you might have an editor at a house that hasn't published you, that bought your work for the house they came from. It gives you a window to market a new manuscript.

30. REVIEWS

I used to say any review is a good review. I said that because a review gives your novel exposure. Most reviews consist of a brief summary of the plot and then a few lines with the reviewer's comments. Be glad that your book has been summarized for you and exposed to the readers of the review. Accept that the reviewer's comments have been written and there is nothing you can do about it.

However, there is no doubt that bad reviews can hurt, not only in terms of ego, but also in terms of sales. One thing that is hard about writing for a living is that the product of your work is out there for anyone to look at and make comments upon. The decision by on-line bookstores to allow anyone with access to a computer to post an anonymous 'review' of any book for all the world to see has been a curious phenomenon and one many writers groups are fighting. What is guaranteed is that someone will not like your book. I'm not a fan of this policy by on-line sellers, even though over 95% of reviews I've gotten have been great. It's a system that is susceptible to abuse and only time will tell how that shakes out. Ultimately it may be needed as more and more books come out in e-format and there is a need to tell quality.

It is a curious phenomenon for many writers that once a book has been published it is no longer as important to them. That is because, as noted above, the writing of that particular work is years in the past and you are presently working on something that is several manuscripts removed. That is fortunate because it allows you to not get as hurt by a negative review.

For example, by the time my third manuscript was released in print, I was working on my ninth. I could hardly remember the entire plot of the third. I certainly felt my writing skills were somewhat better, thus being hit up again for weak characterization didn't hurt as much—indeed, it gave me a focal point to work on improving my writing skills.

Pay attention to responsible reviews. Take what is said seriously and as a learning point. Also, you have to do some work yourself to get reviewed. Your publisher will hit the usual places (Kirkus, Publishers Weekly) but it's up to you to find all those other avenues of exposure such as alumni newsletters, trade magazines, local papers, etc.

You have to target venues for reviews. There are magazines out there for every conceivable subject matter. You have to dig out the ones that relate to the subject matter of your book. Be prepared to purchase copies of your book from your publisher in order to send review copies out.

One last thought on on-line reviews, many posted anonymously. My take on that is to borrow a quote from Richard Russo' excellent book Nobody's Fool: "The best she was able to do was to reflect that people invariably exhibited the very worst side of their flawed natures when invited to put their thoughts into writing, especially when the invitation was sanctioned hit-and-run posing as democracy in action."

31. Numbers & The Entertainment Business

Publishing is a business. I was part of it for ten years before I really understood what I was part of: the entertainment business.

That's a term that most people don't stop to examine. But sort of the way the term 'military intelligence' is considered an oxymoron; I think 'entertainment business' has some built in paradoxes that need to be understood.

To me, it means that there is a joining of emotion and logic to produce a product. I think that too often people focus on one side or the other of this problematic equation without realizing that the two have to exist hand in hand.

I talked early in this book about your manuscript having to appeal to both the intellect and the emotion of the reader. If it were just the former, we could reduce everything to a science, but because the latter comes into play, it becomes something of a guessing game.

How come Hollywood can't accurately predict the next blockbuster? How come publishers cannot accurately predict the next bestseller?

It is theory of mine that publishers throw a hundred books against the wall and hope one or two stick and sell well. I just read that 35 of 40 new TV series from the past season have been canceled, so it's not just the publishing industry that plays this game.

It is a game driven by numbers. When all is said and done, success or failure is determined by number of copies sold. And it is an up or out business.

The first number is how many copies of your book the publisher is going to print. There is absolutely no way you are going to make the NY Times bestseller's list with only 2,500 hardcover copies printed, even if every single one sells.

There are two general ways a publisher determines the print run. For a new author, what I have seen is that your advance will give you a very good idea of how many copies will be printed. (Many editors deny this, but this is my experience)

If you get a $10,000 advance and you're being published in paperback original here's the math:

To earn out a 10K advance, given that you get 8% of the cover price of $5.99 (which comes out to $0.4729 per book), 11,630 copies of your paperback have to sell. Given that the average sell through is about 50% right now on paperbacks, they have to print 23,260 copies of the book. Guess what your print run will approximately be?

For a new author in hardcover, you usually make not a percentage of the cover price, but a percentage of the wholesale price. The average rate is 15%. So if your publisher is giving a 40% discount to the book chain, you make 15% of 60% of the cover price, which usually comes out to about $1.40 a book.

(Don't forget your agent is taking 15% of any of that, but don't worry, only 1 out of 10 books printed sees royalties anyway—i.e. earns out the advance.)

So, you get a 10K advance for your hardcover, then you're looking at $10,000 divided by $1.40 equals 7,142 books have to sell. Given a 50% sell through again, they'd have to print about 14,284 books.

Now that's for a new author. If you are an established author, the numbers are determined by previous sales.

Let me give you a personal example of how to fail in this business and how numbers work:

My first book to be published was a hardcover. The advance was $7,500. The print run was 10,000 copies, which is pretty good for a new author. It sold about 7,500, which is a 75% sell-through. That percentage becomes critical, as you will see.

So, the sales reps for my publisher go out the following year to the book-buyers and say: "Hey, we've got Bob Mayer's second book. How many do you want to order?"

The bookbuyer looks in his computer. He finds that he ordered 10 per store of the first book, sold an average of 7.5. So how many does he order per store? You guessed it. 7.5.

So my print run for my second hardcover was 7,500. It sold about 6,000 copies. An even better sell through percentage but less copies. The third book had a print run of 6,000, sold higher percentage but less copies, etc. etc. etc. By my sixth book with that publisher, I had failed.

Now how do you succeed?

Another personal example: My first paperback original with another publisher was under a new name, thus I was a "new" author. (A good reason for pen names in this business.).

My advance was $12,500. The print run was roughly 55,000 copies. It sold slightly over 30,000 by the end of the first year. Not a bad sell through but nothing to write home to mom about.

So the sales reps went out with the cover of the next book. What should have happened was the chains looked in their computer and ordered slightly less. But here's where something different came into play. The title on this new book, AREA 51, was catchy. The cover design was intriguing. No one went overboard, but the orders came back strong. The initial print run for the second book has been scheduled for 55,000. With the strong orders, it got bumped in the weeks prior to printing. Until it finally settled at 80,000. They shipped 77,000 in the first week.

Within a couple of weeks they had to go back to print for 15,000 more. Then 20,000 more. Then 10,000, then 20,000 more. Totaling 135,000 printed in the first year.

Guess what the print run for the next Area 51 book was? 135,000.

Numbers rule.

People always ask about royalties but the fact is less than ten percent of books published earn royalties. First you have to 'earn back' your advance. Enough books have to sell so that at the royalty rate you have, you make enough money equal to the advance you were given. Once you are past that, then you begin to earn royalties.

A common ploy by publishers is something called 'joint accounting.' When you sign a two-book deal, the publisher stipulates that you will not earn royalties on the first book until you earn out the total advance for *both* books.

Publishers are loath to pay out any quicker than they have to, but it is a two way street. While they tend to hold onto money for a long time after it is earned, they also pay advances long before they publish a book and earn any money. In the long run the two sort of balance out, although in this age of computers, one would think they could account faster than they currently do. Typically publishers do semi-annual accounting. The end of December accounting is credited at the earliest two-month later, and in some case three and a half months later. So technically, a publisher can hold onto money for six months, then an additional three and a half months which is getting pretty close to a year. Also, if you have subrights money coming, it can get bounced another royalty period quite easily.

Another numbers is subrights. My first publisher was strictly a hardcover one. Which meant when they sold paperback rights to my books to another publisher, they got to keep 50% of advances and royalties. You also have to see what the percentage breakdown is for foreign rights between yourself and your US Publisher. Those percentages add up after a while.

If I was a new writer and had a choice—which is highly unlikely—unless my advance was six figures, I would prefer to get published paperback first rather than hardcover. When was the last time you bought a hardcover book from a new author you never heard of?

32. MARKETING & SELF-PROMOTION

Your first book is finally published. You breathe a sigh of relief, lean back from your keyboard and eagerly wait for the author's copies to arrive in the mail, while taking a long awaited break from work. Right? Only if you answer yes to one of the two following questions:

1. You received a large enough advance (that you won't have to pay back if your book does poorly) so that you won't have to ever write again for money. or:

2. You really don't care how many copies of your book sell, and you don't particularly want to make a living as a writer.

If you don't say yes to either of the above questions, then I regret to inform you that your work has only just begun.

158

The greatest failure of most new authors is their lack of marketing their first book. It took me four years to realize that the marketing side of being an author was just as important as the writing side and it was only with my third novel that I finally got into the marketing side of the business.

Marketing yourself: I will only briefly mention (mainly because it was one of my major failures as a novice author) that almost a quarter of a published author's work time has to be spent on marketing yourself. From going to book signings, to workshops, to doing publicity work, whatever. There are several books on the market that give good tips on how to do it.

Remember something very important if you ever do get published: your work has just begun. If you want to make writing your career, you have your foot on the first rung and it's a hard climb up.

Target your market: Unless you are fortunate and skilled enough to have a bestseller, you are fighting for shelf space and time. You may not have noticed it before, but most books stay on the shelf a very short time. The person who cares the most about your book is not your editor or the marketing person (if there is one) at your publisher. It's you.

Book signings: Most new authors tend to overestimate how many books they will sell at a signing. Unless you have a best-seller, or have a book that is of particular interest to the clientele of that particular bookstore, I would say you will be lucky to sell a couple of copies of a hard-cover ($19.95) book. I've sat at signings and sold zero copies of a book.

Because of that simple fact of life, you have to consider very carefully when and where to do signings. Not only is it very boring (and somewhat discouraging.) to sit for six hours and only sell four books, it also takes valuable time away from your writing. When I wrote military techno-thrillers, I feel reasonably comfortable doing book-signings at military post exchanges. Even then though, with a military population of almost 40,000 and twice that many dependents and retirees at a post, I consider a good day, twenty books sold in ten hours.

There are things you can do to help yourself. One is a press release (described below). Another is a professionally done banner (don't expect the bookstore to strain itself by printing up posters and fliers, although many will. If you sell even fifty hardcover books, the bookstore's profit margin is not that great). You can also print up your own fliers (in appendix 7). I've also done my own bookmarks by using a Xerox machine, overhead transparencies, and scissors. They're quite durable. You can also get postcards, fliers, and bookmarks done up professionally.

You should also keep the bookstore manager in mind when deciding whether or not to try and do a signing. I just recently tried setting up a book signing at the Pentagon bookstore. After talking to the people involved though, and being informed that the best signing they ever had was former Secretary of Defense Caspar Weinberger and he sold about a hundred books, I decided it would be a waste not only of my time, but of the store's time to do a signing there. By making that decision I hope I stayed in the good graces of the manager and can now bombard the store with press releases and fliers in the hopes that they will at least order more copies of my next book than they would have.

On the more amusing side, I've found there are basically several types of people you meet at a book signing. One interesting thing I've noted is that the longer someone talks to me, the less likely they are to buy a book. There is also the person who wants to get from me the 'secret' of how to get published. Usually I answer questions for a while, and then tell them about this Toolkit. Since this would cost money they usually depart. There is also the person who wants to make a deal—they have a great idea and if I would only write it for them, they'd give me a certain percentage of the profits.

The biggest advantage of doing a signing is not so much to sell books, though, it is to meet people. Although I sounded negative in the above paragraph, you do meet some interesting people at signings. It's a form of marketing networking.

<u>Press Releases</u>: You need to do your own press releases. The best way to do one is to talk to someone who works at a newspaper and enlist their aid. Another way is to go to the local university and talk to a faculty member in the journalism department.

Basically, a press release is a way to give a newspaper the information you want them to print in a format that they can use almost word for word (thus making it easier for them—and easy makes it more likely you will get printed).

I have three basic press release boilerplates I work off of:
1. A release for a book signing.
2. A release for a new book coming out.
3. A release for my writing seminars.

Some basic rules:
1. Consider who you send it to. Why would they want to run it? A newspaper reports news—it doesn't give away free advertising space. For your local papers, emphasize the local angle. For book signings, often that is a local angle if the store is in the area. Keep in mind the editor who makes the decision on what to run. Give him or her a reason to put it in the paper.
2. Put in a picture or two.

3. Make the actual release very short, but include a full-page copy of your bio, fliers on books released (include reviews), and clips from your previous magazine publications (if you have any).

4. Address it by name to the appropriate editor. Many papers have special Sunday or even daily sections. Call the paper and ask who would be the best person to address the release to.

5. Get it there in **plenty of time** before you would like it to be printed.

6. Follow up with a phone call about two or three days before the time it should go to print (newspapers, even small ones, receive hundreds of releases. Your phone call may make the difference between it getting printed and not getting printed. Also it might help your release to get found out of the slush pile.)

A Marketing Binder is a very useful thing to have: I have a binder that I use to keep most of my marketing resources close at hand. It contains:

1. Fliers for all my books (separate ones for each, and one covering all).

2. Mail order form for my books (sometimes at book signings, people will ask if there is any way they get the books). I also use the same form as an ad in trade publications.

3. A one-page bio sheet. (As noted above, it is very useful in conjunction with press releases. I also use it when interviewed—it answers most of the interviewer's questions up front and allows him to concentrate on the interview rather than writing down basic information. As a bonus, it also makes the interviewer's job easier and everyone I've dealt with appreciates that.)

4. A one page flier for my "How to Write Novels" seminar. (This has come in useful at book fairs and signings—you'd be surprised who walks up to you.)

5. A one page flier for my "How to Get Published" seminar.

6. Clippings of articles I've had published.

7. Advertising fliers for my next book to be published (I give these out with every book I sell, even though the next book might be 8 months away from being published).

8. One page synopsis (sound familiar?) of every published book and every manuscript I have written.

9. Press clippings (articles written about me or my books).

10. Copies of my generic press releases.

11. A master listing of all points of contact.

12. Copies of reviews of all my published books.

13. 8.5 by 11 business card inserts (holds 10 business cards on each side, so you can see them. You'd be surprised at the number of business cards you collect at workshops and signings. That's why it also pays to have your own to exchange.)

As you can see this binder contains quite a bit, but I've found it to be very helpful to have all that material on hand whenever I go anywhere. Indeed, it's quite handy to simply have it all in one place even when I'm working at my desk.

Another place that marketing comes in is the Internet. I have only just begun to do this. That brings up the first point: You can get a free web site when you sign on at America Online and some of those sites are quite well done. The problem is that America Online gives a website to every customer which is now in the millions. So it doesn't do any advertising of your site. Someone either has to know the exact site address or stumble across it by pushing the wrong keys. Also, the URL for that web site will be quite long and not exactly something that people can remember. You also have to design the site yourself and while doing basic text will be easy, adding in scanned photos and covers is another story.

I wimped out and paid for mine to be done. I sell copies of my books off my web site and have managed to pretty much break even in the process. I averaged about 150 hits a week the first year, which isn't bad.

You have to be polite but aggressive when marketing yourself. No one else cares as much about your book as you do.

What about hiring a publicist? I've asked quite a few people about this and the consensus for fiction is: don't bother. Why? Because it's extremely hard to market fiction, which seems to contradict my telling you to market yourself. Let me clarify.

There really are no demographics for readers. I get e-mail from children and from grandparents. I have no clue who is really reading my books. Therefore a publicist has a heck of a time doing one of the most important things they have to do before they can even start a publicity campaign: target your market. Therefore a legitimate publicity firm probably would not even take you on as a client if you have fiction.

But that doesn't mean you don't make the effort yourself. I found doing this very frustrating because you never know what's working or not. And it's a very long-term process. To really succeed in this business lightning has to strike you. Marketing is a form of raising a rod. It's not a guarantee you'll get hit, but it makes the odds better.

Now, to further muddy an already murky picture, let me talk about something I've learned late in my writing career:

Take the following survey:

1. Why did you buy the last novel you bought?
   a. I had read the author before and liked him/her.
   b. Someone recommended the book to me.

c. Never read this author before but I noticed the title/jacket, and read the cover blurb, first couple of pages and thought I might like it.

d. I read a review of the book.

e. The author was doing a book signing locally and I bought it.

f. The author received a six-figure advance.

g. The publisher placed an ad in Publisher's Weekly.

The answers are listed in this order for a specific reason. Surveys have shown that this is the order in which the majority of readers buy books. Most buy books by author name. Then by recommendation.

This survey was put out at a conference by an agent to make a point—authors who get wrapped up in the size of their advance, the 'publicity' effort made by their publisher, etc. etc. oftentimes miss the boat. I know I spent a lot of time spinning my wheels trying to get publishers to allocate money and time to 'publicity' for my books. Much of that was wasted time. That's not to say you shouldn't try to get as much publicity and support as possible, but it is to say that ultimately the book has to sell. The #1 thing a publisher does for a book after it's printed is to get it out to the stores. Once you are on the rack or bookshelf, then readers determine your career.

I used to get very frustrated talking to my editor or publicist because basically what they would say was: "We put the majority of our publishing time and money behind our best-selling books." And my angry reply would be: "How am I going to become one of your best-selling authors if you don't give me any publicity?" That has a certain ring of logic to it, but I've changed that tune. Because publicity is not going to make you a best seller by itself. And many times, much more than most people imagine, most best selling authors work their way into that status by selling a little more of each book, year after year.

There is a thin line that a writer has to follow in terms of making a book a success. The most important factor is to write an interesting, good book. You must do your own publicity work as I've noted before, but you must also be very cognizant of how much time and resources you are going to put into it against the returns you will get. You also have to be careful of crossing the line from being aggressive to being obnoxious. Always, always and always try to be polite in your dealings with people.

There was one radio talk show I tried to get on that took me over three years before I got a call from the host. The day after being on the show my book was an Amazon.com Hot 100. So that worked.

Again, another contradiction, but you never exactly know how effective your efforts are. I've done call-in radio shows where no one calls in. Makes you wonder if you are speaking out to the ethos and no one is listening.

163

In my first ten years I never met anyone from my publishing companies and I have met my two agents only once each face to face. Writing is a lonely business and it is conducted over the phone and through the mail. Because of that, it is important to keep good records and also to be very aware of what is said and written.

One important thing to remember is that, like any business, be professional with everyone you deal with. That includes agents, publishers, booksellers, bookstore owners, writers groups, etc. Networking is very, very important for authors and you will be surprised at what benefits you will reap if you deal courteously and professionally with all you meet.

Just today I received a letter from a man I met at one of my PX book signings—turns out he had his own book in print and also wrote a column in a local paper and he kindly reviewed my book. Every little bit helps.

Keep good records of all your correspondence. Keep a copy of everything and maintain accurate files so you can find documents when needed. Also keep good track of your suspenses and try to beat them when at all possible.

I often get e-mail or letters from people who want help. Some want me to ghostwrite a great idea they have. There are very few writers who would be willing to do this. Most have their own work to do and the odds of such a book getting published are usually slim. Remember one thing from both sides—whether you are trying to get published or you are published—time is money. There is a tendency for people who are self-employed to forget this, but authors have to value their time. Be careful of approaching people cold. Also, if you do make a contact, don't be too aggressive. I told a fellow one time to send me a one-page synopsis and he shipped me the entire manuscript. That was a fast turn-off. Another thing that can be irritating is people who send things like that certified requiring you to go down to the post office and sign for it.

Always remember to thank any contacts you make and remain positive.

The bottom line is to maintain the golden rule in this business, regardless of how others ignore it.

33. HOW TO GET STARTED

This chapter appears to be in the wrong place. Most how-to-write books place it in the beginning—after all, if you don't start, how can you ever do anything?

I place this at the end because I don't think it does you much good to start unless you understand what you're starting. Some of you may already have completed manuscripts; others may not have put word one down on paper. I believe the first half of this book gives you the tools to start and complete a novel. The willpower is up to you. The second half gives you the information you need to submit your completed work and get it published.

What about something in between, though? What about getting some publishing credit before finishing the epic novel (something that may even help the sale of the novel)?

Most creative writing classes focus on the short story as the basic building block. My opinion is that a good short story is much harder to write than a good chapter in a novel. That is because you have to have the complete story in the short story whereas the chapter is just a continuation of a longer story. Also, a short story usually is better written style-wise than a chapter in a novel simply because there is more focus.

The problem is that it is extremely difficult in the present market to sell short fiction. Top-notch freelancers with glittering resumes supply the top of the line magazines. The bottom of the line doesn't pay you for your work. And, like book publishing, there doesn't appear to be much middle of the line in the short fiction magazine world. I've noticed, though, the short story market is starting to pick up a little bit.

One way to get around that is to find a new niche. I listened to a short story freelancer talk one time and his niche was adult Christmas stories. He'd narrowed his subject matter down to that area and focused on it and had been quite successful, not only getting quite a few stories published in reputable magazines, he'd also had a collection of his short stories published. Of course, he also worked full-time as a lawyer.

My recommendation is that if you want to write a novel, then write a novel. Don't spin your wheels writing short stories unless you feel you need the practice in writing. Don't get me wrong—it is certainly excellent practice but don't look at it as a way to make money unless you are very good. Short story writing skills don't necessarily translate into successful novel writing.

If you do want to get published in a magazine, my choice there would be to write non-fiction articles for sale. The first question I always get back is "I'm just a student/housewife/candlestick-maker. What could I write about?" Well, write about school, home or the candlestick business is usually my answer. Pull out your atlas and look around at a hundred mile radius of your home. Is there any place interesting that you might be able to write about? Where I lived in Tennessee, about fifty miles up the road in Kentucky is the Jefferson Davis Memorial—sort of a smaller version of the Washington Monument sitting there in the middle of a small town (Davis's birthplace). Bet most of you don't even know where Davis was born, never mind that there was this large monument to him. That's an article waiting to be written and I've pitched it to several students so far.

165

So far, my articles have been about—you guessed it—writing. But to start with I narrowed my area down. I combined my two careers—writing and the military—and sold an article about writing for military members to Life In The Times, the supplement to the Army/Air Force/Navy Times. You have to know your marketplace. Again, that last line focuses on the business aspect of writing. No matter how great a writer you are, if you don't have an idea how to operate as a businessperson, you aren't going to get very far. I've done this enough that now the editor at Life In The Times calls me every time the supplement comes up.

The economics of becoming a writer is very difficult. Even if you get a manuscript accepted for publication, the odds are very strong that you still won't be making a living off of writing. It will take as long to become a good writer, as it will to become the good architect we talked about earlier. Many people have the talent—not many have the courage and fortitude to go where that talent can take them without any guarantees of success.

The other problem is that not only does it take time, but there are no job openings with salaries in the classified section of the newspaper. (Of course there are some jobs that are writing related, but I've never seen an advertisement for "unpublished author" yet). Novel writers are generally self-employed which is a difficult way to live for many people. If you desire the security of a monthly check and a company health plan and retirement, forget about writing for a living.

I feel that the *life* that someone lives prior to getting published is part of his schooling to be a writer. I spent years in the Special Forces, during which I was not writing novels, but I was experiencing a life that I was able to use in my novels later on. Whatever you are doing now is part of your preparation. The other things you can do to prepare for a writing career is to read extensively.

Another thing that I did wrong in the beginning, and I now recommend, is to network. Go to writers' conferences and workshops. Meet other aspiring authors. Meet published writers. Meet editors and agents. One nice thing about the field of writing is that there is no sense of competition. You aren't going to meet established writers jealously guarding their knowledge because you might steal their contract. As I said before—everyone will be helpful if you have a worthwhile manuscript.

A path many people take is the masters of fine arts (MFA) in creative writing. I know next to nothing about this path so I won't say much. I do wish I had had a better background in literature when I had begun writing. In my third year writing full time I signed up for 6 credit hours in graduate literature courses and found what I learned there to be useful. Another big advantage of the MFA programs is that you are around others who want to write.

166

But sooner or later you do have to start writing. Earlier in this book I mentioned where some famous writers found time to write before they made a living at it. I just read another interview with a young female author who wrote in steno pads that she carried with her everywhere and wrote in every chance she had. Think of all those times you've sat there with time on your hands. Again, like the Nike commercial says: Just do it.

I don't mean to be discouraging but you have to be very realistic when you consider being self-employed. When a publisher cuts you a $5,000 check for signing a contract, it seems in the publisher's eyes, that you just made $5,000 in profit.

The reality?

Your agent takes 15% off the top so you're down to $4,250. You have overhead like your computer, printer, paper, fax, laser cartridges, etc. etc. You have taxes including the 15% up front for being self-employed. You need health insurance. You'd also like to retire some day won't you?

So in reality, in most cases when you get that check, depending on how long it took you to write the book, you've probably *lost* money. No one knows for certain, but I would say there are only a couple hundred people in this country who make their living writing novels.

What would I do if I were an unpublished author with a complete manuscript right now?

First thing I would do is start writing a second manuscript... Too many writers get caught up on marketing their one and only manuscript that they put all their eggs in one basket. You've learned so much from writing the first one, the best thing to do is to put all that to work in writing a second one. Also, remember, the odds are you will get a two book contract. You might want to be well into your second if that does happen.

To market that first manuscript (while I'm putting most of my energy into writing the second one) I would do the following:

1. Write a good cover letter.

2. Write a good one-page synopsis.

3. Research agents and editors and make a list of at least 10 agents (non-fee charging) and 50 publishers (ranging from the big ones in NY, to the one down the street working out of a garage). I would then mail to one agent and ten publishers on week one. Then another agent and ten publishers in a week or two. Then keep that up until I run out of agents and publishers. This way you spread out the rejections—just joking. This way you keep your hopes up.

I would also try to attend a writing conference where I might meet some editors, agents and authors.

And then, I would never quit.

34. ONCE PUBLISHED: STAYING ALIVE IN THE BUSINESS

"I read somewhere that there are only about 200 Americans who can make a living from writing full time. I thought: I can't be one of 200 people in America. That's too hard." The speaker is Michael Crichton in an interview in USA Weekend (Jan 7-9, 1994). He's talking about his early years, when he was faced with the decision between becoming a writer or going to medical school. His choice was medical school. The current state of published writing in America right now is a strange mixture. There are three main areas:

1. Best-selling authors who command mega-bucks and their books are guaranteed to be bestsellers even before they write them.

2. Literary writers. Authors whose works usually sell few copies, are well received critically, and make their living teaching in the University system or off of grants. Most literary writers publicly disdain the first group and ignore the third.

3. The pack. Authors who write mainstream/genre fiction and who scrape their way from $5,000 advance to $5,000 advance; the money received only after the manuscript has been written and rejected on average by fifteen to forty publishers. Most members of the pack strive to become part of the first group and are too busy writing to make much sense of the second group.

I've talked to other midlist writers and many of them harbor some resentment toward the first group, but I think that feeling is misplaced. One friend of mine broke down Stephen King's latest multi-millionaire dollar advance into how much fifty authors could get each, but the fact of the matter is those fifty authors probably wouldn't sell as many books combined as Stephen King.

A writer like Stephen King or John Grisham or Sue Grafton supports a lot of beginning and mid-list writers by helping their publishing house make enough profit on their books to publish all those first novels, which if you remember, nine out of ten fail. The big names pick up that slack financially for the publisher.

Each of the last two lifestyles has different routes to follow, although the "streams can be crossed" to misquote the Ghostbusters, without a nuclear meltdown. The literary/academic world usually requires one of two things: an MFA in writing, or the writer to have won a prestigious award or grant. It is a somewhat closed circle and to enter it, you usually must enter at the bottom—i.e. attend an MFA program. There are various feelings about the MFA programs, but the fact is that it is a doorway into the academic writing life and the most readily accessible one (given you have the time and money to participate).

The pack is also a very difficult world to enter, and an even more difficult one to remain in. An advantage of entering the academic world is that you can gain a certain degree of security as you climb each rung. 95% of writers in the pack perish *after* publishing their first novel. Some hang on by sheer quantity of work—i.e. if the average novel commands a $5,000 to $10,000 advance, then they write several "average" novels per year under that many names to sustain themselves. That sort of living can be quite tasking, though. Most writers in the pack have a job in addition to their writing one.

Others get struck by lightning and break through to the first group. Congratulations. This is often as much due to luck as skill, but I don't begrudge any of those who make it because they did the legwork in order to get "lucky". You don't get lucky in the writing world doing nothing. If you worked hard enough and had a little bit of luck and have finally sold your first novel, there are many traps you have to be aware of. The work has just begun.

The first trap is thinking that you've got it made. Unless your advance was significant, you have to remember one of the rules of the publishing world: advance roughly equals copies printed which roughly equals one-half of copies sold which roughly, hopefully, makes the advance back. If you have a $10,000 advance and think to yourself: "This is going to hit the NY Times Bestseller list and sell 250,000 copies hardcover," you've got a rude awakening coming. A $10,00 advance for a hardcover book might entail a first run of three to four thousand books. You can't sell more books than they print. Keep writing.

Another trap is the track the bookselling and publishing world pushes writers into. If your first three books all do moderately well and each sells, say, 40,000 out of a 75,000 paperback run, guess what? They probably aren't going to print 300,000 copies of your fourth book. In fact, I have found in my experience, that publishers tend to cut down on the print run the longer I am with them as they see that they don't have a best seller but a solid lower level book. Publishers tend to be willing to take more of a risk on a new unknown author than an established mediocre one, which might sound strange to you at first, but actually isn't if you think about it.

Also, bookstores and book suppliers such as Ingram, own computers— those same contraptions that many of us writers use to produce our work. Except, they use their computers differently—they track books and authors and sales and punch all that into the machines and using a toad's eye, a rabbit's foot, blood of a bat, and a few free-lance witches, they (ever notice how there is always a *they* no matter what line of work you are in?) decide how many of each type of book they are going to order, which in turn causes the necromancers at your publisher to decide how many they are going to print. The bottom line is that once you establish a track record, breaking out of it is difficult.

Although I am not an expert on this system, the result I see is that unless you have a best-selling book, the road usually leads down which can be discouraging. But since I don't have a bestseller and am still writing, I do believe the odds can be beat. It takes luck, which to me is the application of hard work.

I have scrambled to make a living at writing through several means. Besides money for the books themselves, I also teach writing wherever and whenever I can; I also do book signings and sold remainders of my novels at military PXs—I used to put almost 30,000 miles a year on my car doing that. The bottom line is that I will do whatever it takes even though sometimes it can get quite tedious and irritating. Nobody said it was going to be easy and it isn't. As a corner man might say to a boxer who is getting beaten and bloodied in the ring—you gotta want it, kid.

There is the classic story of a young fellow who was interested in playing violin. He studied for many years and finally got his big break to play before the "master." He played his heart out and when he was done, he asked the master what he thought. The master replied: "Not enough fire," then left.

The young man was crushed. He put his violin away and pursued another career. Years later, he met the master at a social gathering. He cornered him and reminded him of the event many years ago, saying that the master's somewhat less than inspiring comment had caused him to give up the violin and change his life. The master was surprised. "I tell everyone that," he informed the young man, "regardless of how well they play. If my comment so easily dissuaded you, then you didn't want it bad enough and didn't believe in yourself enough." You will have plenty of opportunities to quit writing and not many to continue. The choice is always yours.

I think you know you're starting to be successful in this business when people start giving you grief. Nobody cares about you when you're a loser, but start getting some success and all of a sudden people come out of the shadows tell you how screwed up your stuff is.

Mid-Career Stumbling Blocks I sometimes meet or hear about writers who are stunned to find themselves 'unemployed.' Their current publisher doesn't offer them a new contract, their agent can't find a new publisher and royalty checks (if any) have dried up.

Remember earlier I mentioned how slow the publishing business is? This is true not only for people trying to break in, but also for those already in. If a writer is not planning at least a year ahead, that writer is in trouble. There are few things worse than watching a panicked writer desperately trying to sell a manuscript because they need to pay that month's mortgage—it isn't going to happen.

Such writers respond with some of the following techniques:

1. They switch agents. The problem with this is that an agent who accepts a client whose career has taken a severe downturn is picking up a ticking bomb. Several agents I've talked to have been so badly scarred by such clients that they won't do it again. It might be very difficult to get a new and better agent in such a situation. Remember, the agent doesn't sell the work, the work sells the work. If the old agent couldn't sell it, the new agent may have just as hard a time. The time to switch agents—if one feels there is a need for change—is when one's career is going well. That's also when it's most difficult to do it. It was extremely hard for me to let go of my first agent. It was also hard to do it in what I consider a fair manner—before I had a new agent lined up. For a while, I was an 'orphan'. I took the chance that I would get an agent I wanted and the gamble paid off.

2. They switch genres. This is something I've both succeeded at and failed at so I look at it both ways. I think writers have to realistically evaluate their skills and capabilities. I sometimes shake my head when I hear writers whose work is selling very well, complain how 'bored' they are with their successful series and want to try something different. I understand the feeling, but sometimes I wonder if that has been thought through. Often writers are successful with certain books because they're good at writing those types of books. Sometimes, when a writer switches genre, they have to switch their writing style to a certain extent and sometimes they don't make that switch successfully. Sometimes they try to apply the format and style they've used in their old genre to the new and it doesn't work.

On the other hand, I think there are plenty of cases of writers who've shifted their path over a notch or two and have been very successful. I start out writing military techno-thrillers. About five books down the line, still doing reasonably well with that, I wrote a science fiction novel on spec. That launched a more successful career in that field. However, my science fiction books features a military person as the protagonist, and the plot revolved around a lot of action, so I wasn't that far afield. When I tried my hand at a first person mystery, with my protagonist a policeman, my agent put up a big flashing red light and asked me to re-evaluate what I was doing.

My experience has been that the market is getting tighter. I think there will be a rebound effect to that in terms of small publishers gaining more prominence. Also, changes in the technology such as on-demand printing and electronic media are going to change the business. However, I still feel it is an up or out business and any writer whose career is not going up better be doing something or else that train coming down the track from behind will run him over.

35. WRITING GROUPS & CONFERENCES

Writing tends to be a solitary profession and, as mentioned earlier, one without an apprenticeship program where you can make a living while learning the craft. Writing groups, conferences, and writing programs try to address some of these problems. There are pros and cons to each—things to be gained and things to be lost in participating in any of them, but that mostly depends on what you want.

Writing groups are usually local—several people who enjoy writing band together and start meeting once a month or so. They read to each other and give feedback. Occasionally they bring in different speakers for presentations.

Groups usually have different focuses—short stories, poetry, novels are the three basic areas. Some groups try to do all, with the resultant problem of having to sit through a type of writing that you might not particularly be interested in—but here lies a hidden advantage: as a novelist you just might learn something by listening to poets or short story writers. Not just might—you will, if you have an open mind. You can learn about perspective and you can also learn about the craft of those other mediums. You can also learn about people—not just through the written word but also by observing those who do the writing. I've found that poets, short story writers, novelists, songwriters—all speak some common language, but there are different angles for each area that can add to your repertoire.

I have found, though, that the people who get the least out of the typical writer's group are the novelist. It is very difficult to read a chapter from a novel and get a good critique, especially if you aren't reading the opening chapter. You have to get people up to speed on the story, then have to weather all the "why didn't you - - -" questions. About one out of ten of those questions are worthwhile. That's not to say as a novelist you shouldn't attend writers' groups and do readings—there are other advantages—it's just to say be aware of the difficulty of reading from a novel in progress at such a group.

An important rule that I believe is necessary for a writers' group (this is also true of writing classes) to survive is: No critiquing of content. Nothing can tear a group apart quicker than people wading into the subject matter—I saw one group run off several writers whose subject matter was religious. The discussion didn't center on the way the person had written the material, but rather became a theological discussion about the material itself. In the same manner, open-mindedness must exist about such things as sex, "profane" language, political views, etc. etc. I think the person who objects to content is the one who has the problem—not the writer. Remember the 1st Amendment.

I was doing a book signing one day and this old lady came up to me and asked me what "language" my books were in. I told her English. She clarified the question by asking me whether I used "profane" language. Since my books were about soldiers, I told her yes, that sort of language fits for those types of characters. She then lectured me that she didn't believe in such language. That's fine for her and anyone else—simply don't buy the book.

However, over the years, I have gotten to the point where for most of my books, I don't use profanity. That's because I get letters from kids every once in a while who read my books. Unless I need it to serve a purpose, I keep it out. Same with sex scenes.

Some writers benefit greatly from critique groups, others not at all. You have to find what works best for you. I am a believer that the best editor for a book is the writer; if the writer is willing to be honest with him or herself.

Conferences and workshops are important. They are the key to networking and publishing is like any other business—who you know is sometimes more important than what you do. There is a difference in the way a cold query is treated versus a query an editor or agent can put a face to. You also get to put a face to editors and agents.

One of my pet peeves—which you probably don't care about anyway, but since I'm writing this book, I get to put down—is the way participants treat editors and agents as if they walk on water and are the source of all valid information. I will spend a week talking about the business of publishing, then they will have a panel of editors and agents on Saturday, and people will ask the same basic questions as if the answers are going to be totally different.

To be honest, that pet peeve stems out of a simple reality of the publishing business—writers are generally at the bottom end of the feeding cycle—especially unpublished writers. Also, just as writers have to pay their dues to earn a place in the business, editors and agents have to do that also. You might feel bad about that rejection slip in your mailbox, but think how that editor who gets a pink slip feels.

A question you should ask yourself when attending a conference is what are the motives of the people who are there. Why are these writers here? I can give you two main reasons—to make some money and to do the same thing you are, network. Usually it's the latter as most conferences only pay enough for the writers to get to the conference, certainly not to make a profit. Writers who are at conferences are there because they like networking also.

Why are these editors here? To look for new writers? Mostly, but I know an editor who has been doing several conferences a year for over a dozen years and has picked up two properties from all that time. To get out of the office? To network with the *other* editors and agents at the conference? To get a free plane ticket and lodging? Whatever. The same is true of agents. I have seen some shysters—fee-charging agents who are there to drum up business. This is not necessarily bad depending on what *you* want. I discussed this topic in the chapter on agents.

One thing to remember is that it is a *writers* conference, not an editor's or agent's conference.

I have quite a bit of respect for people who are willing to take the time and money to attend conferences so that they can learn. My respect goes up even further for those who are willing to truly learn: who are willing to take criticism and suggestions.

Harlan Ellison is well known for eviscerating writers when he holds writing classes. His point is that writing is his profession and those who want to enter it have to be very, very good and he has little patience for those who approach it without the highest standards. In the foreword of one of his novels, Dan Simmons describes attending that class—and being discovered by Harlan Ellison.

I try to be as honest as possible without being rude when working with other writers. Giving false praise wastes everyone's time, but occasionally there are people who do not like hearing anything negative about their project. There are some people who get perturbed that the instructors, editors and agents do not do more to "encourage" the writers. One of the editors responded that that wasn't his job—that was the writers' job.

If you do go to a conference, be prepared. Many have sign-ups where you get to talk to an editor and/or agent for 15 minutes. Have what you are going to say rehearsed. Have your cover letter and one page synopsis in hand. Pitch your idea and story succinctly and in an interesting manner. Don't ever expect to hand the manuscript to them—remember, most are flying home and don't have the space or desire to haul it with them on the plane.

When you get feedback consider it carefully. Don't argue—it won't change their mind about your book, but it will make them think you would be hard to work with.

Use the 'free' time constructively. At a conference I recently attended, I sat for two hours in the bar one evening talking with a fellow who had been Bob Hope's top writer for years, picking up information and advice about the business. What amazed me were all the nights I was there, not a single attendee wandered in and sat down and chatted with the authors, editors and agents who were stuck in the motel. Be willing when the conference director asks for people who want to pick up agents/editors at the airport to volunteer. Take them out to dinner. You might be surprised at what you will reap. I've learned more over a one-hour dinner with editors than sitting for four hours in their lecture during the day.

Treat the people who run the conference with respect and courtesy. They are volunteers who have given tremendously of their time and effort to make sure the conference works. It's not their fault the food the hotel serves is bad or that an author or editor missed a meeting.

Do people actually get 'discovered' at conferences? Yes. I just received an e-mail from a successful writer who told me how he got his first book contract set up at a conference. A few months ago a man who was in my group at the Maui Writers Retreat e-mailed me to tell me of his two book deal.

I'm getting toward the close of this book and this issue of conferences brings up something that dovetails into what I've written on all these pages. I recently listened to an agent talk about mid-career writers and the mistakes they make. The next morning I saw him at breakfast and sat down with him and told him that what he had said the previous day had really struck home. The interesting thing, I continued, was that if I had heard what he'd said a year previously, I would have understood it intellectually but I wouldn't have accepted it emotionally.

I think that is a critical aspect of being a writer. Much of what I've written in this book you might have nodded at and said to yourself "well, that's common sense." But do you really believe it? There is a gap between understanding and acceptance. That gap can cause not just writers, but anyone, great trouble in their life. I've noted that my current agent never really confronts me with anything. Also, he sometimes won't give me advice when I ask for it. I've realized it's not because he's bored or doesn't have time, but rather, like a good psychologist, he can point me in the right direction, but he knows that whether I decide to go there or not is totally up to me. In fact, if he did give me advice I wasn't ready to hear, I could end up reacting and going totally in the wrong direction.

Things I wrote in this book five years ago I've since cut out and replaced with words that are the exact opposite. Yet I believed what I had written five years ago just as much as I believe what I am writing now. What happened? Through experience and some open-mindedness, I learned that I needed to change the way I viewed things.

How to find a conference? The Writers Market has a listing. Also, on the Internet, you can go to Shawguides at: http://writing.shawguides.com/

36. HOLLYWOOD, MOVIE RIGHTS AND SCREENPLAYS

If you've never been to LA, Hollywood in particular, it's hard to describe. There is a rather strange atmosphere in the air there. I love the smell of movie rights in the morning. It smells of—money.

Right. And if pigs had wings they'd fly. Certainly there are big bucks to be made in Hollywood but books being optioned for millions are few and far between. The common option on a book is a couple of thousand and nothing ever happens.

What is an option? An option gives whoever buys it, ownership for the theatrical rights to a work for a given period of time. That person usually then goes around and tries to sell the work to a studio to produce it.

Think of some rather famous books and how long it took for them to get made. Interview With A Vampire made the rounds for many years and several different people, including Julia Phillips, held the option. I recommend reading her book You'll Never Eat Lunch In This Town Again, to get an idea of how Hollywood works. She's the first woman to win an Oscar as producer (Close Encounters Of The Third Kind).

The longer I've worked with various Hollywood types, the more amazed I am that any movie ever gets made. It's a brutal business and the amount of commitment by any involved party to be able to see a project through to completion is just phenomenal.

I've noticed a recent trend where people ask me for free options, contingent on the fact that they will take the work and try to market it. I've done this a couple of times but don't think I will do it any more.

However, you do have to be amenable. The production company that owned the option on one of my books called and said they wanted to renew the option but they didn't want to pay all of the money owed up front. I agreed because I felt they were doing a good job trying to get the film made. Which in my mind generates to about a snowball's chance in hell.

I do recommend reading a book about screenplays. I'm not going to get into it much here since I don't know enough about it, but the way a screenplay is broken down is very interesting and can be helpful to a novelist.

Learning about screenplays can also help you with outlining.

In a nutshell, here are some interesting things to know about screenplays (these are generalities—like novels, there are always exceptions):

-A page in a screenplay should equate to a minute of film. Thus the average feature film screenplay runs 100 to 120 pages, considerably shorter than a novel.

-Each page should be roughly balanced between dialogue and action.

-Screenplays have three acts. The beginning (page 1-30), the middle (pages 30-90) and the end (90-120). The beginning is your set up. Then you have confrontation. Then you have resolution. The two transition points from Act I to II and II to III are known as plot point 1 and plot point 2.

There are exceptions to these rules. For example, <u>Pulp Fiction</u> did not follow this format and was quite a success. That led to many aspiring directors trying to write the "next" Pulp Fiction. The problem is that the non-traditional format wasn't the aspect of that film that made it such a success— Tarantino's deft and snappy dialogue was. The story *without* that dialogue would have been a disaster.

-Screenplays have a very specific form that must be followed. There are programs sold that handle that form, but you must do it right, just as you must do manuscript format correctly.

There are some good things I've learned from dealing with people who work in the movies. There are four major areas to be considered in a screenplay:

1. Character
    -Motivations?
    -Whose point of view?
    -Character arcs—is there development in the character through the course of the movie?
    -What is the conflict?
    -Dialogue—is it believable?
2. Plot
    -Whose point of view?
    -Show it, don't say it.
    -Is the problem to be resolved shown early and clearly enough?
    -Is it 'high concept'?
3. Intent
    -Does it come across?
    -Is it relevant to the audience?
4. Setting

Think about the advantages of film and disadvantages. Then the same for novels. As a writer, you have the advantage of narrative—of being able to give a lot of expository information simply by writing it. A filmmaker has a much more difficult job in this area. However, dialogue in a film is presented realistically while in your book you have only the written word.

These are just a couple of examples. As a writer, you have to start examining every aspect of the craft and art.

37. ELECTRONIC BOOKS, PRINT-ON-DEMAND, AND THE FUTURE

Where is publishing heading? This is an issue that definitely affects everyone from writers through readers.

The biggest problem in publishing right now is inventory. Every time you walk into a store and buy a paperback, you're actually paying for two or three. The average sell-through for paperbacks hovers somewhere around 50% or lower. Sell-through means the number sold of the number printed. What happens to the ones that don't sell? They get the cover torn off for credit, and then recycled. This can result in large losses for the publisher.

It is important to remember that bookstores are a retail business that can return the product, so basically it is a consignment store. Therefore the priority is to move product through shelf space, not necessarily to sell a specific book. The time that stores leave books on their shelves is growing shorter and shorter before they decide to replace it with something else.

Two things have been suggested to alleviate this problem. One is electronic publishing. The book is downloaded, where you can read it on your computer or on specially designed hand-held displays that open one page at a time on the screen. This is a good idea except for a major issue for authors. If a book is in electronic form and can be printed at the push of a button, publishers can rightly claim the book is never out of print. I talk more about that a little further on.

The second is print-on-demand where bookstores will be able to quickly print and bind books as they are needed. This will alleviate the problem of large inventory and returns.

Another interesting trend is the resurgence of small presses. As the larger publishing houses become more concerned with the bottom line and bestsellers, it opens the door for smaller houses to take over the mid-list. With on-line bookstores and the possibility of print-on-demand, the future is looking better for these smaller publishers to take a piece of the market.

Publishing is on the edge of a big changes and anyone who wants to be an author should stay on top of these changes, because they will affect everyone involved in the business.

<u>Electronic books</u>.

I'm writing this while e-books is a very small market with only 10,000 Rocket Books sold. For a while I've been listening to, and reading about, e-books and frankly I think most people are seriously underestimating the effect this will have on publishing.

Let me begin by saying we will always have the printed book. It is the traditional medium and the one most people prefer by far. But e-books are more than just a book. They are a living book. In an e-book you can cross-reference, underline, make notes, have a dictionary handy, highlight, and even have video/pictures to supplement the story. You can also increase the size of fonts so that any book can be a large print book.

The Rocket Book came out in 1998. That same year print on demand was demonstrated. A few individuals have seen the connection between e-books and print-on-demand, but so far most have missed the boat.

I believe the first area where e-books will grow by leaps and bounds very quickly is in textbooks. Instead of lugging around fifty pounds of books, a student will soon be able to load all his or her texts into one hand-held device.

I think the true breakthrough in the popularity will come when all the various pieces of hardware: the e-book, laptop, Palm Pilot, cell phone, etc. will be scrunched into one device. Think about the possibilities then. With one machine you will be able to:

-book your flight and room.

-read an e-book on the flight

-bring up a map to make sure you know where you are (and probably use a ground positioning receiver built into the device to pinpoint your location)

-look up references for various sites you visit.

-type in notes about what you see (so you can tax-deduct the trip)

The real key for writers about e-books is that the business will be, as agent Richard Curtis puts it, author centric. This is true not only of publishing, but many other businesses. Think about travelers. The trend is for them to book their own arrangements over the Internet, making the travel agent a dinosaur. In the same way, we may see publishers and agents become outmoded as the author can reach the reader directly without middlemen.

The biggest issue right now is quality control. Since practically anyone has access to the Internet, dozens of e-book publishers are springing up in the virtual world. How will potential readers be able to distinguish between quality work and junk? This will take time to sort out.

As this goes to print Random House has just made a rather dramatic step in e-books. First, they've announced that they will give 50% royalties to authors, which is what agents and authors have been asking for. Second, and more importantly for the reader, they are going to lower the price of an e-book below that of a bound book.

Another issue for e-books will be 'branding.' Any person who is willing to pay a couple of hundred dollars to one of the many sites that are springing up on the Internet can be 'published' in both e-book and print on demand. Their book can also be listed at Amazon. However who will determine which of these many, basically self-published, books have any quality?

Earlier in the chapter on reviews I indicated I was not particularly thrilled with the posted reviews at Amazon. However, I've had to reconsider this. Who better than the reader to 'brand' books?

179

How to write books: Go to the bookstore or library and you will find numerous books in the same vein as this book telling you how to write. Read them. Study them. Take what you can use and don't worry about what you can't. One thing I've noticed in all of them is that most authors think you have to write the same way they do. One said you simply <u>must</u> learn Latin, as it is the only way you can understand and use English. Right—I don't think Dean Koontz knows Latin (OK, maybe he does). Write *your* way—just do it well. Use how to write books as another tool. I do suggest reading a few though, just to get the common themes. It's like the commercial—if eight out of ten how-to-get-published books say it, then it's probably true.

Self-publishing: They're called "vanity presses" for a reason. Pay if you simply want to feel good about having a bound book. A tiny fraction of self-published books turn a profit. If it was such a good book the odds are a regular publisher would have taken it on. Like literary agencies that charge a fee, vanity presses make their money off of you—not the book.

The real trap in self-publishing is marketing your book. Most bookstore chains won't even give you the time of day. For 99.9% of you reading this article forget about self-publishing.

I recently sat next to a self-published author at a book fair. He was an example of where self-publishing was a good idea. He was a sports columnist for a local paper who took a bunch of his articles and made a book out of them. The first thing he did right was not expend a whole lot of energy in writing a book, since the work was already done. He had five hundred copies printed up and sold them at local book fairs across Kentucky and was doing all right. He also visited local bookstores and had his book placed in there on commission.

If you are sure you can market and sell your book, then self-publishing might be for you—this mostly applies to specific non-fiction markets. I've never heard of a fiction self-published book that did well. Books with titles like <u>How To Satisfy Your Woman Every Time</u> might make it.

I've read several articles recently about how self-publishing is one of the fastest growing businesses and that's true. But that doesn't mean the books that are self-published are making money, it means the people who get paid to publish those books have more clients. Big difference.

Another time self-publishing is good is when you simply want to have a book in hand that you want to give to people, perhaps your family. If you've written your memoirs, it might be a good idea to get it published and bound so you can give it to your children and great-grandchildren.

Multiple book contracts: Publishers are investing in your name when they publish your manuscript. Because of that, they tend to want more than a one

shot deal. Initially that sounds great—you get to sign two or three book contracts right from the get-go. The disadvantage, though, is that you lock yourself into that publisher at a price range that may not be your true worth two
or three years down the line.

Unfortunately, most writers who are scrambling around down in the pack,
don't really have too much choice in this area—you need the advance money
in order to continue writing. Just be aware, though, that there are disadvantages to signing several book contracts at the same time.

One disadvantage is something called "joint accounting." That's where the
publisher ties both your advances together for two books. Even if your first
one earns out its advance, you don't see royalties until you earn out the
advances for both, even though the second one hasn't been published yet.

Being self-employed. Publishers seem to be of the opinion that if they give
a $5,000 advance then the writer just "made" $5,000. They don't seem to
understand that the writer probably *lost* around $10,000 on the deal when you
take into account the amount of time spent on the manuscript; investment in
equipment such as computer and printer; time and money spent on research;
agent's fee; taxes; food (yes most of us do have to eat those days we write;
rent; etc. etc. etc.).

I got to the point on marketing one manuscript where I simply told my
agent I could not let it go for the offer a publisher was making because I
couldn't afford to write and live at the price they were offering. Even with the
offer being doubled it just about broke me even on the work.

There are many writers whose writing income is above and beyond their
"normal" income. Many retired people write simply for the pleasure and
when they are published are very happy with the extra money. But for those
of you with your literary dagger clenched between your teeth as you try to
infiltrate the shores of the publishing world, do not underestimate the cost
of staying in business.

How long should a manuscript be? This is an often-asked question and
one that is dangerous to answer. The standard answer is: As long as the quality of writing can support.

If you have to wheel your manuscript in to an editor's office in a wheel-
barrow, you might get an initial negative impression, but if the quality of the
writing and story makes it a magnificent opus, then they'll buy it.

On the other end of the spectrum, The Bridges Of Madison County was
perhaps 50,000 words?

Generally, though, I say the normal manuscript length is between 75,000
and 100,000 words. Most of mine seem to be around 100,000 words or 400

manuscript pages. My longest so far was 580 manuscript pages and my short-est just over 300.

The manuscript has to be long enough to tell the story well.

A question I am asked surprisingly often (I say surprisingly because it's something I never really worried about) is how to protect your story idea and the manuscript from being "stolen."

I am not a lawyer and am not too familiar with copyright law, but from my experience I don't think that is something most of us need to worry about. The first question I ask people who ask that question is why would someone want to steal their idea? Although probably not the most polite thing I could ask, it is one that should be considered. If the idea is so good, then it will be bought legitimately.

I have not heard of one single case in the writing business (although I am sure it has happened) where a submission idea was stolen.

Also, if it is *your* idea, who knows it better than you? Agents and editors accept that fact and would be foolish to try to take your idea and give it to someone else. If you and I started with the exact same original idea, when we finished our manuscript, the results would be two very different books.

The bottom line is, in my opinion, don't worry too much about your idea or manuscript getting stolen. If you are really that concerned, seal it in an envelope and mail it to yourself and let it remain sealed. The postmark will help prove dating.

Pen Names or who the hell are you anyway?

This is a question I am asked constantly. Why do I write under so many names? Currently, I am published under four names besides my own and have a manuscript on the market under a fifth name. The reasons are:

1. Normally, once you are under contract with a publisher, they "own" the next work under that name. They have right of refusal on any new work using that name. So to free yourself, you have to use a different name.

2. You might be writing in a different genre. Readers and publishers are very picky. If you've been writing horror under your name for five years and suddenly write a romance, it would behoove you to use a different name to try to get it published. Very few authors have ever managed to switch genres under the same name.

I heard Dan Simmons at a signing the other day say he had just gotten a very unique contract—two books, any subject. That's very rare in the business. But Simmons has written horror and science fiction so well, that the publisher felt whatever he wrote would work.

3. I mentioned earlier in the chapter under numbers that this is an up or out business. Using a new name gives you a new opportunity to succeed.

Many authors have written under various pen names. I think Dean Koontz had eight.

Are there guidelines for picking pen names? Not really. It's recommended you go early in the alphabet, since books are usually shelved according to authors' last names. I've started grouping my pen names in the D's—Doherty, Donegan, Dalton. Makes it easier to look for the books in a store.

The Chains versus The Independents. This is a very hot topic currently. Personally, to me a bookstore is a bookstore.

I recently received e-mail from a fellow author urging me to write to the FCC about supporting the independent bookstores against one of the major chains. I had to look at this carefully. My reply to this author was that in my local town, there were four bookstores—two indies, two chain stores. The two chain stores carried his book. The two indies didn't. I suggested that he re-evaluate where he is putting his loyalty.

As part of my marketing campaign I sent out over 3,500 personal letters to independent bookstores with about 45 signed bookplates in each. This was a considerable investment of time and money. I received zero replies. The stores I checked had not used the bookplates. My motto as an author to both the independents and the chains is let's support the independent author.

It goes back to what I mentioned earlier about perspective. Different stores have different focuses. I've been treated quite well by both independent storeowners and chain store managers. The bottom line for both is that they want to sell books. So do I.

IN CLOSING

Quite a bit of what you just read won't make very much sense—or too much sense—to you if you are just beginning to write manuscripts. But reread it every once in a while and you will find that the more you write, the more sense it makes. I read numerous writing books when I first began and got quite frustrated because a lot of it seemed very simple or I didn't agree with some of the things that were said. But I didn't truly understand until I tried writing. Then it all begins clicking into place.

Remember—writing is work. You must put the time and effort into it to succeed.

So, although I said there is no right or wrong, I will leave you with one simple rule:

WRITE.

Then.

WRITE SOME MORE.

Then. Yep. WRITE EVEN MORE.

Appendixes

Appendix 1:
Sample Chapter Outline

<u>Chapter 1</u>:
<u>Nashville/ 9 Nov/ 11 PM/ 0400 Zulu</u>
-Kelly Reynolds gets tape and letter in mail from a male reporter friend
as she comes home late at night.

-she listens to tape—intercepted radio conversation between AF jet pilot
participating in Red Flag (US vs. "Soviet" simulation fight out of Nellis AFB) getting caught by tower (Dreamland—Nellis AFB call sign) for violating restricted
air space over Area 51. Pilot reports being forced down by strange object, then
goes off air suddenly. Male friend says he is going to investigate—will be there
on such and such night—the same night she is listening to the tape.

<u>Nellis Air Force Base Range/ 9 Nov/ 10 PM/ 0600 Zulu</u>
-shift to male reporter infilling site 51 in Nevada

<u>The Cube, Area 51/ 9 Nov/ 10:30 PM/ 0630 Zulu</u>
-shift to underground govt building (the Cube= C3= CCC, Command
and Control Central) where they pick up the man infilling on IR scope from
nearby mountain and track him coming in. Introduce General Gullick; refer
to pending Nightscape mission; start recall.

Purpose: introduces Kelly, Area 51 site mystery.

Appendix 2:
Sample Cover Letter

Bob Mayer
PO Box 3604
Boulder, CO 80307
(303) XXX-XXXX

Presidio Press   29 April 2000
31 Pamaron Way
Novato, CA 94949

Dear Ms.—
What if a secret organization of West Point Graduates has been covertly manipulating our government's policies for the past fifty years and now appears to be planning a coup against the President?

THE LINE is the story of Boomer Watson, an officer in the Army's elite Delta Force and Major Benita Trace, assigned to a headquarters in Hawaii where the President will be arriving in one week to give a speech at the 56th anniversary of the attack on Pearl Harbor. Each stumbles across clues point-ing to both the existence of The Line and the apparent coup—when they get together they realize it is up to them to stop the impending assassination.

But all is not as it appears—from an apparently botched covert mission into the Ukraine to stop nuclear terrorism; to underwater fights to the death in the waters off Hawaii; to murder on the sidelines of the Army-Navy game in Philadelphia; to the movement of shadowy military forces to Oahu; to the recovery of a secret diary buried in Custer' grave at West Point—it soon becomes clear that more is going on than even Boomer and Trace suspect and the novel builds to a shattering climax on the morning of December 7th as the President prepares to make his speech over the watery grave of the *Arizona* .

I have eight novels accepted for publication, three of which have been published. As specific background for this novel I graduated from West Point in 1981 and served in the Green Berets as A-Team Leader and Battalion Operations Officer for ten years.

This is a 120,000 word thriller. I appreciate your taking the time to review this submission and look forward to hearing from you.

Sincerely,

Appendix 3:
Example Synopsis

THE LINE

What if a secret military organization has been covertly manipulating our government's policies for the past fifty years and now appears to be planning a coup?

In 1995 Boomer Watson is a member of the elite Delta Force on a classified mission into the Ukraine when everything goes wrong—the target, instead of radical Ukrainian politicians, turns out to be NATO nuclear inspectors. Returning from the apparently botched mission, Boomer is relieved of his command and sent to Hawaii to get him out of the way. In Hawaii he links up with a former lover and fellow West Pointer, Major Benita Trace, who is working on a novel about an organization she calls THE LINE, referring to the long gray line of West Point graduates.

Working at Fort Shafter, Boomer becomes aware that strange events are occurring. A commander in the 1st Special Forces Group is relieved and a right wing officer takes his place; a covert special operations mission is being planned to coincide with the President's visit to Pearl Harbor on December 7th, a visit where the President will make a speech on his Military Reform Act, which is violently opposed by the military; the Colonel from the office of the Joint Chiefs of Staff who ordered the ill-fated mission in the Ukraine suddenly shows up in Hawaii; a Sergeant Major (Skibicki) tells Boomer the story of Boomer's father's death in Vietnam, a story that coincides with Trace's suspicions about The Line.

When Trace's house is broken into and the manuscript is stolen, Boomer begins to take action, going to the north shore of Oahu and observing a classified military operation that isn't supposed to be occurring, while at the same time Trace goes back to the mainland US to talk to the former commander of Special Forces in Vietnam (Rison) to confirm whether or not The Line exists. Boomer barely escapes with his life and comes to the conclusion that a military coup against the President is planned during a practice commander and control exercise during the President's visit to the Islands.

While Trace meets Rison at the Army-Navy game, Boomer and Skibicki come into conflict with shadowy military forces on the island of Oahu and in the waters offshore. Just before Rison is shot, he gives Trace the location of a diary that holds the key to the Line—the only problem is that to recover it, Trace will have to return to West Point. It becomes a race against time, as December 7th looms closer. The Command and Control exercise is cancelled but it appears that The Line will now attack the President at dawn on the 7th at the *Arizona* Memorial as he commemorates the 54th anniversary of the Japanese attack.

Not only is the question of the coup to be answered, but further, what is to be done if The Line does indeed exist—an organization that appears to have been responsible for such events as the devastating defeat at Pearl Harbor in 1941; the downing of Gary Power's U-2; the Bay of Pigs; the morass in Vietnam; the debacle of Desert One; and numerous other events. Can the plot be stopped and can such an organization be allowed to exist?

But through the long night of December 6th Boomer learns that what appears to be is *and isn't* and he is caught in a moral dilemma with a decision to make that will affect the future of the country. For there are more than two sides to this conflict and secrecy and lies surround Boomer and Trace as they try to unravel the truth while at the same time foil the plot against the President. The initial coup that Boomer thought he saw was actually forces moving in to protect the President and the real coup threatens in another direction.

They discover that there is a person on the President's side trying to get the diary for his own purposes and both Boomer and Trace were set up from the very beginning to play their roles in both stopping the coup and recovering the diary.

At the last second, the coup is stopped and the major plotters from The Line are killed. But there is still the loose end of the diary and the person close to the President who got Trace and Boomer involved in the first place without their knowledge. Skibicki kills the President's man and retrieves the diary. In the end, Boomer and Trace go back to West Point and in an address to the Corps of Cadets, make public the contents, shredding the veil of secrecy all sides wove.

Appendix 4:
Resources

SUGGESTED RESOURCES

The Authors Guild Inc. 330 West 42nd St. New York, N.Y. 10036. 212-563-5904

Sisters In Crime. They put out a pamphlet called: *Shameless Promotion for Brazen Hussies* which is very good for learning how to market your material, additionally, it lists prices for printing of marketing material (cards, bookmarks, postcards, etc.) by Black Mountain Press.
Rowan Mountain Literary Association/ POB 10111, Blacksburg, VA. 24062/703-961-3315

Novel & Short Story Writer's Market Published yearly by Writer's Digest Books: 1507 Dana Ave. Cincinnati, Ohio 45207. A good source to locate markets. Includes listings for Literary and Small Circulation Magazines; Commercial Periodicals; Small Press; Commercial Publishers. Agents are now listed separately in another book by Writer's Digest Books. Also out on CD-ROM.

Beyond The Bestseller: A Literary Agent Takes You Inside The Book Business. by Richard Curtis. Penguin Books USA Inc. 375 Hudson St. New York, N.Y. 10014.

As the title suggests, this is written by a person with years of experience as an agent. A good source for writers to gain an understanding of an agents perspective and to gain insight on the entire business side of publishing—something many new writers ignore to their future misfortune.

1001 Ways To Market Your Books. by John Kremer. Ad-Lib Publications. 51 N. Fifth St. PO Box 1102. Fairfield, Iowa. 52556-1102. 800-669-0773. A smorgasbord of ideas to help you in marketing your books once they are published. A good resource book when you really want to put the effort into self-promotion.

Rotten Rejections. Edited by Andre Bernard. Pushcart Press. PO Box 380, Wainscott, NY 11975. When those rejection slips pile up and you get depressed, pull this out and read a few. Then get back to work.

Writer's Digest 1507 Dana Avenue. Cincinnati, Ohio 45207. 800-333-0133. A good source of information with articles covering areas of interest to the author struggling to get published. Also covers markets for writers.

National Writers Club 1450 South Havana, Suite 620. Aurora, CO 80012. 303-751-7844

Associated Writing Programs 804-683-3839

Mystery Writers of America 17 East 47th St. 6th Floor. New York, N.Y. 10017.

Romance Writers of America 713-440-6885

Science Fiction Writers of America PO Box 4335. Spartanburg, SC 29305

Western Writers of America 416 Bedford. El Paso, TX 79922

National Writers Union 873 Broadway, Suite 203. New York, N.Y. 10003. 212-254-0279

International Women's Writing Guild 212-737-7536

Web sites of interest:

www.amazon.com/ An on-line bookstore. You can give your own reviews of books listed.

www.bookatoz.com/ Information on publishing, industry resources, and book resources.

www.bookwire.com/ "The 1st place to look for book information." Author tours. Publishers Weekly and other good links.

www.barnesandnoble.com/ Barnes and Noble bookstore on-line.

www.enews.com/ Search 200 magazines.

www.nypl.org/index.html New York Public Library on-line

lcweb.loc.gov/homepage/lchp.html Library of Congress

www.encyclopedia.com Encyclopedia.com

www.bocklabs.wisc.edu/ims/agents Directory of literary agents

www.literaryagent.com directory of literary agents

www.sfwa.org Science Fiction Writers Association

www.pageonelit.com great site with author interviews and you can sign up for
 Pageone newsletter. Lots of very good links.
www.shawguides.com good site to look up <u>**conferences**</u>
To subscribe to <u>PW Daily for Booksellers</u> fill out the form at http://www.pub-
 lishersweekly.com/pwdaily
www.authorsden.com good site for author, event, information

Appendix 5:
Example Story Grid

Chapter	Start	End	Date	Local	Zulu	Location	Action
Chapter number							
	Start page number						
		End page number					
			Date chapter takes place				
				Local Time			
					Zulu or Greenwich mean time		
						Location of action	
							Brief summary of what happens
1	1	12	Mon	9:12am		Antarctica	Plane leaves, crashes

List out all actions as they occur. This allows you to refer back quickly and find information.

196

Appendix 6:
Plot Line

Time   Protagonist   Antagonist   Major Supporting   Misc.

Timeline in real time
        Actions of protagonist in order
                Actions of antagonist in order
                        Actions of major supporting charac
                        ters—as many as needed
                                    Miscellaneous action,
                                    backdrop

Go down each column one at a time. Then once all actions as far as you know are listed, you draw arrows between the various columns to indicate the order that you will write them in your story.

About the Author

BOB MAYER is a West Point graduate, Special Forces veteran and author of over seventeen novels. Under the pen name Robert Doherty he has written the best-selling AREA 51 and PSYCHIC WARRIOR series. Under the pen name Greg Donegan he has written the ATLANTIS series. For more information check www.nettrends.com/mayer.

Printed in the United States
1908